Selenium Testing Tools Cookbook

Over 90 recipes to build, maintain, and improve test automation with Selenium WebDriver

Unmesh Gundecha

BIRMINGHAM - MUMBAI

Selenium Testing Tools Cookbook

First published: November 2012

Production Reference: 1161112

Published by Packt Publishing Ltd.
Livery Place
35 Livery Street
Birmingham B3 2PB, UK.

ISBN 978-1-84951-574-0

www.packtpub.com

Cover Image by Faiz Fattohi (faizfattohi@gmail.com)

Credits

Author
Unmesh Gundecha

Project Coordinator
Yashodhan Dere

Reviewers
V.Vamsi Chandra

Dave Hunt

Proofreaders
Matthew Humphries

Lydia May Morris

Acquisition Editor
Usha Iyer

Indexer
Hemangini Bari

Lead Technical Editor
Azharuddin Sheikh

Graphics
Valentina D'silva

Aditi Gajjar

Technical Editors
Mayur Hule

Ankita Shashi

Veronica Fernandes

Prashant Salvi

Production Coordinator
Arvindkumar Gupta

Cover Work
Arvindkumar Gupta

Copy Editors
Brandt D'Mello

Laxmi Subramanian

Alfida Paiva

About the Author

Unmesh Gundecha has a Master's Degree in Software Engineering and around 10 years of experience in Software Development and Testing. Unmesh has architected functional test automation projects using industry standard, in-house and custom test automation frameworks along with leading commercial and open source test automation tools. Presently he is working as Test Architect with a multinational company in Pune, India.

We would be remiss if we did not thank all of the people who helped make this book a reality. This includes the wonderful people at Packt Publishing, in particular Usha Iyer – Acquisition Editor, who proposed that I write this book. I'm grateful for all the help I got from the editorial staff at Packt Publishing in reviewing this book, particularly, Azharuddin Sheikh, Sonali Tharwani, Mayur Hule, Veronica Fernandes, Prashant Salvi, and especially Yashodhan Dere – Project Coordinator, who coordinated the progress of this book, by ensuring that I stayed on track.

This book has benefited a lot from a great team of technical reviewers. I'd like to thank each of them for volunteering their time reviewing drafts of this book and providing valuable feedback – Dave Hunt who is Selenium contributor, for his insight into some key areas; Vamsi Chandra for making sure the code samples for all chapters work by executing each and every sample; and Tarun Kumar for his early feedback.

I would like to thank my wife Punam, for supporting me while I was writing this book and making sure I did things on time, and my friends and colleagues at work for supporting me for all these years.

Finally, a big thanks to Selenium Development and User Community for building this wonderful tool.

About the Reviewers

V.Vamsi Chandra is a QA Automation Lead at the technology company Everlution Ltd. and has overall five years of experience in the software industry. He has completed his Masters in Mobile Computing and Networking, and has studied Bachelor of Technology in Computer Science and Engineering. He holds various certifications such as ISEB-ISTQB, MCP, MCSE, MCITP, and ITIL v3. He has been involved in to improving the quality of the product by testing with various tools, using Automation and Manual, works of **Software Development Life Cycle** (**SDLC**), **Software Testing Life Cycle** (**STLC**), and Agile (scrum) testing methodology to deliver high standard/complex products to the client.

He has worked in various sectors in Everlution Ltd. such as financial, banking, commercial, and retail, has handled complex projects, and designed customized frameworks for Fifth Third Bank-USA, Sainsbury's, Myindospace, Nationwide Building Society, and Mergermarket. The company also delivers web-based products.

> I would like to thank Mr. Unmesh Gundecha for this wonderful and exciting opportunity to reveal my thoughts in my own platform and to explore a bit beyond technologies. I am also thankful to the team for supporting and communicating fully to achieve this success.

Dave Hunt lives in Kent, UK with his wife and young son. He has always had a passion for turning mundane tasks into one-click solutions, and when he discovered Selenium back in 2005, his career in software testing and automation development was sealed. He works from home for Mozilla Corporation, where he assists teams in creating automated tests for their projects – ranging from Mozilla's web properties to the Firefox web browser and Thunderbird e-mail client.

www.PacktPub.com

Support files, eBooks, discount offers and more

You might want to visit www.PacktPub.com for support files and downloads related to your book.

Did you know that Packt offers eBook versions of every book published, with PDF and ePub files available? You can upgrade to the eBook version at www.PacktPub.com and as a print book customer, you are entitled to a discount on the eBook copy. Get in touch with us at service@packtpub.com for more details.

At www.PacktPub.com, you can also read a collection of free technical articles, sign up for a range of free newsletters and receive exclusive discounts and offers on Packt books and eBooks.

http://PacktLib.PacktPub.com

Do you need instant solutions to your IT questions? PacktLib is Packt's online digital book library. Here, you can access, read and search across Packt's entire library of books.

Why Subscribe?

- ▸ Fully searchable across every book published by Packt
- ▸ Copy and paste, print and bookmark content
- ▸ On demand and accessible via web browser

Free Access for Packt account holders

If you have an account with Packt at www.PacktPub.com, you can use this to access PacktLib today and view nine entirely free books. Simply use your login credentials for immediate access.

I would like to dedicate this book to my parents, who have raised me to be the person I am today and to my loving wife Punam for giving me the support and encouragement to write this book!

Table of Contents

Preface

This book will help you in learning advanced techniques for testing web applications with Selenium WebDriver API and related tools. In this book you will learn how to test web applications effectively and efficiently with Selenium WebDriver on desktops, mobile web browsers, and in a distributed environment.

This book covers design patterns such as data-driven testing, page objects, and object map for designing a highly maintainable and reliable test automation framework. You will also learn how to integrate Selenium WebDriver with Behavior-driven Development frameworks such as Cucumber-JVM, SpecFlow.NET, and Capybara.

This book also covers techniques to extend Selenium for your specific needs. There are more than 90 recipes that you can use to build or extend your existing test automation framework.

What this book covers

Chapter 1, Locating Elements, introduces you to locator techniques supported by Selenium WebDriver, for locating elements on pages in your web applications. Selenium WebDriver provides one of the advanced techniques for locating elements on web pages with multiple locator strategies such as XPath, CSS, and DOM. We can also implement custom locator strategies for locating elements. This chapter will also help you in getting started with Selenium WebDriver locator API.

Chapter 2, Working with Selenium API, demonstrates how to use Selenium WebDriver API for building tests. We will explore API and investigate advanced user interactions for performing complex mouse and keyboard operations, working with various types of UI elements used in web applications.

Chapter 3, Controlling the Test Flow, demonstrates how to use Selenium WebDriver API for building a reliable test automation framework. The tenants of good test automation are robustness, reliability, recovery from unexpected events, and unhandled execution. This chapter covers recipes on handling synchronization with implicit and explicit waits, multiple windows, and pop-ups and alerts that are displayed during the test execution.

Chapter 4, Data-driven Testing, introduces the data-driven testing approach, a widely used methodology in test automation. Selenium WebDriver does not have built-in features to support data driven testing. However we can extend Selenium WebDriver API to support data-driven testing. This chapter covers recipes to support data-driven testing using JUnit/Apache POI and JDBC technologies.

Chapter 5, Using the Page Object Model, introduces the Page Object model pattern, which is widely used for structuring Selenium WebDriver tests. This chapter provides tips on building testing frameworks using Page Object model.

Chapter 6, Extending Selenium, demonstrates how to extend Selenium WebDriver API and add features for building a scalable test automation framework. This chapter covers some of the important recipes in extending Selenium WebDriver for various practical scenarios such as supporting custom UI controls, capturing images of elements, and performing image-based verifications.

Chapter 7, Testing on Mobile Browsers, introduces you to testing mobile web applications with the Apple iOS and Android platform. This chapter covers recipes for configuring and using Selenium WebDriver to test a mobile application on the iPhone and Android based devices/simulators.

Chapter 8, Client-side Performance Testing, demonstrates how to measure client-side performance with Selenium WebDriver. Client-side performance can be measured in different ways with Selenium WebDriver. We can use tools such as dynaTrace and HttpWatch, along with Selenium WebDriver to collect, measure, and monitor client-side performance of web applications.

Chapter 9, Testing HTML 5 Web Applications, introduces you to using Selenium WebDriver to test web applications using HTML5 standard. This chapter explains how to test video and canvas elements and web storage API of HTML5.

Chapter 10, Recording Videos of Tests, briefly describes how to record videos of test runs using tools such as Monte Media Library in Java, Microsoft Expression Encode SDK in .NET, and Castro in Python.

Chapter 11, Behavior-driven Development, introduces Behavior-driven Development with Selenium WebDriver using tools such as Cucumber-JVM, JBehave for Java, SpecFlow.NET for .NET, and Capybara for Ruby.

Integration with Other Tools, demonstrates how to set up Selenium WebDriver with Eclipse and IntelliJ IDEA. We will also set up Maven and ANT along with Selenium WebDriver and Jenkins for running tests in Continuous Integration. This chapter also covers recipes for using tools such as AutoIt and Sikuli for testing non-web UI.

This chapter is not present in the book but is available as a free download from `http://www.packtpub.com/sites/default/files/downloads/Integration_ with_Other_Tools.pdf`.

Distributed Testing with Selenium Grid, demonstrates how to set up a distributed test environment with Selenium Grid. We will add nodes with various browser and operating system combinations. We will run tests in parallel using TestNG, which helps in reducing the time of test execution and increases the test coverage.

This chapter is not present in the book but is available as a free download from `http://www.packtpub.com/sites/default/files/downloads/Distributed_ Testing_with_Selenium_Grid.pdf`.

What you need for this book

You will need the following software to follow the recipes in this book:

- ▶ Browsers: Microsoft Internet Explorer, Google Chrome, or Mozilla Firefox
- ▶ Selenium browser drivers: Chrome Driver, InternetExplorer Driver
- ▶ Selenium tools: Selenium WebDriver client driver (based on your preference of programming language) and Selenium Standalone Server
- ▶ IDE: Eclipse, IntelliJ IDEA, and Microsoft Visual Studio (for .NET)
- ▶ BDD framework tools: Cucumber-JVM, JBehave (for Java), SpecFlow.NET (for .NET), and Capybara (for Ruby)
- ▶ Build and integration tools: Maven, ANT, and Jenkins
- ▶ Performance tools: dynaTrace AJAX Edition, HttpWatch, and BrowserMob Proxy
- ▶ Other tools: AutoIt and Sikuli
- ▶ Video capture tools: Monte Media Library (for Java), Microsoft Expression Encoder SDK (for .NET), and Castro (for Python)
- ▶ Mobile tools: Apple Xcode (for iOS mobile browser testing), Android SDK, Android Server APK, and iWebDriver for iOS
- ▶ Language runtimes: JDK 1.6 (for Java), Ruby 1.9 (for Ruby), and Python 2.7 (for Python)

Who this book is for

This book is for software quality assurance/testing professionals, test managers, or software developers with prior experience in using Selenium and Java for testing web-based applications. This book also provides examples for C#, Python, and Ruby users.

Conventions

In this book, you will find a number of styles of text that distinguish between different kinds of information. Here are some examples of these styles, and an explanation of their meaning.

Code words in text are shown as follows: "The `WebElement` class also supports find methods to find child elements."

A block of code is set as follows:

```
<form name="loginForm">
    <label for="username">UserName: </label> <input type="text"
        class="username" /></br>
    <label for="password">Password: </label> <input
        type="password" class="password" /></br>
    <input name="login" type="submit" value="Login" />
</form>
```

When we wish to draw your attention to a particular part of a code block, the relevant lines or items are set in bold:

```
//Locate all the Checkbox which are checked by calling jQuery
//find() method.
//find() method returns elements in array
List<WebElement> elements = (List<WebElement>)
    js.executeScript("return jQuery.find(':checked')");
```

Any command-line input or output is written as follows:

```
mvn clean test
```

New terms and **important words** are shown in bold. Words that you see on the screen, in menus or dialog boxes for example, appear in the text like this: "Right-click to open the pop-up menu and select the **Inspect element** option."

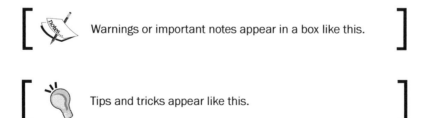

Warnings or important notes appear in a box like this.

Tips and tricks appear like this.

Reader feedback

Feedback from our readers is always welcome. Let us know what you think about this book—what you liked or may have disliked. Reader feedback is important for us to develop titles that you really get the most out of.

To send us general feedback, simply send an e-mail to feedback@packtpub.com, and mention the book title through the subject of your message.

If there is a topic that you have expertise in and you are interested in either writing or contributing to a book, see our author guide on www.packtpub.com/authors.

Customer support

Now that you are the proud owner of a Packt book, we have a number of things to help you to get the most from your purchase.

Downloading the example code

You can download the example code files for all Packt books you have purchased from your account at http://www.packtpub.com. If you purchased this book elsewhere, you can visit http://www.packtpub.com/support and register to have the files e-mailed directly to you.

Errata

Although we have taken every care to ensure the accuracy of our content, mistakes do happen. If you find a mistake in one of our books—maybe a mistake in the text or the code—we would be grateful if you would report this to us. By doing so, you can save other readers from frustration and help us improve subsequent versions of this book. If you find any errata, please report them by visiting http://www.packtpub.com/support, selecting your book, clicking on the **errata submission form** link, and entering the details of your errata. Once your errata are verified, your submission will be accepted and the errata will be uploaded to our website, or added to any list of existing errata, under the Errata section of that title.

Piracy

Piracy of copyright material on the Internet is an ongoing problem across all media. At Packt, we take the protection of our copyright and licenses very seriously. If you come across any illegal copies of our works, in any form, on the Internet, please provide us with the location address or website name immediately so that we can pursue a remedy.

Please contact us at `copyright@packtpub.com` with a link to the suspected pirated material.

We appreciate your help in protecting our authors, and our ability to bring you valuable content.

Questions

You can contact us at `questions@packtpub.com` if you are having a problem with any aspect of the book, and we will do our best to address it.

1
Locating Elements

In this chapter, we will cover:

- ▶ Using browser tools for inspecting elements and page structure
- ▶ Locating an element using the findElement method
- ▶ Locating elements using findElements method
- ▶ Locating links
- ▶ Locating elements by tag name
- ▶ Locating elements using CSS selectors
- ▶ Locating elements using XPath
- ▶ Locating elements using text
- ▶ Locating elements using advanced CSS selectors
- ▶ Using jQuery selectors
- ▶ Locating table rows and cells
- ▶ Locating child elements in a table

Introduction

The success of automated **GUI** (**Graphical User Interface**) tests depends on identifying and locating GUI elements from the application under test and then performing operations and verifications on these elements to achieve the test flow. This boils down to the test tool's ability to recognize various GUI elements effectively.

Selenium WebDriver provides one of the advanced techniques for locating elements on web pages. Selenium's feature-rich API provides multiple locator strategies such as Name, ID, CSS selectors, XPath, and so on. We can also implement custom locator strategies for locating elements.

In this chapter, we will explore more on how to use locator strategies by starting with ID, Name, and Class.

In any web development project, it is always a good practice to assign attributes such as Name, IDs, or Class to GUI elements. This makes the application more testable and conforms to accessibility standards. However, following these practices is not always possible. For such scenarios, we have to use advanced locator strategies such as CSS selector and XPath.

While CSS selector and XPath are popular among Selenium users, CSS selector is highly recommended over XPath due to its simplicity, speed, and performance.

Using browser tools for inspecting elements and page structure

Before we start exploring locators, we need to analyze the page and elements to understand how these are structured in the application, what properties or attributes are defined for the elements, how JavaScript or AJAX calls are made from the application, and so on.

Browsers render visual elements of the application for end users by hiding the HTML code and other resources. When we want to automate interaction with the application using Selenium WebDriver, we need to look carefully at the background code written to render pages and elements in browsers. We need to identify information such as attribute values and elements structure for locating elements and perform user actions using Selenium WebDriver API.

Here is an example of a BMI Calculator application page and HTML code written to render this page in a browser as displayed in the following screenshots:

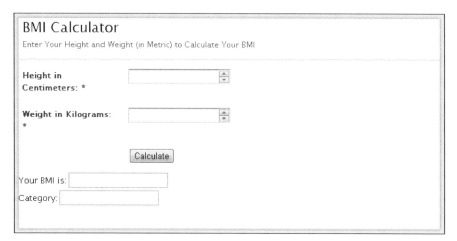

```
108  <header id="header" class="info">
109  <h2>BMI Calculator</h2>
110  <div>Enter Your Height and Weight (in Metric) to Calculate Your BMI</div>
111  </header>
112
113  <ul>
114
115  <li id="foli1" class="notranslate          ">
116  <label class="desc" id="title1" for="heightCMS">
117  Height in Centimeters:
118  <span id="req_1" class="req">*</span>
119  </label>
120  <div>
121  <input name="heightCMS" id="heightCMS" type="number" class="field text medium" value="" maxlength="255" tabindex="1"
       onkeyup=""/>
122  </div>
123  </li><li id="foli2" class="notranslate          ">
124  <label class="desc" id="title2" for="weightKg">
125  Weight in Kilograms:
126  <span id="req_2" class="req">*</span>
127  </label>
128  <div>
129  <input name="weightKg" id="weightKg" type="number" class="field text medium" value="" maxlength="255" tabindex="2"
       onkeyup=""/>
130  </div>
131  </li>
132
133    <li class="buttons ">
134          <div>
```

You can view the code written for a page by right-clicking in the browser window and selecting the **View Page Source** option from the pop-up menu. This will display the HTML code of the page in a separate window. This might look messy and difficult to understand.

We need special tools that can display this information in a structured and easy to understand format. In this recipe we will briefly explore few of these tools before we dive into locators.

How to do it...

In the following sections we will explore some of the tools which are in-built in browsers and plugins to analyze elements and page structure. These tools will help us to understand how elements and their attributes are defined on a page, DOM structure, JavaScript calls, CSS Style attributes, and so on.

Inspecting pages and elements with Firefox using Firebug add-in

The newer versions of Firefox provide in-built ways to analyze the page and elements; however, we will use the Firebug add-in which has more powerful features. You need to install the Firebug add-in in Firefox from `https://addons.mozilla.org/en-us/firefox/addon/firebug/`.

To inspect an element from the page, move the mouse over the desired element and right-click to open the pop-up menu. Select the **Inspect Element with Firebug** option as shown in the following screenshot:

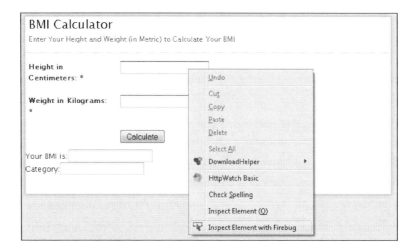

This will display Firebug with HTML code in a tree format as shown in the following screenshot:

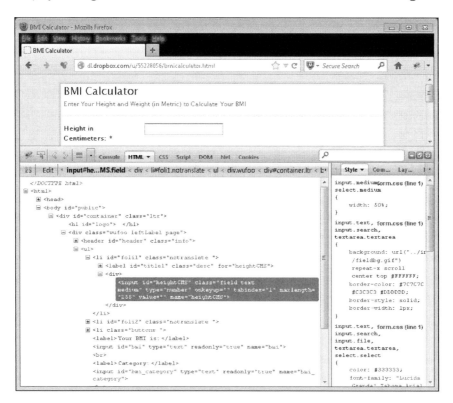

Firebug provides various other debugging features. It also generates XPath and CSS selectors for elements. For this, select the desired element in the tree and right-click and select **Copy XPath** or **Copy CSS Path** option from the pop-up menu as shown in the following screenshot:

This will paste the possible XPath or CSS selector value on the clipboard.

Inspecting pages and elements with Google Chrome

Google Chrome provides an in-built feature to analyze pages and elements. This is very similar to Firebug. You can move the mouse over a desired element on the page and right-click to open the pop-up menu, then select **Inspect element** option. This will open Developer Tools in the browser, which displays information similar to that of Firebug, as shown in the following screenshot:

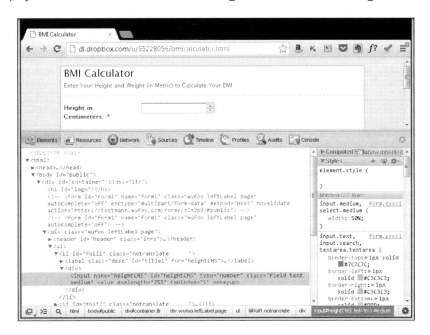

Chrome Developer Tools also provide a feature where you can get XPath for an element by right-clicking on the desired element in the tree and selecting the **Copy XPath** option from the pop-up menu.

Inspecting pages and elements with Internet Explorer

Similar to Google Chrome, Microsoft Internet Explorer also provides an in-built feature to analyze pages and elements.

To open the Developer Tools, press the *F12* key. The Developer Tools section will be displayed as shown in the following screenshot:

To inspect an element, click on the pointer (⬚) icon and hover over the desired element on the page. Developer Tools will highlight the element with a blue outline and display the HTML code in a tree as shown in the following screenshot:

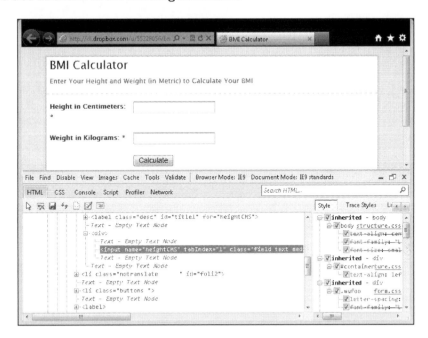

How it works...

Browser Developer Tools come in handy during test development. These tools will help you in finding the locator details for elements. These tools parse the code for a page and display the information in a hierarchal tree. These tools also provide information on how styles have been applied, page resources, page DOM (Document Object Model), JavaScript code, and so on.

Some of these tools also provide the ability to run JavaScript code for debugging and testing.

In the following recipes we will explore various types of locators that are supported by Selenium WebDriver and these tools will help you in finding and deciding various locator strategies or methods provided by Selenium WebDriver API.

Locating an element using the findElement method

Locating elements in Selenium WebDriver is done by using the `findElement()` and `findElements()` methods provided by WebDriver and WebElement class.

The `findElement()` method returns a `WebElement` object based on a specified search criteria or throws up an exception if it does not find any element matching the search criteria.

The `findElements()` method returns a list of `WebElements` matching the search criteria. If no elements are found, it returns an empty list.

Find methods take a locator or query object as an instance of `By` class as an argument. Selenium WebDriver provides `By` class to support various locator strategies. The following table lists various locator strategies supported by Selenium WebDriver:

Strategy	Syntax	Description
By ID	Java: `driver.findElement(By. id(<element ID>))`	Locates an element the using ID attribute
	C#: `driver.FindElement(By. Id(<elementID>))`	
	Python: `driver.find_element_by_ id(<elementID>)`	
	Ruby: `driver.find_ element(:id,<elementID>)`	
By name	Java: `driver.findElement(By. name(<element name>))`	Locates an element using the Name attribute
	C#: `driver.FindElement(By. Name(<element name>))`	
	Python: `driver.find_element_by_ name(<element name>)`	
	Ruby: `driver.find_ element(:name,<element name>)`	
By class name	Java: `driver.findElement(By. className(<element class>))`	Locates an element using the Class attribute
	C#: `driver.FindElement(By. ClassName(<element class>))`	
	Python: `driver.find_element_by_ class_name(<element class>)`	
	Ruby: `driver.find_ element(:class,<element class>)`	

Strategy	Syntax	Description
By tag name	Java: `driver.findElement(By.tagName(<htmltagname>))`	Locates an element using the HTML tag
	C#: `driver.FindElement(By.TagName(<htmltagname>))`	
	Python: `driver.find_element_by_tag_name(<htmltagname >)`	
	Ruby: `driver.find_element(:tag_name,< htmltagname >)`	
By link text	Java: `driver.findElement(By.linkText(<linktext>))`	Locates link using it's text
	C#: `driver.FindElement(By.LinkText(<linktext >))`	
	Python: `driver.find_element_by_link_text(<linktext >)`	
	Ruby: `driver.find_element(:link_text,< linktext >)`	
By partial link text	Java: `driver.findElement(By.partialLinkText(<linktext>))`	Locates link using it's partial text
	C#: `driver.FindElement(By.PartialLinkText(<linktext >))`	
	Python: `driver.find_element_by_partial_link_text(<linktext >)`	
	Ruby: `driver.find_element(:partial_link_text,< linktext >)`	
By CSS	Java: `driver.findElement(By.cssSelector(<css selector>))`	Locates element using the CSS selector
	C#: `driver.FindElement(By.CssSelector(<css selector >))`	
	Python: `driver. find_elements_by_css_selector (<css selector>)`	
	Ruby: `driver.find_element(:css,< css selector >)`	

Strategy	Syntax	Description
By XPath	Java: `driver.findElement(By.xpath (<xpath query expression>))`	Locates element using XPath query
	C#: `driver.FindElement(By. XPath(<xpath query expression>))`	
	Python: `driver. find_elements_by_ xpath (<xpath query expression>)`	
	Ruby: `driver.find_ element(:xpath,<xpath query expression>)`	

In this recipe, we will use the `findElement()` method to locate elements.

How to do it...

Locating elements using `id`, `name`, or `class` attributes is the preferred way to find elements. Let's try using these methods to locate elements as described in the following sections.

Finding elements by the ID attribute

Using the `id` attribute is the most preferable way to locate elements on a page. The W3C standard recommends that developers provide an `id` attribute for elements that are unique to each element. Having a unique `id` attribute provides a very explicit and reliable way to locate elements on the page.

While processing the DOM, browsers use `id` as the preferred way to identify the elements and this provides the fastest locator strategy.

Let's now look at how to use `id` attributes for locating elements on a login form.

```
<form name="loginForm">
    <label for="username">UserName: </label> <input type="text"
        id="username" /><br/>
    <label for="password">Password: </label> <input
        type="password" id="password" /><br/>
    <input name="login" type="submit" value="Login" />
</form>
```

Downloading the example code

You can download the example code files for all Packt books you have purchased from your account at http://www.packtpub.com. If you purchased this book elsewhere, you can visit http://www.packtpub. com/support and register to have the files e-mailed directly to you.

To locate the **User Name** and **Password** fields, we can use the id attribute in the following way:

```
WebElement username = driver.findElement(By.id("username"));
WebElement password = driver.findElement(By.id("password"));
```

Finding elements by the Name attribute

Locating elements with the id attribute is the most preferred locator strategy, but you might find situations where you cannot use the id attribute due to the following reasons:

- Not all elements on a page have the id attribute specified
- The id attributes are not specified for key elements on a page
- The id attribute values are dynamically generated

In this example, the login form elements use the name attribute instead of the id attribute:

```
<form name="loginForm">
    <label for="username">UserName: </label> <input type="text"
        name="username" /><br/>
    <label for="password">Password: </label> <input
        type="password" name="password" /><br/>
    <input name="login" type="submit" value="Login" />
</form>
```

We can use the name attribute to locate elements in the following way:

```
WebElement username = driver.findElement(By.name("username"));
WebElement password = driver.findElement(By.name("password"));
```

Unlike id, the name attribute may not be unique on a page. You might find multiple elements with similar name attributes and in such a case, the first element on the page with the specified value will be selected, which may not be the element you are looking for. This may cause the test to fail.

When building a testable application, you should recommend that the developers add the id attribute for key elements as well as other unique attributes to enable the easy location of elements.

Finding elements by the Class attribute

Apart from using the `id` and `name` attributes, you can also use the `class` attribute to locate elements. The `class` attribute is provided to apply CSS to an element.

In this example, the login form elements use the `class` attribute instead of the `id` attribute:

```
<form name="loginForm">
    <label for="username">UserName: </label> <input type="text"
        class="username" /></br>
    <label for="password">Password: </label> <input
        type="password" class="password" /></br>
    <input name="login" type="submit" value="Login" />
</form>
```

We can use the `class` attribute to locate elements in the following way:

```
WebElement username =
    driver.findElement(By.className("username"));
WebElement password =
    driver.findElement(By.className("password"));
```

How it works...

Selenium WebDriver API provides the `findElement()` method to locate the elements that are required in a test from the page under test.

When locating an element matching specified criteria, it looks through the **DOM (Document Object Model)** for matching elements and returns the first matching element to the test.

There's more...

The `WebElement` class also supports find methods that find child elements. For example, imagine that there are some duplicate elements on a page. However, they are located in separate `<div>` elements. We can first locate the parent `<div>` element and then locate the child element within the context of the `<div>` element in the following way:

```
WebElement div = driver.findElement(By.id("div1"));
WebElement topLink = div.findElement(By.linkText("top"));
```

You can also a use a shortcut method in the following way:

```
WebElement topLink = driver.findElement
    (By.id("div1")).findElement(By.linkText("top"));
```

NoSuchElementFoundException

The `findElement()` and `FindElements()` methods throw up the
`NoSuchElementFoundException` exception when they fail to find the desired
element using the specified locator strategy.

See also

▶   The *Locating elements using findElements method* recipe

Locating elements using findElements method

Selenium WebDriver provides the `findElements()` method, which enables the acquisition
of a list of elements matching the specified search criteria. This method is useful when we
want to work with a group of similar elements. For example, we can get all the links displayed
on a page or get rows from a table, and so on.

In this recipe, we will get all the links and print their targets by using the `findElements()`
method.

How to do it...

Let's create a test which will get all the links from a page and verify the count of links and
print target for each link as follows:

```java
@Test
public void testFindElements()
{
    //Get all the links displayed on Page
    List<WebElement> links = driver.findElements(By.tagName("a"));

    //Verify there are four links displayed on the page
    assertEquals(4, links.size());

    //Iterate though the list of links and print
    //target for each link
    for(WebElement link : links)
        System.out.println(link.getAttribute("href"));

}
```

How it works...

The `findElements()` method returns all the elements matching with the locator specified as a list of `WebElements`. In Java, we can use the `List` class to create an instance of list of `WebElements`.

```
List<WebElement> links = driver.findElements(By.tagName("a"));
```

The `size()` method of the `List` class will tell us how many elements are there in the list.

```
assertEquals(4, links.size());
```

We can iterate using this list in the following way, getting a link and printing its target value:

```
for(WebElement link : links)
    System.out.println(link.getAttribute("href"));
```

See also

> ▶ The *Locating an element using the findElement method* recipe

Locating links

Selenium WebDriver provides multiple ways to locate links. You can locate a link either by its text or by partial text.

Locating links with partial text comes in handy when links have dynamic text. In this recipe, we will see how to use these methods to locate the links on page.

How to do it...

Let's create a sample test to see how locating links work in Selenium WebDriver with the following options.

Finding a link by its text

Selenium WebDriver's `By` class provides the `linkText()` method to locate links using the text displayed for the link. In the following example, we will locate the GMail link:

```
WebElement gmailLink = driver.findElement(By.linkText("GMail"));
assertEquals("http://mail.google.com/",
    gmailLink.getAttribute("href"));
```

Finding a link by partial text

Selenium WebDriver's `By` class also provides a method to locate links using partial text. This method is useful where developers create links with dynamic text. In this example, a link is provided to open inbox. This link also displays the number of new e-mails which may change dynamically. Here we can use the `partialLinkText()` method to locate the link using a fixed or known portion of the link text, in this case it would be inbox.

```
WebElement inboxLink =
    driver.findElement(By.partialLinkText("Inbox"));
System.out.println(inboxLink.getText());
```

How it works...

The `linkText` and `partialLinkText` locator methods query the driver for all the links that meet the specified text and returns the matching link(s).

There's more...

You can also locate links using `id`, `name`, or `class` attributes if developers have provided these attributes.

 Locating elements based on text can cause issues while testing applications in multiple locales. Using parameterized text locator value could work in such applications.

See also

- ▶ The *Locating an element using the findElement method* recipe
- ▶ The *Locating elements using findElements method* recipe

Locating elements by tag name

Selenium WebDriver's `By` class provides a `tagName()` method to find elements by their HTML tag name. This is similar to the `getElementsByTagName()` DOM method in JavaScript.

This comes in handy when you want to locate elements using their tag name. For example, locating all `<tr>` tags in a table and so on.

In this recipe, we will briefly see how to use the `tagName` locator method.

How to do it...

Let's assume you have a single button element on a page. You can locate this button by using its tag in the following way:

```
WebElement loginButton = driver.findElement(By.tagName("button"));
loginButton.click();
```

Take another example where we want to count how many rows are displayed in `<table>`. We can do this in the following way:

```
WebElement table = driver.findElement(By.id("summaryTable"));
List<WebElement> rows = table.findElements(By.tagName("tr"));
assertEquals(10, rows.size());
```

How it works...

The `tagName` locator method queries the DOM and returns a list of matching elements for the specified tag name. This method may not be reliable while locating individual elements and the page might have multiple instances of these elements.

See also

▶ The *Locating elements using findElements method* recipe

Locating elements using CSS selectors

Cascading Style Sheets (**CSS**) is a style sheet language used for describing the presentation semantics (the look and formatting) of a document written in a markup language such as HTML or XML.

Major browsers implement CSS parsing engines for formatting or styling the pages using CSS syntax. CSS was introduced to keep the presentation information separate from the markup or content. For more information on CSS and CSS selectors, visit `http://en.wikipedia.org/wiki/Cascading_Style_Sheets`.

In CSS, pattern-matching rules determine which style should be applied to elements in the DOM. These patterns, called selectors, may range from simple element names to rich contextual patterns. If all conditions in the pattern are true for a certain element, the selector matches the element and the browser applies the defined style in CSS syntax.

Selenium WebDriver uses same principles of CSS selectors to locate elements in DOM. This is a much faster and more reliable way to locate the elements when compared with XPaths.

In this recipe, we will explore some basic CSS selectors and then later on we will dive into advanced CSS selectors.

How to do it...

Let's explore some basic CSS selectors that can be used in Selenium WebDriver. Selenium WebDriver's By class provides the cssSelector() method for locating elements using CSS selectors.

Finding elements with absolute path

CSS absolute paths refer to the very specific location of the element considering its complete hierarchy in the DOM. Here is an example where the **Username Input** field is located using the absolute path. While providing absolute path, a space is given between the elements.

```
WebElement userName = driver.findElement(By.cssSelector("html body
    div div form input"));
```

You can also use the previous selector in the following way by describing the direct parent to child relationships with > separator:

```
WebElement userName = driver.findElement(By.cssSelector("html >
    body > div > div > form > input"));
```

However, this strategy has limitations as it depends on the structure or hierarchy of the elements on a page. If this changes, the locator will fail to find the element.

Finding elements with relative path

With relative path we can locate an element directly, irrespective of its location in the DOM. For example, we can locate the **Username Input** field in the following way, assuming it is the first <input> element in the DOM:

```
WebElement userName = driver.findElement(By.cssSelector("input"));
```

The following CSS selectors use the Class and ID attributes to locate the elements using relative paths. This is same as the className() and id() locator methods. However, there is another strategy where we can use any other attribute of the element that is not covered in the By class.

Finding elements using the Class selector

While finding elements using the CSS selector, we can use the Class attribute to locate an element. This can be done by specifying the type of HTML tag, then adding a dot followed by the value of the class attribute in the following way:

```
WebElement loginButton =
    driver.findElement(By.cssSelector("input.login"));
```

This will find the **Login** button's `<input>` tag whose Class attribute is `login`.

There is also a shortcut where you can put a . and class attribute value and ignore the HTML tag. However, this will return all the elements with class as `login` and the test may not return the correct element.

```
WebElement loginButton = driver.findElement(By.cssSelector(".login"));
```

This method is similar to the `className()` locator method.

Finding elements using ID selector

We can locate the element using the IDs assigned to elements. This can be done by specifying the type of HTML tag, then entering a hash followed by the value of the Class attribute, as shown:

```
WebElement userName =
    driver.findElement(By.cssSelector("input#username"));
```

This will return the username `<input>` element using its `id` attribute.

There is also a shortcut where you can enter # and a class attribute value and ignore the HTML tag. However, this will return all the elements with the `id` set as `username` and the test may not return the correct element. This has to be used very carefully.

```
WebElement userName =
    driver.findElement(By.cssSelector("#username"));
```

This method is similar to the `id` locator strategy.

Finding elements using attributes selector

Apart from the `class` and `id` attributes, CSS selectors also enable the location of elements using other attributes of the element. In the following example, the Name attribute is used to locate an `<input>` element.

```
WebElement userName =
    driver.findElement(By.cssSelector("input[name=username]"));
```

Using the `name` attribute to locate an element is similar to the `name()` locator method of the By class.

Let's use some other attribute to locate an element. In the following example, the `<img>` element is located by using its `alt` attribute.

```
WebElement previousButton =
    driver.findElement(By.cssSelector("img[alt='Previous']"));
```

You might come across situations where one attribute may not be sufficient to locate an element and you need to combine additional attributes for a precise match. In the following example, multiple attributes are used to locate the **Login** button's `<input>` element:

```
WebElement previousButton = driver.findElement(By.cssSelector("input[t
ype='submit'][value='Login']"));
```

Finding elements using Attributes Name Selector

This strategy is a bit different from the earlier strategy where we want to locate elements based on only the specific attribute defined for them but not attribute values. For example, we want to lookup all the `<img>` elements which have `alt` attribute specified.

```
List<WebElement> imagesWithAlt =
    driver.findElements(By.cssSelector("img[alt]"));
```

A Boolean `not()` pseudo-class can also be used to locate elements not matching the specified criteria. For example, to locate all the `<img>` elements that do not have the `alt` attribute, the following method can be used:

```
List<WebElement> imagesWithoutAlt =
    driver.findElements(By.cssSelector("img:not([alt])"));
```

Performing partial match on attribute values

CSS selector provides a way to locate elements matching partial attribute values. This is very useful for testing applications where attribute values are dynamically assigned and change every time a page is requested. For example, ASP.NET applications exhibit this kind of behavior, where IDs are generated dynamically. The following table explains the use of CSS partial match syntax:

Syntax	Example	Description
`^=`	`input[id^='ctrl']`	Starting with:
		For example, if the ID of an element is `ctrl_12`, this will locate and return elements with `ctrl` at the beginning of the ID.
`$=`	`input[id$='_userName']`	Ending with:
		For example, if the ID for an element is `a_1_userName`, this will locate and return elements with `_userName` at the end of the ID.
`*=`	`Input[id*='userName']`	Containing:
		For example, if the ID of an element is `panel_login_userName_textfield`, this will use the `userName` part in the middle to match and locate the element.

How it works...

CSS selector is a pattern and the part of a CSS rule that matches a set of elements in an HTML or XML document.

The majority of browsers support CSS parsing for applying styles to these elements. Selenium WebDriver uses CSS parsing engine to locate the elements on a page. CSS selectors provide various methods, rules, and patterns to locate the element from a page. This is also a more reliable and fast method when compared with XPath locators.

Using CSS selector, the test can locate elements in multiple ways using Class, ID, attribute values, and text contents as described in this recipe.

See also

▸   The *Locating elements using advanced CSS selectors* recipe

Locating elements using XPath

XPath, the XML path language, is a query language for selecting nodes from an XML document. All the major browsers support XPath as HTML pages are represented as XHTML documents in DOM.

The XPath language is based on a tree representation of the XML document and provides the ability to navigate around the tree, selecting nodes using a variety of criteria.

Selenium WebDriver supports XPath for locating elements using XPath expressions or queries.

Locating elements with XPath works very well with a lot of flexibility. However, this is the least preferable locator strategy due its slow performance.

One of the important differences between XPath and CSS is, with XPath we can search elements backward or forward in the DOM hierarchy while CSS works only in a forward direction. This means that with XPath we can locate a parent element using a child element.

In this recipe, we will explore some basic XPath queries to locate elements and then examine some advanced XPath queries.

How to do it...

Let's explore some basic XPath expressions that can be used in Selenium WebDriver. Selenium WebDriver provides the xpath() method for locating elements using XPaths.

Finding elements with absolute path

Similar to CSS absolute paths, XPath absolute paths refer to the very specific location of the element, considering its complete hierarchy in the DOM. Here is an example where **Username Input** field is located using the absolute path. While providing absolute path a space is given between the elements.

```
WebElement userName =
    driver.findElement(By.xpath("html/body/div/div/form/input"));
```

However, this strategy has limitations as it depends on the structure or hierarchy of the elements on a page. If this changes, the locator will fail to get the element.

Finding elements with relative path

With relative path, we can locate an element directly irrespective of its location in the DOM. For example, we can locate the **Username Input** field in the following way, assuming it is the first <input> element in the DOM:

```
WebElement userName = driver.findElement(By.xpath("//input"));
```

Finding elements using index

In the previous example, the XPath query will return the first <input> element that it finds in the DOM. There could be multiple elements matching the specified XPath query. If the element is not the first element, we can also locate the element by using its index in DOM. For example in our login form, we can locate the **Password** field which is the second <input> element on the page in the following way:

```
WebElement userName = driver.findElement(By.xpath("//input[2]"));
```

Finding elements using attributes values with XPath

Similar to CSS, we can also locate elements using their attribute values in XPath. In the following example, the **Username** field is located using the ID attribute:

```
WebElement userName =
    driver.findElement(By.xpath("//input[@id='username']"));
```

Here is another example where the image is located using the alt attribute:

```
WebElement previousButton =
    driver.findElement(By.xpath("img[@alt='Previous']"));
```

You might come across situations where one attribute may not be sufficient to locate an element and you need combined additional attributes for a precise match. In the following example, multiple attributes are used to locate the <input> element for the **Login** button:

```
WebElement previousButton =
    driver.findElement(By.xpath
    ("//input[@type='submit'][@value='Login']"));
```

The same result can be achieved by using XPath and operator.

```
WebElement previousButton = driver.findElement
    (By.xpath("//input[@type='submit'and @value='Login']"));
```

In the following example, either of the attributes is used to locate the elements using XPath or operator:

```
WebElement previousButton = driver.findElement
    (By.xpath("//input[@type='submit'or @value='Login']"));
```

Finding elements using attributes with XPath

This strategy is a bit different from the earlier strategy where we want to locate elements based only on the specific attribute defined for them but not attribute values. For example, we want to lookup all the <img> elements that have the alt attribute specified.

```
List<WebElement> imagesWithAlt = driver.findElements
    (By.xpath ("img[@alt]"));
```

Performing partial match on attribute values

Similar to CSS selector, XPath also provides a way to locate elements matching partial attribute values using XPath functions. This is very useful for testing applications where attributes values are dynamically assigned and change every time a page is requested. For example, ASP.NET applications exhibit this kind of behavior where IDs are generated dynamically. The following table explains the use of these XPath functions:

Syntax	Example	Description
starts-with()	input[starts-with(@ id,'ctrl')]	Starting with:
		For example, if the ID of an element is ctrl_12, this will locate and return elements with ctrl at the beginning of the ID.
ends-with()	input[ends-with(@id, '_ userName')]	Ending with:
		For example, if the ID of an element is a_1_userName, this will locate and return elements with _userName at the end of the ID.
contains()	Input[contains(@ id,'userName')]	Containing:
		For example, if the ID for an element is panel_login_userName_textfield, this will use the userName part in the middle to match and locate the element.

Matching any attribute using a value

XPath matches the attribute for all the elements for a specified value and returns the element. For example, in the following XPath query, `'userName'` is specified. XPath will check all the elements and their attributes to see if they have this value and return the matching element.

```
WebElement userName =
    driver.findElement(By.xpath("//input[@*='username']"));
```

Locating elements with XPath axis

XPath axes help to locate elements based on the element's relationship with other elements in a document. Here are some examples for some common XPath axes used to locate elements from a `<table>` element. This can be applied to any other element structure from your application.

Product	Price	Qty
Product 1	$100	12
Product 2	$150	5

Here is the graphical representation of the HTML elements:

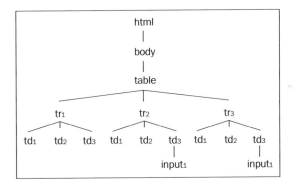

Axis	Description	Example	Result
ancestor	Selects all ancestors (parent, grandparent, and so on) of the current node.	`//td[text()='Product 1']/ancestor::table`	This will get the table element.
descendant	Selects all descendants (children, grandchildren, and so on) of the current node.	`/table/ descendant::td/input`	This will get the input element from the third column of the second row from the table.
following	Selects everything in the document after the closing tag of the current node.	`//td[text()='Product 1']/following::tr`	This will get the second row from the table.
following-sibling	Selects all siblings after the current node.	`//td[text()='Product 1']/following-sibling::td`	This will get the second column from the second row immediately after the column that has `Product 1` as the text value.
preceding	Selects all nodes that appear before the current node in the document, except ancestors, attribute nodes, and namespace nodes.	`//td[text()='$150']/ preceding::tr`	This will get the header row.
preceding-sibling	Selects all siblings before the current node.	`//td[text()='$150']/ preceding-sibling::td`	This will get the first column of third row from the table.

You can find more about XPath axis at `http://www.w3schools.com/xpath/xpath_axes.asp`.

How it works...

XPath is a powerful language for querying and processing DOM in browsers. XPath is used to navigate through elements and attributes in a DOM. XPath provides rules, function, and syntax to locate the elements.

The majority of browsers support XPath and Selenium WebDriver provides the ability to locate elements using the XPath language.

Using the `xpath()` method of the `By` class we can locate elements using XPath syntax. XPath is little slower than the CSS selectors as XPath provides the ability to search elements bi-directionally. You can search for the parent element if you know the child or you can locate a child element using its relationship with the parent and siblings.

Using XPath, a test can locate elements in multiple ways based on the structure of the document, attribute values, text contents and so on, as described in this recipe.

Locating elements using text

While testing web applications, you will also encounter situations where developers don't assign any attributes to the elements and it becomes difficult to locate elements.

Using the CSS selectors or XPath, we can locate elements based on their text contents. In this recipe, we will explore methods to locate elements using text values.

How to do it...

For locating elements by using their text contents, CSS selectors and XPath provide methods to find text within the elements. If an element contains specific text, this will return the element back to the test.

Using CSS selector Contains Pseudo-Class

CSS selectors provide the `contains()` pseudo-class which can be used to see if an element contains the specified text. For example, a test wants to locate the cell of a table using its contents in the following way:

```
WebElement cell =
    driver.findElement(By.cssSelector("td:contains('Item 1')"));
```

The `contains()` pseudo-class accepts the text to be searched as a parameter. It then checks all the `<td>` elements in DOM for the specified text.

 The `contains()` pseudo-class may not work with browsers that don't natively support CSS selectors. Also, it has been deprecated from CSS3 specification.

As an alternative for `contains()` pseudo-class, you can use the `innerText` attribute (does not work with Firefox) or `textContent` attribute (for Firefox) in the following ways:

```
WebElement cell =
    driver.findElement(By.cssSelector("td[innerText='Item 1']"));
```

Or

```
WebElement cell = driver.findElement
    (By.cssSelector("td[textContent='Item 1']"));
```

You can also use jQuery selectors which support the `contains()` pseudo-class.

Using XPath text function

XPath provides the `text()` function which can be used to see if an element contains the specified text in the following way:

```
WebElement cell = driver.findElement
    (By.xpath("//td[contains(text(),'Item 1')]"));
```

Here we are using the `contains` function along with the `text()` function. The `text()` function returns the complete text from the element and the `contains()` function checks for the specific value that we have mentioned.

Finding elements using exact text value in XPath

With XPath, elements can be located by exact text value in the following way:

```
WebElement cell = driver.findElement
    (By.xpath("//td[.='Item 1']"));
```

This will locate the `<td>` element matching with exact text.

How it works...

CSS selector and XPath provide methods with which to locate elements based on their text contents. This approach comes in handy when *elements don't have enough attributes or when no other strategies work when attempting to locate these elements.*

For locating elements using their text, both CSS selector and XPath search through the DOM for elements that have the specified text value and return the matching element(s).

Locating elements using advanced CSS selectors

We saw some basic CSS selectors in earlier recipes. In this recipe, we will explore some advanced CSS selectors for locating elements.

How to do it...

In the *Locating elements using CSS selectors* recipe, we explored some basic CSS selectors. Let's explore advanced CSS selectors such as adjacent sibling combinators and pseudo-classes as described in the following sections.

Finding child elements

CSS selectors provide various ways to locate child elements from parent elements.

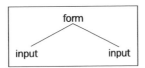

For example, to locate the **Username Field** in the login form, we can use the following selector. Here, > is used denote the parent and child relationship.

```
WebElement userName =
    driver.findElement(By.cssSelector("form#loginForm > input"));
```

Similarly the nth-child() method can be used in the following way:

```
WebElement userName = driver.findElement
    (By.cssSelector("form#loginForm :nth-child(2)"));
```

Here, the second element in <form> is the **Username** field. The following table shows some of the structural pseudo-classes used to locate child elements:

Pseudo-class	Example	Description
:first-child	form#loginForm :first-child	This will locate the first element under the form, that is, the label for username.
:last-child	form#loginForm :last-child	This will locate the last element under the form, that is, the **Login** button.
:nth-child(2)	form#loginForm :nth-child(2)	This will locate the second child element under the form, that is, the **Username** field.

Finding sibling elements

With CSS selector, we can locate sibling elements using the + operator. For example, on the sample page the <p> element with Description for Product 2 text is selected in the following way:

```
WebElement productDescription =
    driver.findElement(By.cssSelector("div#top5 > p + p"));
```

In this example, the first child of div#top5 will be <p> with Description for Product 1 and its immediate sibling will be Description for Product 2. Here are few more adjacent sibling combinators for locating siblings:

p + p	div#top5 > p + p	Immediately following sibling. This will locate Description for Product 2.
p + * + p	div#top5 > p + * + p	Following sibling with one intermediary. This will locate Description for Product 3.

Using user action pseudo-classes

Using the user action :focus pseudo-class, we can locate the element which has current input focus in the following way:

```
WebElement productDescription =
    driver.findElement(By.cssSelector("input:focus"));
```

This will locate any element that currently has the input focus. You can also locate elements using :hover and :active pseudo-classes.

Using UI state pseudo-classes

Using UI state pseudo-classes, we can locate elements for various states such as control is enabled, disabled, and checked. The following table describes these in detail:

Pseudo-class	Example	Description
:enabled	input:enabled	This will locate all the elements that are enabled for user input.
:disabled	input:enabled	This will locate all the elements that are disabled for user input.
:checked	input:checked	This will locate all the elements (checkboxes) that are checked.

How it works...

Apart from the basic CSS selectors, you can also use various advanced CSS selector methods such as pseudo-classes or adjacent sibling combinators to locate the elements with Selenium WebDriver API.

Visit http://www.w3schools.com/cssref/css_selectors.asp for an exhaustive list of CSS selectors and their usage.

See also

▶ The *Locating elements using CSS selectors* recipe

Using jQuery selectors

jQuery selectors is one of the important feature of the jQuery library. jQuery Selectors are based on CSS1-3 selectors along with some additional selectors. These selectors use the familiar CSS Selector syntax to allow developers to quickly and easily identify page elements to operate upon with the jQuery library methods. Similar to CSS selectors, these selectors allow us to locate and manipulate HTML elements as a single element or list of elements.

jQuery selectors can be used where CSS selectors are not supported natively by the browsers.

In this recipe, we will explore in brief how to use jQuery selectors with Selenium WebDriver.

How to do it...

Let's create a test which checks that specified checkboxes are selected when page is displayed, as follows:

```
@SuppressWarnings("unchecked")
@Test
public void testDefaultSelectedCheckbox() {

    WebDriver driver = new ChromeDriver();
    driver.get("http://dl.dropbox.com/u/55228056/Locators.html");

    //Expected list of selected Checkbox
    List<String> checked =  Arrays.asList(new
        String[]{"user1_admin", "user3_browser"});

    //Create an instance of JavaScript Executor from driver
    JavascriptExecutor js = (JavascriptExecutor) driver;

    //Locate all the Checkbox which are checked by calling jQuery
    //find() method.
    //find() method returns elements in array
    List<WebElement> elements = (List<WebElement>)
        js.executeScript("return jQuery.find(':checked')");

    //Verify two Checkbox are selected
```

```
        assertEquals(elements.size(),2);

        //Verify correct Checkbox are selected
        for (WebElement element : elements)
            assertTrue(checked.contains(element.getAttribute("id")));

        driver.close();
    }
```

How it works...

Selenium WebDriver can be enhanced by jQuery selectors using the jQuery API. However, we need to make sure that the page has jQuery API loaded before using these selectors. The jQuery API provides the `find()` function through which we can search for elements. We need to use the `JavaScriptExecutor` class to use jQuery's `find()` method. In this example, we will locate all the selected checkboxes on a page by calling the `find()` method.

```
    //Locate all the Checkbox which are checked by calling jQuery
        find() method.
    //find() method returns elements in array
    List<WebElement> elements = (List<WebElement>)
        js.executeScript("return jQuery.find(':checked')");
```

The `find()` method returns a WebElement or list of WebElements matching the selector criteria back to the test. For more details and a list of available jQuery selectors, please visit `http://api.jquery.com/category/selectors/`.

You can also use the CSS Selectors described in this chapter with the jQuery `find()` method.

There's more...

For using jQuery selectors, the page under test should have jQuery library loaded. If your application does not use jQuery, you can load the jQuery on the page by attaching jQuery library at runtime with the following utility methods:

```
    private void injectjQueryIfNeeded() {
        if (!jQueryLoaded())
            injectjQuery();
    }

    public Boolean jQueryLoaded() {
        Boolean loaded;
        try {
            loaded = (Boolean) driver.executeScript("return
                jQuery()!=null");
```

```
    } catch (WebDriverException e) {
        loaded = false;
    }
    return loaded;
}

public void injectjQuery() {
    driver.executeScript(" var headID =
        document.getElementsByTagName(\"head\")[0];"
    + "var newScript = document.createElement('script');"
    + "newScript.type = 'text/javascript';"
    + "newScript.src = 'http://ajax.googleapis.com/
        ajax/libs/jquery/1.7.2/jquery.min.js';"
    + "headID.appendChild(newScript);");
}
```

The `injectjQueryIfNeeded()` method will internally call the `jQueryLoaded()` method to see if the jQuery object is available on the page. If the page does not have the jQuery object defined, the `injectjQueryIfNeeded()` method will call the `injectjQuery()` method to attach the jQuery library to the page header at runtime. This is done by adding a `<script>` element, which refers the Google CDN (Content Delivery Network) for jQuery library file, to the page. You may change the version used in this example to the latest version of the jQuery library.

Locating table rows and cells

While working with tables, we can locate the rows and cells effectively by using a set of the `By` class methods.

In this recipe, we will see how to locate rows and columns in table.

How to do it...

Let's create a simple test that will print data from a table, locating its rows and columns as follows:

```
@Test
public void testTable() {

    WebElement simpleTable = driver.findElement(By.id("items"));

    //Get all rows
    List<WebElement> rows =
        simpleTable.findElements(By.tagName("tr"));
    assertEquals(3, rows.size());
```

```
            //Print data from each row
            for (WebElement row : rows) {
                List<WebElement> cols =
                    row.findElements(By.tagName("td"));
                for (WebElement col : cols) {
                    System.out.print(col.getText() + "\t");
                }
                System.out.println();
            }
        }
```

How it works...

A table in HTML is a collection of `<tr>` and `<td>` elements for rows and cells, respectively. In the sample test, the table can be located as a WebElement using its ID as follows:

```
WebElement simpleTable = driver.findElement(By.id("items"));
```

To get all the rows from a table, the `findElements()` method is called on `simpleTable` and the `tagName` strategy is used to get all `<tr>` elements. These are rows of a table.

```
List<WebElement> rows =
    simpleTable.findElements(By.tagName("tr"));
```

Each `<tr>` element then holds the `<td>` elements, which are the columns or cells of the table. The test iterates through the row and columns to print the data in the following way:

```
//Print data from each row
for (WebElement row : rows) {
    List<WebElement> cols = row.findElements(By.tagName("td"));
    for (WebElement col : cols) {
        System.out.print(col.getText() + "\t");
    }
    System.out.println();
}
```

This method comes in handy when you have a test that needs to verify data in a table.

There's more...

We can also use CSS selectors or XPath for locating table rows and cells using index matching. In the following example, CSS selector is used to locate the first cell of the second row in the table:

```
WebElement cell = driver.findElement
    (By.cssSelector("table#items tbody tr:nth-child(2) td"));
```

Similarly using XPath, it can be done in the following way:

```
WebElement cell = driver.findElement
    (By.xpath("//table[@id='items']/tbody/tr[2]/td"));
```

See also

▶ The *Locating child elements in a table* recipe

▶ The *Locating elements using FindElements method* recipe

Locating child elements in a table

Working with simple tables is relatively easy. However, you will come across complex tables where other than data, table cells have child elements for user interaction. For example, in an e-commerce application when you open the shopping cart page, it looks a simple table but inside there are many complex elements.

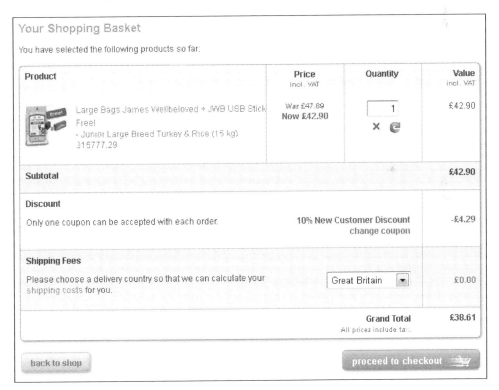

Furthermore, these elements are dynamically created based on user actions and may have attribute values generated at runtime. Locating these elements may become a challenging task.

In this recipe, we will explore strategies to locate child elements within tables using CSS and XPath.

How to do it...

Here is sample table that lists users of a system and their details including what access rights are assigned to these users. A test needs to select a given checkbox and see if the selected access is granted to the user.

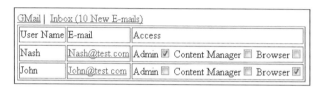

If we look at the code for this table, each record or row has the following code:

```
<tr>
    <td>Nash</td>
    <td><a href="mailto:nash@test.com">Nash@test.com</a></td>
    <td>
        <div>
            <label for="user128_admin">Admin</label>
            <input type="checkbox" id="user128_admin"
                checked="true"/>
            <label for="user128_cm">Content Manager</label>
            <input type="checkbox" id="user128_cm"/>
            <label for="user128_browser">Browser</label>
            <input type="checkbox" id="user128_browser"/>
        </div>
    </td>
</tr>
```

The checkbox has dynamic IDs that we cannot correlate to a user. However, we can deal with such issues by using CSS selectors or XPath. In this example, we want to grant user Nash with admin access. This can be done using CSS selectors in the following way:

```
WebElement adminCheckBox = driver.findElement
    (By.cssSelector("td:contains('Nash')+td+td>div>label:contains
    ('Admin')+input"));

adminCheckBox.click();
```

We can also use XPath in the following way:

```
WebElement adminCheckBox = driver.findElement
    (By.xpath("//td[contains(text(),'Nash')]/following-
    sibling::td/descendant::div/label
    [contains(text(),'Admin')]/following-sibling::input"));


adminCheckBox.click();
```

How it works...

Parent, child, and sibling in CSS or XPath axes become a great help in correlating users with roles and developing a generic locator strategy for this feature. In simple terms, these strategies help to locate elements based on the element's relationship with other elements in a document.

Coming back to the problem, first we need to find a unique way to identify a user in the table. For this, we will locate a cell which contains username. We will locate this cell using its inner text in the following way:

CSS	XPath
`td:contains('Nash')`	`//td[contains(text(),'Nash')]`

Next, we need to find the cell which contains the child elements. This is the second cell from the cell containing username.

CSS	XPath
`td:contains('Nash')+td+td`	`//td[contains(text(),'Nash')]/` `following-sibling::td/`

In the next step, we need to locate the label with the correct option. The next sibling of this label will be the checkbox we are looking for.

CSS	XPath

`td:contains('Nash')+td+td>div>lab`
`el:contains('Admin')+input`
	`//td[contains(text(),'Nash')]/`
	`following-sibling::td/`
	`descendant::div/`
	`label[contains(text(),'Admin')]/`
	`following-sibling::input`

See also

▶   The *Locating elements using CSS selectors* recipe

▶   The *Locating elements using advanced CSS selectors* recipe

▶   The *Locating elements using XPath* recipe

2
Working with Selenium API

In this chapter, we will cover:

- ▶ Checking an element's text
- ▶ Checking an element's attribute values
- ▶ Checking an element's CSS values
- ▶ Using Advanced User Interactions API for mouse and keyboard events
- ▶ Performing double-click on an element
- ▶ Performing drag-and-drop operations
- ▶ Executing JavaScript code
- ▶ Capturing screenshots with Selenium WebDriver
- ▶ Capturing screenshots with RemoteWebDriver/Grid
- ▶ Maximizing the browser window
- ▶ Automating dropdowns and lists
- ▶ Checking options in dropdowns and lists
- ▶ Checking selected options in dropdowns and lists
- ▶ Automating radio buttons and radio groups
- ▶ Automating checkboxes
- ▶ Controlling a Windows process
- ▶ Reading a Windows registry value from Selenium WebDriver
- ▶ Modifying a Windows registry value from Selenium WebDriver

Introduction

Selenium WebDriver implements a very comprehensive API for working with web elements, Advanced User Interactions, executing JavaScript code, and support for various types of controls such as List, Dropdown, Radio Button, and Checkbox.

In this chapter, we will explore how these APIs can be used to build simple to complex test steps. This chapter will also help in overcoming some common issues while building tests with Selenium WebDriver. The chapter examples are created with Selenium WebDriver Java bindings. The sample code for this chapter contains some of these recipes implemented with C#, Ruby, and Python.

Checking an element's text

While testing a web application, we need to verify that elements are displaying correct values or text on the page. Selenium WebDriver's WebElement API provides various ways to retrieve and verify text. Sometimes, we need to retrieve text or value from an element into a variable at runtime and later use it at some other place in the test flow.

In this recipe, we will retrieve and verify text from an element by using the WebElement class' `getText()` method.

How to do it...

Here, we will create a test that locates an element and then retrieves text from the element in a string variable. We will verify contents of this string for correctness.

```
@Test
public void testElementText()
{
  //Get the message Element
  WebElement message = driver.findElement(By.id("message"));

  //Get the message elements text
  String messageText = message.getText();

  //Verify message element's text displays "Click on me and my
    //color will change"
  assertEquals("Click on me and my color will change",
    messageText);

  //Get the area Element
```

```
WebElement area = driver.findElement(By.id("area"));

//Verify area element's text displays "Div's Text\nSpan's Text"
assertEquals("Div's Text\nSpan's Text",area.getText());
}
```

How it works...

The WebElement class' getText() method returns value of the innerText attribute
of the element.

```
String messageText = message.getText();
```

If the element has child elements, the value of the innerText attribute of child elements
will also be returned along with parent element. In the following example, we have a <span>
element within a <div> element. While we are retrieving the innerText from <div>
element it also appends innerText of <span> element.

```
//Get the area Element
WebElement area = driver.findElement(By.id("area"));

//Verify element's text displays "Div's Text\nSpan's Text"
assertEquals("Div's Text\nSpan's Text",area.getText());
```

There's more...

We can also perform a partial match using Java String API methods such as contains(),
startsWith(), and endsWith(). We can use these methods in the following way:

```
assertTrue(messageText.contains("color"));
assertTrue(messageText.startsWith("Click on"));
assertTrue(messageText.endsWith("will change"));
```

Checking an element's attribute values

Developers configure various attributes of elements displayed on the web page during design or
at runtime to control the behavior or style of elements when they are displayed in the browser.
For example, the <input> element can be set to read-only by setting the readonly attribute.

There will be tests that need to verify that element attributes are set correctly. We can
retrieve and verify an element's attribute by using the getAttribute() method of the
WebElement class.

In this recipe, will check the attribute value of an element by using the getAttribute()
method.

How to do it...

Create a test which locates an element and check its attribute value as follows:

```
@Test
public void testElementAttribute()
{
  WebElement message = driver.findElement(By.id("message"));
  assertEquals("justify",message.getAttribute("align"));
}
```

How it works...

By passing the name of the attribute to the `getAttribute()` method, it returns the value of the attribute back to the test. In this example, we are checking that the `align` attribute of the `<p>` element is set to justify.

```
assertEquals("justify",message.getAttribute("align"));
```

Checking an element's CSS values

Various styles are applied on elements displayed in a web application, so they look neat and become more usable. Developers add these styles using CSS (also known as Cascading Style Sheets). There may be tests that need to verify that correct styles have been applied to the elements. This can be done using `WebElement` class's `getCSSValue()` method, which returns the value of a specified style attribute.

In this recipe, we will use the `getCSSValue()` function to check the style attribute defined for an element.

How to do it...

Let's create a test which reads the CSS `width` attribute and verifies the value.

```
@Test
public void testElementStyle()
{
  WebElement message = driver.findElement(By.id("message"));
  String width = message.getCssValue("width");
  assertEquals("150px",width);
}
```

How it works...

By passing the name of CSS attribute to the `getCSSValue()` method, it returns the value of the CSS attribute. In this example, we are checking that the width attribute of the `<div>` element is set to `150px`.

```
WebElement message = driver.findElement(By.id("message"));
String width = message.getCssValue("width");
assertEquals("150px",width);
```

See also

▶ The *Checking an element's attribute values* recipe

Using Advanced User Interactions API for mouse and keyboard events

The Selenium WebDriver's Advanced User Interactions API allows us to perform operations from keyboard events and simple mouse events to complex events such as dragging-and-dropping, holding a key and then performing mouse operations by using the `Actions` class, and building a complex chain of events exactly like a user doing these manually.

The `Actions` class implements the builder pattern to create a composite action containing a group of other actions.

In this recipe, we will use the `Actions` class to build a chain of events to select rows in a table.

How to do it...

Let's create a test to select the multiple rows from different positions in a table using the *Ctrl* key. We can select multiple rows by selecting the first row, then holding the *Ctrl* key, and then selecting another row and releasing the *Ctrl* key. This will select the desired rows from the table.

```
@Test
public void testRowSelectionUsingControlKey() {

    List<WebElement> tableRows = driver.findElements
      (By.xpath("//table[@class='iceDatTbl']/tbody/tr"));

    //Select second and fourth row from table using Control Key.
    //Row Index start at 0
    Actions builder = new Actions(driver);
```

```
builder.click(tableRows.get(1))
        .keyDown(Keys.CONTROL)
        .click(tableRows.get(3))
        .keyUp(Keys.CONTROL)
        .build().perform();

//Verify Selected Row table shows two rows selected
List<WebElement> rows = driver.findElements
    (By.xpath("//div[@class='icePnlGrp
    exampleBox']/table[@class='iceDatTbl']/tbody/tr"));
assertEquals(2,rows.size());
}
```

How it works...

We need to create an instance of the `Actions` class by passing the instance of `driver` class to the constructor in the following way:

```
Actions builder = new Actions(driver);
```

We will build a chain of events that we need to perform for selecting the rows. This will require performing a `click()` operation on the first row, then holding the *Ctrl* key using `keyDown()`, clicking on the end row, and then releasing the *Ctrl* key by calling `keyUp()`. The `Actions` class provides various methods to perform keyboard and mouse operations.

```
Actions builder = new Actions(driver);
builder.click(tableRows.get(1)).keyDown(Keys.CONTROL)
        .click(tableRows.get(3)).keyUp(Keys.CONTROL)
        .build().perform();
```

We can create a composite action that is ready to be performed by calling the `build()` method. Finally the test will perform this composite action by calling the `perform()` method of the `Actions` class.

The `Keys` class will represent all non-textual keys on the keyboard, for example Control Key, Shift Key, Function Keys, and so on. In the previous example, we used `keyDown(Keys. CONTROL)` to press and hold the *Ctrl* key until next operation is completed.

 Actions may not work properly for elements that are not visible or enabled. Before using these events, make sure that elements are visible and enabled.

See also

▶   The *Performing double-click on an element* recipe

Performing double-click on an element

There will be elements in a web application that need double-click events fired for performing some actions. For example, double-clicking on a row of a table will launch a new window. The Advanced User Interaction API provides a method to perform double-click.

In this recipe, we will use the `Actions` class to perform double-click operations.

How to do it...

Let's create a test that locates an element for which a double-click event is implemented. When we double-click on this element, it changes its color.

```
@Test
public void testDoubleClick() throws Exception
{
  WebDriver driver = new ChromeDriver();
  driver.get
     ("http://dl.dropbox.com/u/55228056/DoubleClickDemo.html");

  WebElement message = driver.findElement(By.id("message"));

  //Verify color is Blue
  assertEquals("rgb(0, 0, 255)",
    message.getCssValue("background-color").toString());

  Actions builder = new Actions(driver);
  builder.doubleClick(message).build().perform();

  //Verify Color is Yellow
  assertEquals("rgb(255, 255, 0)",
    message.getCssValue("background-color").toString());

  driver.close();
}
```

How it works...

For performing double-click on an element, `doubleClick()` method of the `Actions` class is called. For calling this method, we need to create an instance of `Actions` class as follows:

```
Actions builder = new Actions(driver);
```

The `doubleClick()` method needs the element on which the double-click event will be fired. We can call the `doubleClick()` method by passing the element as follows:

```
builder.doubleClick(message).build().perform();
```

See also

► The *Using Advanced User Interactions API for mouse and keyboard events* recipe

► The *Performing drag-and-drop operations* recipe

Performing drag-and-drop operations

Selenium WebDriver implements Selenium RC's `dragAndDrop` command using `Actions` class. As seen in earlier recipes the `Actions` class supports advanced user interactions such as firing various mouse and keyboard events. We can build simple or complex chains of events using this class.

In this recipe, we will use the `Actions` class to perform drag-and-drop operations.

How to do it...

Let's implement a test which will perform a drag-and-drop operation on a page using the `Actions` class.

```
@Test
public void testDragDrop() {

  driver.get
    ("http://dl.dropbox.com/u/55228056/DragDropDemo.html");

  WebElement source = driver.findElement(By.id("draggable"));
  WebElement target = driver.findElement(By.id("droppable"));

  Actions builder = new Actions(driver);
  builder.dragAndDrop(source, target).perform();
  try
  {
    assertEquals("Dropped!", target.getText());
  } catch (Error e) {
    verificationErrors.append(e.toString());
  }
}
```

How it works...

For dragging an element on to another element and dropping it, we need to locate these elements and pass them to the dragAndDrop() method of the Actions class. For calling this method, we need to create an instance of the Actions class in the following way:

```
Actions builder = new Actions(driver);
```

The dragAndDrop() method needs the source element and target element where the source element will be dragged-and-dropped. We can call the dragAndDrop() method in the following way:

```
builder.dragAndDrop(source, target).perform();
```

See also

▸ The *Using Advanced User Interactions API for mouse and keyboard events* recipe

▸ The *Performing double-click on an element* recipe

Executing JavaScript code

Selenium WebDriver API provides the ability to execute JavaScript code with the browser window. This is a very useful feature where tests need to interact with the page using JavaScript. Using this API, client-side JavaScript code can also be tested using Selenium WebDriver. Selenium WebDriver provides a JavascriptExecutor interface that can be used to execute arbitrary JavaScript code within the context of the browser.

In this recipe, we will explore how to use JavascriptExecutor for executing JavaScript code. This book has various other recipes where JavascriptExecutor has been used to perform some advanced operations that are not yet supported by the Selenium WebDriver.

How to do it...

Let's create a test that will call JavaScript code to return title and count of links (that is a count of Anchor tags) from a page. Returning a page title can also be done by calling the driver.getTitle() method.

```
@Test
public void testJavaScriptCalls() throws Exception
{
    WebDriver driver = new ChromeDriver();
    driver.get("http://www.google.com");
```

```
JavascriptExecutor js = (JavascriptExecutor) driver;

String title = (String) js.executeScript
  ("return document.title");
assertEquals("Google", title);

long links = (Long) js.executeScript
  ("var links = document.getElementsByTagName
  ('A'); return links.length");
assertEquals(42, links);

driver.close();
}
```

How it works...

By casting the WebDriver instance to a `JavascriptExecutor` interface we can execute the JavaScript code in Selenium WebDriver.

```
JavascriptExecutor js = (JavascriptExecutor) driver;
```

In the following example, a single line of JavaScript code is executed to return the title of the page displayed in the driver. The `JavascriptExecutor` interface provides the `executeScript()` method to which we need to pass the JavaScript code.

```
String title = (String) js.executeScript("return document.title");
```

 While returning values from the JavaScript code, we need to use the `return` keyword. Based on the type of return value, we need to cast the `executeScript()` method. For decimal values, `Double` can be used, for non-decimal numeric values `Long` can be used, and for Boolean values `Boolean` can be used. If JavaScript code is returning an HTML element, then `WebElement` can be used. For text values, `String` can be used. If a list of objects is returned, then any of the values will work based on type of objects. Otherwise, a null will be returned.

In the following example, we execute a multiline JavaScript code to retrieve count of links on a page:

```
long links = (Long) js.executeScript("var links =
  document.getElementsByTagName('A'); return links.length");
```

There's more...

Arguments can also be a passed to the JavaScript code being executed by using the `executeScript()` method. In the following example, we want to set the value of an element. A special `arguments` array will be used inside the JavaScript code.

```
js.executeScript("document.getElementByID('name').value =
    arguments[0]","John");
```

Capturing screenshots with Selenium WebDriver

Selenium WebDriver provides the `TakesScreenshot` interface for capturing a screenshot of a web page. This helps in test runs, showing exactly happened when an exception or error occurred during execution, and so on. We can also capture screenshots during verification of element state, values displayed, or state after an action is completed.

Capturing screenshots also helps in verification of layouts, field alignments, and so on where we compare screenshots taken during test execution with baseline images.

In this recipe, we will use the `TakesScreenshot` interface to capture a screenshot of the web page under test.

How to do it...

Let's create a test that will open our test application and take a screenshot of the page in PNG format.

```
@Test
public void testTakesScreenshot()
{
  try {
    File scrFile =
      ((TakesScreenshot)driver).getScreenshotAs(OutputType.FILE);
    FileUtils.copyFile(scrFile, new
      File("c:\\tmp\\main_page.png"));
  } catch (Exception e) {
    e.printStackTrace();
  }
}
```

How it works...

The `TakesScreenshot` interface provides the `getScreenshotAs()` method to capture a screenshot of the page displayed in the `driver` instance. In the following example, we specified `OutputType.FILE` as an argument to the `getScreenshotAs()` method, so that it will return the captured screenshot in a file:

```
File scrFile =
  ((TakesScreenshot)driver).getScreenshotAs(OutputType.FILE);
```

We can save the file object returned by the `getScreenshotAs()` method using the `copyFile()` method of the `FileUtils` class from the `org.apache.commons.io.FileUtils` class.

 The `TakesScreenshot` relies on the browser API for capturing the screenshots. The HtmlUnit Driver does not support the `TakesScreenshot` interface.

There's more...

The `OutputType` class provides multiple ways in which to output the screenshot data using the `getScreenshotAs()` method. In the previous example we saw a screenshot captured in a file. Screenshots can also be captured in a Base64 string format or in raw bytes. In the following example, a screenshot is captured as Base64 string:

```
String base64 =
  ((TakesScreenshot)driver).getScreenshotAs(OutputType.BASE64);
```

Capturing screenshots in C#

For capturing screenshots with .NET bindings, a similar ITakesScreenshot interface is available. In the following example, the `ITakesScreenshot` interface is used for capturing the screenshot using the `Screenshot` class:

```
IWebDriver driver = new FirefoxDriver();
driver.Navigate().GoToUrl("http://www.google.com");
Screenshot screenshot =
  ((ITakesScreenshot)driver).GetScreenshot();
screenshot.SaveAsFile("c:\\temp\\main_page.png",
  System.Drawing.Imaging.ImageFormat.Png);
```

The `Screenshot` class provides the `SaveAsFile()` method. We can specify the desired format using `System.Drawing.Imaging.ImageFormat`.

See also

▶ The *Capturing screenshots with RemoteWebDriver/Grid* recipe

▶ The *Capturing screenshots of elements in the Selenium WebDriver* recipe in *Chapter 6, Extending Selenium*

▶ The *Comparing images in Selenium* recipe in *Chapter 6, Extending Selenium*

Capturing screenshots with RemoteWebDriver/Grid

While running tests with RemoteWebDriver or Grid it is not possible to take the screenshots, as the `TakesScreenshot` interface is not implemented in RemoteWebDriver.

However, we can use the `Augmenter` class which adds the `TakesScreenshot` interface to the remote driver instance.

In this recipe, we will use the `Augmenter` class to capture a screenshot from RemoteWebDriver.

Getting ready

Create a test which uses RemoteWebDriver.

How to do it...

Add the following code to the test using RemoteWebDriver:

```
driver = new Augmenter().augment(driver);
File scrFile =
   ((TakesScreenshot)driver).getScreenshotAs(OutputType.FILE);
FileUtils.copyFile(scrFile, new File("c:\\tmp\\screenshot.png"));
```

How it works...

The `Augmenter` class enhances the RemoteWebDriver by adding to it various interfaces including the `TakesScreenshot` interface.

```
driver = new Augmenter().augment(driver);
```

Later we can use the `TakesScreenshot` interface from RemoteWebDriver to capture the screenshot.

Maximizing the browser window

Selenium RC's `windowMaximize()` command was missing in Selenium WebDriver. However starting from release 2.21, Selenium WebDriver supports maximizing the browser window.

In this short recipe, we will see how to maximize the browser window.

Getting ready

Create a new test which will get an instance of `WebDriver`, navigate to a site and perform some basic actions and verifications.

How to do it...

To maximize a browser window, we need to call the `maximize()` method of the `Window` interface of the `driver` class. Add the second line right below where you define an instance of `FirefoxDriver`.

```
driver = new FirefoxDriver();
driver.manage().window().maximize();
```

How it works...

The `WebDriver` class provides the `window` interface for setting up the browser window size, state, and so on. When we call the `maximize()` method, the browser window will be maximized from normal or minimized state.

```
driver.manage().window().maximize();
```

Automating dropdowns and lists

Selenium WebDriver supports testing Dropdown and List controls using a special `Select` class instead of the `WebElement` class.

The `Select` class provides various methods and properties to interact with dropdowns and lists created with the HTML `<select>` element.

In this recipe, we will automate Dropdown and List control using `Select` class.

How to do it...

Let's create a test for a Dropdown control. This test will perform some basic checks and then call various methods to select options in dropdown.

```
@Test
public void testDropdown()
{
    //Get the Dropdown as a Select using its name attribute
    Select make = new Select(driver.findElement(By.name("make")));

    //Verify Dropdown does not support multiple selection
    assertFalse(make.isMultiple());
    //Verify Dropdown has four options for selection
    assertEquals(4, make.getOptions().size());

    //With Select class we can select an option in Dropdown using
    //Visible Text
    make.selectByVisibleText("Honda");
    assertEquals("Honda", make.getFirstSelectedOption().getText());

    //or we can select an option in Dropdown using value attribute
    make.selectByValue("audi");
    assertEquals("Audi", make.getFirstSelectedOption().getText());

    //or we can select an option in Dropdown using index
    make.selectByIndex(0);
    assertEquals("BMW", make.getFirstSelectedOption().getText());
}
```

Create another test for a List control which has multi-selection enabled. The test will perform some basic checks and then call methods to select multiple options in a list. The test will verify the selection and then deselect the options by calling various deselection methods, namely by visible text, by value, and by index, respectively.

```
@Test
public void testMultipleSelectList()
{
    //Get the List as a Select using its name attribute
    Select color = new Select(driver.findElement(By.name("color")));

    //Verify List support multiple selection
    assertTrue(color.isMultiple());

    //Verify List has five options for selection
```

```
assertEquals(5, color.getOptions().size());

//Select multiple options in the list using visible text
color.selectByVisibleText("Black");
color.selectByVisibleText("Red");
color.selectByVisibleText("Silver");

//Deselect an option using visible text
color.deselectByVisibleText("Silver");

//Deselect an option using value attribute of the option
color.deselectByValue("rd");

//Deselect an option using index of the option
color.deselectByIndex(0);
}
```

How it works...

The Selenium WebDriver provides the `Select` class for working with Dropdown or List controls. We can identify and locate these controls in a way that is similar to how we locate WebElements. However, we will use the `Select` class instead of the `WebElement` class. This is done in the following way:

```
Select color = new Select(driver.findElement(By.name("color")));
```

The HTML `<select>` element supports dropdown or list with multi-select options. We can check if the control supports multi-select by calling the `isMultiple()` method of the `Select` class. It returns `true` if the control supports multi-selection and `false` if it does not.

```
assertFalse(make.isMultiple());
```

We can check number of options available in the dropdown or list by calling the `getOptions()` method of the `Select` class and querying the size of the returned collection of WebElements.

```
assertEquals(4, make.getOptions().size());
```

The `Select` class provides three different ways to select and deselect the options from dropdown and lists.

Selection/deselection by visible text

We can select an option by its visible text. For example, here is code snippet for the `<select>` element:

```
<select name="color" size="6" multiple="multiple"
  style="width:100px">
  <option value="bl">Black</option>
  <option value="wt">White</option>
  <option value="rd">Red</option>
  <option value="br">Brown</option>
  <option value="sl">Silver</option>
</select>
```

Each option in this `<select>` element has a value property as well as text label specified between `<option>` and `</option>`. This will be displayed to the user for selection. We can select an option using this text label by calling the `selectByVisibleText()` method of the `Select` class.

```
color.selectByVisibleText("Black");
```

Similarly you can deselect an already selected option by calling the `deselectByVisibleText()` method.

```
color.deselectByVisibleText("Black");
```

Selection/deselection by value

We can also select an option by using its value attribute. For example, the following option has value attribute `"bl"` and text label `"Black"`:

```
<option value="bl">Black</option>
```

To select this option by value, we need to call the `selectByValue()` method of the `Select` class.

```
color.selectByValue("bl");
```

Similarly you can deselect an already selected option by calling the `deselectByValue()` method.

```
color.deselectByValue("bl");
```

Selection/deselection by index

This is another way by which we can select an option by using its index. When options are displayed on the page, they are indexed in DOM in the order in which these are defined on a page. We can call the `selectByIndex()` method of the `Select` class by specifying the index value.

```
color.selectByIndex("0");
```

Similarly you can deselect an already selected option by calling the `deselectByIndex()` method.

```
color.deselectByIndex(0);
```

 This method may cause problems where options are dynamic and their index changes frequently.

There's more...

We can select/deselect multiple options from a dropdown or list by calling the select/deselect methods in a sequence. For example, in the Color list that supports multiple selections, we can select options in the following way:

```
color.selectByVisibleText("Black");
color.selectByVisibleText("Red");
color.selectByVisibleText("Silver");
```

This will select `Black`, `Red`, and `Silver` options in the list.

See also

  ▶ The *Checking options in dropdowns and lists* recipe
  ▶ The *Checking selected options in dropdowns and lists* recipe

Checking options in dropdowns and lists

While testing the dropdowns and lists created with the `<select>` element, there will be a need to check that correct options are displayed for user selection. These options may be static or populated from a database.

In this recipe we will see how options can be checked against the expected values.

Getting ready

This recipe will need the test created from the earlier *Automating dropdowns and lists* recipe. We will add additional steps for checking the options.

How to do it...

Let's modify the `testDropdown()` test method for checking the options. Add the following highlighted code to the test:

```java
@Test
public void testDropdown()
{
    //Get the Dropdown as a Select using its name attribute
    Select make = new Select(driver.findElement(By.name("make")));

    //Verify Dropdown does not support multiple selection
    assertFalse(make.isMultiple());
    //Verify Dropdown has four options for selection
    assertEquals(4, make.getOptions().size());

    //We will verify Dropdown has expected values as listed in a array
    List<String> exp_options = Arrays.asList(new String[]{"BMW",
        "Mercedes", "Audi","Honda"});
    List<String> act_options = new ArrayList<String>();

    //Retrieve the option values from Dropdown using getOptions() method
    for(WebElement option : make.getOptions())
        act_options.add(option.getText());

    //Verify expected options array and actual options array match
    assertArrayEquals(exp_options.toArray(),act_options.toArray());

    //With Select class we can select an option in Dropdown
    //using Visible Text
    make.selectByVisibleText("Honda");
    assertEquals("Honda", make.getFirstSelectedOption().getText());

    //or we can select an option in Dropdown using value attribute
    make.selectByValue("audi");
    assertEquals("Audi", make.getFirstSelectedOption().getText());

    //or we can select an option in Dropdown using index
    make.selectByIndex(0);
}
```

How it works...

Checking options in a dropdown or list needs a slightly different approach as there is no inbuilt method available in the `Select` class. In this approach, we create a list of expected values that we want to check in the dropdown or list.

```
List<String> exp_options = Arrays.asList(new String[]{"BMW",
    "Mercedes", "Audi","Honda"});
```

The text labels for all the options will be retrieved in a similar list. For this, we will iterate through all the options using the `getOptions()` method of the `Select` class. The `getOptions()` method returns all the options as instances of the `WebElement` class in a list. Using the `getText()` method of the `WebElement` class, the text label of all the options will be added in the `act_options` array list.

```
List<String> act_options = new ArrayList<String>();

    //Retrieve the option values from Dropdown using getOptions()
    //method
    for(WebElement option : make.getOptions())
        act_options.add(option.getText());
```

We will compare the `exp_options` list with `act_options` for any mismatch at the end.

```
assertArrayEquals(exp_options.toArray(),act_options.toArray());
```

There's more...

For checking whether a specific option is available for selection, we can simply perform a check on the `act_options` array list in the following way:

```
assertTrue(act_options.contains("BMW"));
```

See also

▶   The *Automating dropdowns and lists* recipe
▶   The *Checking selected options in dropdowns and lists* recipe

Checking selected options in dropdowns and lists

In earlier recipes, we saw how to select options in the Dropdown and List controls as well as check what options are available for selection. We also need to verify that the correct options are selected in these controls, either by default or by the user.

In this recipe, we will see how to check options which are selected in a dropdown or list.

Getting ready

This recipe will need the test created from the earlier *Automating dropdowns and lists* recipe. We will add additional steps for checking the options.

How to do it...

Let's modify the `testDropdown()` test method for checking the options. Add the following highlighted code to the test:

```
@Test
public void testDropdown()
{
    ...

    //With Select class we can select an option in Dropdown using
    //Visible Text
    make.selectByVisibleText("Honda");
    assertEquals("Honda", make.getFirstSelectedOption().getText());

    //or we can select an option in Dropdown using value attribute
    make.selectByValue("audi");
    assertEquals("Audi", make.getFirstSelectedOption().getText());

    //or we can select an option in Dropdown using index
    make.selectByIndex(0);
    assertEquals("BMW", make.getFirstSelectedOption().getText());
}
```

Also modify the `testMultipleSelectList ()` test method for checking the options. Add the following highlighted code to the test:

```java
@Test
public void testMultipleSelectList()
{
    ...

    //Select multiple options in the list using visible text
    color.selectByVisibleText("Black");
    color.selectByVisibleText("Red");
    color.selectByVisibleText("Silver");

    //We will verify list has multiple options selected as listed
    //in a array
    List<String> exp_sel_options = Arrays.asList
        (new String[]{"Black", "Red", "Silver"});
    List<String> act_sel_options = new ArrayList<String>();

    for(WebElement option : color.getAllSelectedOptions())
        act_sel_options.add(option.getText());

    //Verify expected array for selected options match with actual
    //options selected
    assertArrayEquals
        (exp_sel_options.toArray(),act_sel_options.toArray());

    //Verify there 3 options selected in the list
    assertEquals(3,color.getAllSelectedOptions().size());

    //Deselect an option using visible text
    color.deselectByVisibleText("Silver");
    //Verify selected options count
    assertEquals(2,color.getAllSelectedOptions().size());

    //Deselect an option using value attribute of the option
    color.deselectByValue("rd");
    //Verify selected options count
    assertEquals(1,color.getAllSelectedOptions().size());

    //Deselect an option using index of the option
    color.deselectByIndex(0);
    //Verify selected options count
    assertEquals(0,color.getAllSelectedOptions().size());
}
```

How it works...

When the user selects an option from a dropdown or list, which supports only single option selection, the selected option can be queried through the getFirstSelectedOption() method of the Select class. It returns the option as an instance of WebElement. For example, in the Make dropdown we selected the Honda option using the selectByVisible() method. To check this selection, we can use the getFirstSelectedOption() and the getText() methods in the following way:

```
//With Select class we can select an option in Dropdown using Visible
Text
    make.selectByVisibleText("Honda");
    assertEquals("Honda", make.getFirstSelectedOption().getText());
```

Checking selected options in a multi-select dropdown or list

For checking selected options in a multi-select dropdown or list we can use the getAllSelectedOptions() method of the Select class. It returns all the selected options as a list of WebElement. In this test we created a list of expected selected items and then retrieved the selected options in a list by iterating WebElement returned by getAllSelectedOptions():

```
//We will verify list has multiple options selected as listed in a
//array
List<String> exp_sel_options = Arrays.asList(new String[]{"Black",
    "Red", "Silver"});
List<String> act_sel_options = new ArrayList<String>();

for(WebElement option : color.getAllSelectedOptions())
    act_sel_options.add(option.getText());
```

Using the assertArrayEquals() method of JUnit we will compare both exp_sel_options and act_sel_options to check that correct options are selected in the list.

```
//Verify expected array for selected options match with actual
//options selected
assertArrayEquals(exp_sel_options.toArray(),
    act_sel_options.toArray());
```

We can also check the number of options selected in a list by querying the size from the getAllSelectedOptions() method. For example, we selected three options in the list, so the getAllSelectedOptions().size() method should return 3.

```
assertEquals(3,color.getAllSelectedOptions().size());
```

There's more...

For checking whether a specific option is selected, we can simply perform a check on the `act_sel_options` array list in the following way:

```
assertTrue(act_sel_options.contains("Red"));
```

See also

- ▸ The *Checking options in dropdowns and lists* recipe
- ▸ The *Checking selected options in dropdowns and lists* recipe

Automating radio buttons and radio groups

Selenium WebDriver supports Radio Button and Radio Group controls using the `WebElement` class. We can select and deselect the radio buttons using the `click()` method of the `WebElement` class and check whether a radio button is selected or deselected using the `isSelected()` method.

In this recipe, we will see how to work with the Radio Button and Radio Group controls.

How to do it...

Let's create a test which gets Radio Button and Radio Group controls. We will perform select and deselect operations.

```
@Test
public void testRadioButton()
{
  //Get the Radiobutton as WebElement using it's value attribute
  WebElement petrol =
    driver.findElement(By.xpath("//input[@value='Petrol']"));

  //Check if its already selected? otherwise select the Radiobutton
  //by calling click() method
  if (!petrol.isSelected())
    petrol.click();

  //Verify Radiobutton is selected
  assertTrue(petrol.isSelected());

  //We can also get all the Radiobuttons from a Radio Group in a list
```

```
//using findElements() method along with Radio Group identifier
List<WebElement> fuel_type =
    driver.findElements(By.name("fuel_type"));
for (WebElement type : fuel_type)
{
    //Search for Diesel Radiobutton in the Radio Group and select
    //it
    if(type.getAttribute("value").equals("Diesel"))
    {
        if(!type.isSelected())
            type.click();

        assertTrue(type.isSelected());
        break;
    }
}
}
```

How it works...

We can locate a radio button similar to any other element as a `WebElement` class. In this example, XPath is used to locate the radio button using its `value` attribute.

```
//Get the Radiobutton as WebElement using it's value attribute
WebElement petrol = driver.findElement(By.xpath
    ("//input[@value='Petrol']"));
```

We can select or deselect a radio button by using the `WebElement` class's `click()` method. There are no separate methods to perform these operations. When we want to select a radio button, we need to be careful that it's not already selected otherwise calling the `click()` method will deselect the radio button. We can check if a radio button is already selected by calling the `isSelected()` method, which returns `true` if its selected and `false` if it's not selected. Here the `click()` method will be called only when the radio button is not selected.

```
//Check if its already selected? otherwise select the Radiobutton
//by calling click() method
if (!petrol.isSelected())
    petrol.click();
```

Working with radio group

Instead of just locating a single radio button we can also work with a group of radio buttons by locating all the radio buttons from a group as list of `WebElement` using the `findElements()` method. In the following example, radio button from `fuel_type` radio group is retrieved in a list of `WebElement`:

```
//We can also get all the Radiobuttons from a Radio Group in a
//list using findElements() method along with Radio Group
//identifier
List<WebElement> fuel_type =
  driver.findElements(By.name("fuel_type"));
```

We can then iterate through this list to find a specific radio button and select or deselect a radio button.

```
for (WebElement type : fuel_type)
{
  //Search for Diesel Radiobutton in the Radio Group and select it
  if(type.getAttribute("value").equals("Diesel"))
  {
    if(!type.isSelected())
      type.click();

    assertTrue(type.isSelected());
    break;
  }
}
```

Automating checkboxes

Selenium WebDriver supports Checkbox control using the `WebElement` class. We can select or deselect a checkbox using the `click()` method of the `WebElement` class and check whether a checkbox is selected or deselected using the `isSelected()` method.

In this recipe, we will see how to work with the Checkbox control.

How to do it...

Here is a test which gets a Checkbox control. We will perform select and deselect operations.

```
@Test
public void testCheckBox()
{
  //Get the Checkbox as WebElement using it's value attribute
```

```
WebElement airbags = driver.findElement
   (By.xpath("//input[@value='Airbags']"));

//Check if its already selected? otherwise select the Checkbox
//by calling click() method
if (!airbags.isSelected())
   airbags.click();

//Verify Checkbox is Selected
assertTrue(airbags.isSelected());

//Check Checkbox if selected? If yes, deselect it
//by calling click() method
if (airbags.isSelected())
   airbags.click();

//Verify Checkbox is Deselected
assertFalse(airbags.isSelected());
}
```

How it works...

We can locate a checkbox in a way similar to that in which we locate any other element on a page. In this example, XPath is used to locate the checkbox by its value attribute.

```
//Get the Checkbox as WebElement using it's value attribute
WebElement airbags = driver.findElement
   (By.xpath("//input[@value='Airbags']"));
```

We can select or deselect a checkbox by using the WebElement class's click() method. There are no separate methods to perform these operations. When we want to select a checkbox, we need to be careful that it's not already selected otherwise calling the click() method will deselect the checkbox. We can check if a checkbox is already selected by calling the isSelected() method which returns true if its selected and false if it's not selected. Here the click() method will be called only when the checkbox is not selected.

```
//Check if its already selected? otherwise select the Checkbox
//by calling click() method
if (!airbags.isSelected())
    airbags.click();
```

Similarly, for deselecting the checkbox, we need to see if it is already selected.

```
//Check Checkbox if selected? If yes, deselect it
//by calling click() method
if (airbags.isSelected())
   airbags.click();
```

Controlling Windows processes

Selenium WebDriver Java bindings provide the `WindowsUtils` class with methods to interact with the Windows operating system. During test runs, there might be a need to close open instances of browser windows or processes at the beginning of the test. By using the `WindowsUtils` class, we can control the process and perform tasks, such as killing an open process, and so on.

In this recipe, we will use the `WindowsUtils` class to kill the open browser window.

How to do it...

Let's close an open instance of Firefox by using the `WindowsUtils` class in the `setUp()` method as follows:

```
@Before
public void setUp()
{
  WindowsUtils.tryToKillByName("firefox.exe");
  driver = new FirefoxDriver();
  driver.get("http://www.google.com");
  driver.manage().window().maximize();
}
```

How it works...

We can close or kill any process running on the Windows OS by using the `tryToKillByName()` function of the `WindowsUtils` class. We need to pass the name of process we wish to close.

```
WindowsUtils.tryToKillByName("firefox.exe");
```

The `WindowsUtils` class will search the specified process and kill any running instances. If the process does not exist, an exception will be thrown up. However, the test will continue with the next steps.

Reading a Windows registry value from Selenium WebDriver

The `WindowsUtils` class provides various methods to interact with the registry on the Windows operating system. While running tests on the Windows operating system and Internet Explorer, the test might need to read and modify IE settings or there may be a need to get some settings related to the web server or database from the registry in tests. The `WindowsUtils` class comes handy in these situations.

In this recipe, we will use `WindowsUtil` to read the exact name of the operating system on which the test is running. We might need this information printed in our test logs.

How to do it...

We need to import the `org.openqa.selenium.os.WindowsUtils` class and use the `readStringRegistryValue()` method for reading a registry value that is represented as a `String`.

```
String osname = WindowsUtils.readStringRegistryValue
    ("HKEY_LOCAL_MACHINE\\SOFTWARE\\Microsoft\\Windows
    NT\\CurrentVersion\\ProductName");
System.out.println(osname);
```

How it works...

The `WindowsUtils` class provides multiple methods by which to read Windows registry values based on different data types. The `WindowsUtils` class interacts with the OS to get these values from registry keys. In this example, we are reading the name of the OS, which is represented as a `String`. We need to pass the complete path of the registry key to the `readStringRegistryValue()` function:

```
String osname =
    WindowsUtils.readStringRegistryValue
    ("HKEY_LOCAL_MACHINE\\SOFTWARE\\Microsoft\\Windows
    NT\\CurrentVersion\\ProductName");
```

If the data type is `Integer` then we can use the `readIntegerRegistryValue()` method and for Boolean, we can use `readBooleanRegistryValue()`.

See also

▶ The *Modifying a Windows registry value from Selenium WebDriver* recipe

Modifying a Windows registry value from Selenium WebDriver

The `WindowsUtils` class also provides methods to update existing Windows registry values or create new registry keys and values. Similar to reading registry values, `WindowsUtils` class provides multiple methods to modify keys and values.

In this recipe, we will use the `WindowsUtils` class to create a new registry key with a string value.

How to do it...

Use the `writeStringRegistryValue()` method for modifying existing Windows registry value or creating a new key and value represented as a string.

```
WindowsUtils.writeStringRegistryValue("HKEY_CURRENT_USER\\SOFTWARE
    \\Selenium\\SeleniumVersion", "2.24");
assertEquals("2.24",WindowsUtils.readStringRegistryValue
    ("HKEY_CURRENT_USER\\SOFTWARE\\Selenium\\SeleniumVersion"));
```

How it works...

When the `writeStringRegistryValue()` method is executed along with the path, a new registry key will be created in `HKEY_CURRENT_USER\SOFTWARE` with Selenium and a new value will be stored in `SeleniumVersion`.

```
WindowsUtils.writeStringRegistryValue("HKEY_CURRENT_USER\\SOFTWARE
    \\Selenium\\SeleniumVersion", "2.24");
```

The `WindowsUtils` class provides multiple methods based on value type such as `writeIntegerRegistryValue()` for integer values and `writeBooleanRegistryValue()` for Boolean data type.

 The `writeStringRegistryValue()` method creates a new registry key if it does not exist in the registry.

See also

▸ The *Reading a Windows registry value from Selenium WebDriver* recipe

3
Controlling the Test Flow

In this chapter, we will cover the following:

- ▶ Synchronizing a test with an implicit wait
- ▶ Synchronizing a test with an explicit wait
- ▶ Synchronizing a test with custom-expected conditions
- ▶ Checking an element's presence
- ▶ Checking an element's status
- ▶ Identifying and handling a pop-up window by its name
- ▶ Identifying and handling a pop-up window by its title
- ▶ Identifying and handling a pop-up window by its content
- ▶ Handling a simple JavaScript alert
- ▶ Handling a confirm box alert
- ▶ Handling a prompt box alert
- ▶ Identifying and handling frames
- ▶ Identifying and handling frames by their content
- ▶ Working with IFRAME

Introduction

While building test automation for a complex web application using Selenium WebDriver, we need to ensure that the test flow is maintained for reliable test automation.

When tests are run, the application may not always respond with the same speed. For example, it might take a few seconds for a progress bar to reach 100 percent, a status message to appear, a button to become enabled, and a window or pop-up message to open.

You can handle these anticipated timing problems by synchronizing your test to ensure that Selenium WebDriver waits until your application is ready before performing a certain step. There are several options that you can use to synchronize your test. Selenium RC has various waitFor methods; however, being a pure web automation API, Selenium WebDriver provides very limited methods for synchronization. In this chapter, you will see how to use the `WebDriverWait` class to implement synchronization in tests.

Pop ups and Alerts

For building a great user interface, developers use features similar to desktop applications in the form of pop-up windows and alerts. While testing complex workflows, tests need to flow from the browser window to a pop-up window in order to alert the user and perform operations as needed. This chapter also explains common issues that pertain to the handling of pop-up windows and alerts, and how best we can use Selenium WebDriver API for this.

Synchronizing a test with an implicit wait

The Selenium WebDriver provides an implicit wait for synchronizing tests. When an implicit wait is implemented in tests, if WebDriver cannot find an element in the **Document Object Model (DOM)**, it will wait for a defined amount of time for the element to appear in the DOM.

In other terms, an implicit wait polls the DOM for a certain amount of time when trying to find an element or elements if they are not immediately available. The default setting is 0.

Once set, the implicit wait is set for the life of the WebDriver object's instance. However, an implicit wait may slow down your tests when an application responds normally, as it will wait for each element appearing in the DOM and increase the overall execution time.

In this recipe, we will briefly explore the use of an implicit wait; however, it is recommended to avoid or minimize the use of an implicit wait.

How to do it...

Let's create a test on a demo AJAX-enabled application as follows:

```
public void testWithImplicitWait()
{
    //Go to the Demo AJAX Application
    WebDriver driver = new FirefoxDriver();
    driver.get("http://dl.dropbox.com/u/55228056/AjaxDemo.html");

    //Set the Implicit Wait time Out to 10 Seconds
    driver.manage().timeouts().implicitlyWait(10, TimeUnit.SECONDS);

    try {

        //Get link for Page 4 and click on it
        WebElement page4button = driver.findElement(By.linkText("Page
4"));
        page4button.click();

        //Get an element with id page4 and verify it's text
        WebElement message = driver.findElement(By.id("page4"));
        assertTrue(message.getText().contains("Nunc nibh tortor"));

    } catch (NoSuchElementException e) {
        fail("Element not found!!");
        e.printStackTrace();
    } finally {
        driver.close();
    }
}
```

How it works...

The Selenium WebDriver provides the `Timeouts` Interface for configuring the implicit wait. The `Timeouts` Interface provides an `implicitlyWait()` method, which accepts the time the driver should wait when searching for an element. In this example, a test will wait for an element to appear in DOM for `10` seconds:

```
driver.manage().timeouts().implicitlyWait(10, TimeUnit.SECONDS);
```

Until the end of a test or an implicit wait is set back to 0, every time an element is searched using the `findElement()` method, the test will wait for 10 seconds for an element to appear.

Minimize or avoid using an implicit wait in your tests and try to handle synchronization issues with an explicit wait, which provides more control when compared with an implicit wait.

See also

▶ *Synchronizing a test with an explicit wait*

▶ *Synchronizing a test with custom-expected conditions*

Synchronizing a test with an explicit wait

The Selenium WebDriver also provides an explicit wait for synchronizing tests, which provides a better control when compared with an implicit wait. Unlike an implicit wait, you can write custom code or conditions for wait before proceeding further in the code.

An explicit wait can only be implemented in cases where synchronization is needed and the rest of the script is working fine.

The Selenium WebDriver provides `WebDriverWait` and `ExpectedCondition` classes for implementing an explicit wait.

The `ExpectedCondition` class provides a set of predefined conditions to wait before proceeding further in the code. The following table shows some common conditions that we frequently come across when automating web browsers supported by the `ExpectedCondition` class:

Predefined condition	Selenium method
An element is visible and enabled	`elementToBeClickable(By locator)`
An element is selected	`elementToBeSelected(WebElement element)`
Presence of an element	`presenceOfElementLocated(By locator)`
Specific text present in an element	`textToBePresentInElement(By locator, java.lang.String text)`
Element value	`textToBePresentInElementValue(By locator, java.lang.String text)`
Title	`titleContains(java.lang.String title)`

For more conditions, visit `http://selenium.googlecode.com/svn/trunk/docs/api/java/org/openqa/selenium/support/ui/ExpectedConditions.html`.

In this recipe, we will explore some of these conditions with the `WebDriverWait` class.

How to do it...

Let's implement a test that uses the `ExpectedConditions.titleContains()` method to implement an explicit wait as follows:

```
@Test
public void testExplcitWaitTitleContains()
{
    //Go to the Google Home Page
    WebDriver driver = new FirefoxDriver();
    driver.get("http://www.google.com");

    //Enter a term to search and submit
    WebElement query = driver.findElement(By.name("q"));
    query.sendKeys("selenium");
    query.click();

    //Create Wait using WebDriverWait.
    //This will wait for 10 seconds for timeout before title is
    //updated with search term
    //If title is updated in specified time limit test will move to
    //the text step
    //instead of waiting for 10 seconds
    WebDriverWait wait = new WebDriverWait(driver, 10);
    wait.until(ExpectedConditions.titleContains("selenium"));

    //Verify Title
    assertTrue(driver.getTitle().toLowerCase().
startsWith("selenium"));

    driver.quit();
}
```

How it works...

We can create a wait for a set of common conditions using the `ExpectedCondition` class. First, we need to create an instance of the `WebDriverWait` class by passing the driver instance and timeout for a wait as follows:

```
WebDriverWait wait = new WebDriverWait(driver, 10);
```

Next, `ExpectedCondition` is passed to the `wait.until()` method as follows:

```
wait.until(ExpectedConditions.titleContains("selenium"));
```

The `WebDriverWait` object will call the `ExpectedCondition` class object every 500 milliseconds until it returns successfully.

See also

▸ *Synchronizing a test with custom-expected conditions*

▸ *Synchronizing a test with an implicit wait*

Synchronizing a test with custom-expected conditions

The Selenium WebDriver also provides a way to build custom-expected conditions along with common conditions using the `ExpectedCondition` class. This comes in handy when a wait can be handled with a common condition supported by the `ExpectedCondition` class.

In this recipe, we will explore how to create a custom condition.

How to do it...

We will create a test that will create a wait until an element appears on the page using the custom `ExpectedCondition` class as follows:

```
@Test
public void testExplicitWait()
{
    //Go to Sample Application
    WebDriver driver = new FirefoxDriver();
    driver.get("http://dl.dropbox.com/u/55228056/AjaxDemo.html");

    try {
        //Get the link for Page 4 and click on it, this will call AJAX
code
        //for loading the contents for Page 4
        WebElement page4button = driver.findElement(By.linkText("Page
4"));

        page4button.click();

        //Create Wait using WebDriverWait.
        //This will wait for 5 seconds for timeout before page4
        //element is found
        //Element is found in specified time limit test will move to
        //the text step
        //instead of waiting for 10 seconds
```

```
//Expected condition is expecting a WebElement to be returned
//after findElement finds the
//element with specified locator
WebElement message = (new WebDriverWait(driver, 5))
        .until(new ExpectedCondition<WebElement>(){
            @Override
            public WebElement apply(WebDriver d) {
                return d.findElement(By.id("page4"));
            }});
assertTrue(message.getText().contains("Nunc nibh tortor"));

} catch (NoSuchElementException e) {
    fail("Element not found!!");
    e.printStackTrace();
} finally {
    driver.close();
}
}
```

How it works...

The Selenium WebDriver provides the ability to implement the custom `ExpectedCondition` class along with the `WebDriverWait` class for creating a custom-wait condition, as needed by a test. In this example, we created a custom condition, which returns a `WebElement` object once the inner `findElement()` method locates the element within a specified timeout as follows:

```
WebElement message = (new WebDriverWait(driver, 5))
.until(new ExpectedCondition<WebElement>(){
    @Override
    public WebElement apply(WebDriver d) {
    return d.findElement(By.id("page4"));
}});
```

There's more...

A custom wait can be created in various ways. In the following section, we will explore some common examples for implementing a custom wait.

Waiting for element's attribute value update

Based on the events and action performed, the value of an element's attribute might change at runtime. For example, a disabled textbox gets enabled based on the user's rights. A custom wait can be created on the attribute value of the element. In the following example, the ExpectedCondition class waits for a Boolean return value, based on the attribute value of an element:

```
(new WebDriverWait(driver, 10)).until(new ExpectedCondition<Boolean>()
{
    public Boolean apply(WebDriver d) {
        return d.findElement(By.id("userName")).
getAttribute("readonly").contains("true");
}});
```

Waiting for an element's visibility

Developers hide or display elements based on the sequence of actions, user rights, and so on. The specific element might exist in the DOM, but are hidden from the user, and when the user performs a certain action it appears on the page. A custom-wait condition can be created based on the element's visibility as follows:

```
(new WebDriverWait(driver, 10)).until(new ExpectedCondition<Boolean>()
{
    public Boolean apply(WebDriver d) {
        return d.findElement(By.id("page4")).isDisplayed();
}});
```

Waiting for DOM events

The web application may be using a JavaScript framework such as jQuery for AJAX and content manipulation. For example, jQuery is used to load a big JSON file from the server asynchronously on the page. While jQuery is reading and processing this file, a test can check its status using the active attribute. A custom wait can be implemented by executing the JavaScript code and checking the return value as follows:

```
(new WebDriverWait(driver, 10)).until(new ExpectedCondition<Boolean>()
{
    public Boolean apply(WebDriver d) {
        JavascriptExecutor js = (JavascriptExecutor) d;
        return (Boolean)js.executeScript("return jQuery.active == 0");
}});
```

Checking an element's presence

The Selenium WebDriver doesn't implement Selenium RC's `isElementPresent()` method for checking if an element is present on a page. This method is useful for building a reliable test where you can check an element's presence before performing any action on it.

In this recipe, we will write a method similar to the `isElementPresent()` method.

How to do it...

For implementing the `isElementPresent()` method, follow these steps:

1. Create a method `isElementPresent()` and keep it accessible to your tests as follows:

```
private boolean isElementPresent(By by) {
    try {
        driver.findElement(by);
        return true;
    } catch (NoSuchElementException e) {
        return false;
    }
}
```

2. Implement a test which calls the `isElementPresent()` method. It will check if the desired element is present on a page; if found then it clicks on the element, else fails the test. This is done as follows:

```
@Test
public void testIsElementPresent()
{
    //Check if element with locator criteria exists on Page
    if (isElementPresent(By.name("airbags"))) {
        //Get the checkbox and select it
        WebElement airbag = driver.findElement(By.
name("airbags"));
        if (!airbag.isSelected())
            airbag.click();
    }
    else {
        fail("Airbag Checkbox doesn't exists!!");
    }
}
```

How it works...

The isElementPresent() method takes a locator using an instance of By. It then calls the findElement() method. If the element is not found, a NoSuchElementException exception will be thrown. Using the try and catch block, the isElementPresent() method will return true if the element is found and no exception is thrown; otherwise it will return false if NoSuchElementException is thrown by the findElement() method.

See also

▸ *Checking an element's status*

Checking an element's status

Many a time a test fails to click on an element or enter text in a field as the element is disabled or exists in the DOM, but is not displayed on the page; this will result in an error being thrown and the test resulting in failures. For building reliable tests that can run unattended, a robust exception and error handling is needed in the test flow.

We can handle these problems by checking the state of elements. The WebElement class provides the following methods to check the state of an element:

Method	Purpose
isEnabled()	This method checks if an element is enabled. Returns true if enabled, else false for disabled.
isSelected()	This method checks if element is selected (radio button, checkbox, and so on). It returns true if selected, else false for deselected
isDisplayed()	This method checks if element is displayed.

In this recipe, we will use some of these methods to check the status and handle possible errors.

How to do it...

We will create a test where a checkbox for the LED head lamp option needs to be selected on a page. This checkbox will be enabled or disabled based on the previously selected option. Before selecting this checkbox, we will make sure that it's enabled for selection as follows:

```
@Test
public void testElementIsEnabled()
{
    //Get the Checkbox as WebElement using it's name attribute
```

```
    WebElement ledheadlamp = driver.findElement(By.xpath("//input[@
name='ledheadlamp']"));

    //Check if its enabled before selecting it
    if (ledheadlamp.isEnabled())
    {
        //Check if its already selected? otherwise select the Checkbox
        if (!ledheadlamp.isSelected())
            ledheadlamp.click();
    }
    else
    {
        fail("LED Lamp Checkbox is disabled!!");
    }

}
```

How it works...

We are selecting a checkbox by checking two states of an element—first, it is enabled and second it is not selected. We can use the `isEnabled()` function of the `WebElement` class, which returns `true` if the element is enabled or `false` if it's disabled. The test will fail if the checkbox is disabled. If we don't check this condition, the test will possibly throw an exception saying the object is disabled, as follows:

```
//Check if its enabled before selecting it
if (ledheadlamp.isEnabled())
{
    //Check if its already selected? otherwise select the Checkbox
    if (!ledheadlamp.isSelected())
        ledheadlamp.click();
}
else
{
    fail("LED Lamp Checkbox is disabled!!");
}
```

Identifying and handling a pop-up window by its name

In Selenium WebDriver, testing pop-up windows involves identifying a pop-up window, switching the driver context to the pop-up window, then executing steps on the pop-up window, and finally switching back to the parent window.

The Selenium WebDriver allows us to identify a pop-up window by its `name` attribute or window handle and switching between the pop-up window and the browser window is done using the `Webdriver.switchTo().window()` method.

In this recipe, we will identify and handle a pop-up window by using its `name` attribute. Developers provide the `name` attribute for a pop-up window that is different from its title. In the following example, a user can open a pop-up window by clicking on the **Help** button. In this case, the developer has provided `HelpWindow` as its name:

```
<button id="helpbutton" onClick='window.open("help.html","HelpWindow",
"width=500,height=500");'>Help</button>
```

How to do it...

Let's implement a test that identifies a pop-up window using its `name` attribute as follows:

```
@Test
public void testWindowPopup()
{
    //Save the WindowHandle of Parent Browser Window
    String parentWindowId = driver.getWindowHandle();

    //Clicking Help Button will open Help Page in a new Popup Browser
Window
    WebElement helpButton = driver.findElement(By.id("helpbutton"));
    helpButton.click();

    try {
        //Switch to the Help Popup Browser Window
        driver.switchTo().window("HelpWindow");
    } catch (NoSuchWindowException e) {
        e.printStackTrace();
    }

    //Verify the driver context is in Help Popup Browser Window
    assertTrue(driver.getTitle().equals("Help"));

    //Close the Help Popup Window
```

```
driver.close();


    //Move back to the Parent Browser Window
    driver.switchTo().window(parentWindowId);
    //Verify the driver context is in Parent Browser Window
    assertTrue(driver.getTitle().equals("Build my Car -
Configuration"));
    }
```

How it works...

The Selenium WebDriver provides a way to switch between the browser windows and change the context of a driver. For moving to a pop-up window from the parent or the browser window, the `driver.switchTo().window()` method is used. This method accepts the `name` or `handle` attribute of the pop-up window. In the following example, the `name` attribute is used as follows:

```
//Switch to the Help Popup Browser Window
driver.switchTo().window("HelpWindow");
```

Now we can perform actions or verifications on the pop-up window through the driver instance as usual.

During a test, when you want to move to a pop-up window called from a parent window, save the parent window's `handle` attribute in a variable so that when operations on the pop-up window are over and we want to switch back to the parent window, we can use the `handle` as follows:

```
//Save the WindowHandle of Parent Browser Window
String parentWindowId = driver.getWindowHandle();
```

A test can switch back to the parent window using its `handle` attribute as follows:

```
//Move back to the Parent Browser Window
driver.switchTo().window(parentWindowId);
```

There is more...

The pop-up windows can be closed by calling the `driver.close()` method. However, developers might implement the closing of a pop-up window by clicking on a button or a link. In this case, closing a pop-up window directly might lead to errors or exceptions.

NoSuchWindowException

The `driver.switchTo().window()` method throws the `NoSuchWindowException` exception when it fails to identify the desired pop-up window. Handling this exception helps to build a robust test, which would otherwise run into errors.

See also

▶ *Identifying and handling a pop-up window by its title*

▶ *Identifying and handling a pop-up window by its content*

Identifying and handling a pop-up window by its title

Many a times developers don't assign the `name` attribute to pop-up windows. In such cases, we can use its window `handle` attribute. However, the `handle` attributes keep changing and it becomes difficult to identify the pop-up window, especially when there is more than one pop-up window open. Using the `handle` and `title` attributes of the page displayed in a pop-up window, we can build a more reliable way to identify the pop-up windows.

In this recipe, we will use the `title` attribute to identify the pop-up window and then perform operations on it.

How to do it...

We will create a test that retrieves the handles of all the open windows in the current driver context. We will iterate through this list and check the title matching the criteria as follows:

```
@Test
public void testWindowPopupUsingTitle() {
    //Save the WindowHandle of Parent Browser Window
    String parentWindowId = driver.getWindowHandle();

    //Clicking Visit Us Button will open Visit Us Page in a new Popup
    //Browser Window
    WebElement visitButton = driver.findElement(By.id("visitbutton"));
    visitButton.click();

    //Get Handles of all the open Popup Windows
    //Iterate through the set and check if tile of each window matches
    //with expected Window Title
    Set<String> allWindows = driver.getWindowHandles();
    if(!allWindows.isEmpty()) {
        for (String windowId : allWindows) {
```

```
        try {
                if(driver.switchTo().window(windowId).getTitle().
equals("Visit Us")) {
                        //Close the Visit Us Popup Window
                        driver.close();
                        break;
                }
        }
        catch(NoSuchWindowException e) {
                e.printStackTrace();
        }
    }
}

//Move back to the Parent Browser Window
driver.switchTo().window(parentWindowId);
//Verify the driver context is in Parent Browser Window
assertTrue(driver.getTitle().equals("Build my Car -
Configuration"));
}
```

How it works...

The `driver.getWindowHandles()` method returns the handles of all the open pop-up windows in a list as follows:

```
Set<String> allWindows = driver.getWindowHandles();
```

We can then iterate through this list and find out the matching pop-up window by checking the title of each window by using the `handle` attribute as follows:

```
if(!allWindows.isEmpty()) {
    for (String windowId : allWindows) {

        try {
                if(driver.switchTo().window(windowId).getTitle().
equals("Visit Us")) {
                        //Close the Visit Us Popup Window
                        driver.close();
                        break;
                }
        }
        catch(NoSuchWindowException e) {
                e.printStackTrace();
        }
    }
}
```

You can create a reusable function for identifying pop-up windows using the `title` attribute.

See also

▸ *Identifying and handling a pop-up window by its name*

▸ *Identifying and handling a pop-up window by its content*

Identifying and handling a pop-up window by its content

In certain situations, developers neither assign the `name` attribute nor provide a title to the page displayed in a pop-up window. This becomes more complex when a test needs to deal with multiple pop-up windows open at the same time—to identify the desired pop-up window.

Ideally, you should reach out to developers and recommend that they add either the `name` attribute or title for better testability and accessibility.

As a workaround to this problem, we can check the contents of each window returned by the `driver.getWindowHandles()` method to identify the desired pop-up window.

How to do it...

Let's create a test that retrieves the handles of all the open windows in the current driver context. It will then iterate through this list, switching to the window and then checking for the content, which will help in identifying the correct window as follows:

```
@Test
public void testWindowPopupUsingContents()
{
    //Save the WindowHandle of Parent Browser Window
    String currentWindowId = driver.getWindowHandle();

    //Clicking Chat Button will open Chat Page in a new Popup Browser
    //Window
    WebElement chatButton = driver.findElement(By.id("chatbutton"));
    chatButton.click();

    //There is no name or title provided for Chat Page Popup
    //We will iterate through all the open Windows and check the
    //contents to find
    //out if it's Chat Window
```

```
Set<String> allWindows = driver.getWindowHandles();
if(!allWindows.isEmpty()) {
    for (String windowId : allWindows) {
        driver.switchTo().window(windowId);

        if(driver.getPageSource().contains("Build my Car -
Configuration - Online Chat")) {
            try {

                //Find the Close Button on Chat Popup Window and
close the Popup
                //by clicking Close Button instead of closing it
directly
                WebElement closeButton = driver.findElement(By.
id("closebutton"));
                closeButton.click();
                break;
            } catch(NoSuchWindowException e) {
                e.printStackTrace();
            }
        }
    }
}
//Move back to the Parent Browser Window
driver.switchTo().window(currentWindowId);
//Verify the driver context is in Parent Browser Window
assertTrue(driver.getTitle().equals("Build my Car -
Configuration"));
}
```

How it works...

After retrieving all the open windows by calling the `driver.getWindowHandles()` method, the test will iterate through each item, switching to the window and then checking if the desired content is present in the window with the help of the following code snippet:

```
if(!allWindows.isEmpty()) {
    for (String windowId : allWindows) {
        driver.switchTo().window(windowId);

        if(driver.getPageSource().contains("Build my Car -
Configuration - Online Chat")) {
            try {
```

```
                            //Find the Close Button on Chat Popup Window and close
                            //the Popup
                            //by clicking Close Button instead of closing it
                            //directly
                            WebElement closeButton = driver.findElement(By.
   id("closebutton"));
                            closeButton.click();
                            break;
                    } catch(NoSuchWindowException e) {
                            e.printStackTrace();
                    }
                }
            }
}}
```

In this example, it checks for specific text appearing on a page by calling the `driver.getPageSource()` method.

If a window is found with the specific text, it will be closed by clicking on the **Close** button instead of calling the `driver.close()` method. You can implement this in your test when pop-up windows cannot be identified by using the `name` attribute or the title. This will help in building more reliable tests.

See also

> ▸ *Identifying and handling a pop-up window by its name*

> ▸ *Identifying and handling a pop-up window by its title*

Handling a simple JavaScript alert

Web developers use JavaScript alerts for informing users about validation errors, warnings, getting a response for an action, accepting an input value, and so on.

Tests will need to verify that the user is shown correct alerts while testing. It would also be required to handle alerts while performing an end-to-end workflow. The Selenium WebDriver provides an `Alert` class for working with JavaScript alerts.

In this recipe, we will handle a simple alert box using Selenium WebDriver's `Alert` class. A simple alert box is often used to notify the user with information such as errors, warnings, and success. When an alert box pops up, the user will have to click on the **OK** button to proceed, as shown in the following screenshot:

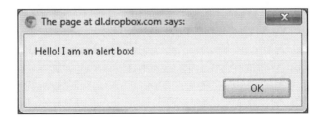

How to do it...

We will create a test a page on which, when a button is clicked, a simple alert box is displayed to the user. This test will also check that correct information is displayed in the alert box as follows:

```java
@Test
public void testSimpleAlert()
{
    //Clicking button will show a simple Alert with OK Button
    WebElement button = driver.findElement(By.id("simple"));
    button.click();

    try {

        //Get the Alert
        Alert alert = driver.switchTo().alert();

        //Get the Text displayed on Alert using getText() method of
Alert class
        String textOnAlert = alert.getText();

        //Click OK button, by calling accept() method of Alert Class
        alert.accept();

        //Verify Alert displayed correct message to user
        assertEquals("Hello! I am an alert box!",textOnAlert);

    } catch (NoAlertPresentException e) {
        e.printStackTrace();
    }
}
```

How it works...

The Selenium WebDriver provides an `Alert` class for handling alerts. To get the alert box displayed on the screen as an instance of the `Alert` class, the `driver.switchTo().alert()` method is used as follows:

```
Alert alert = driver.switchTo().alert();
```

A test might need to verify what message is displayed in an alert box. We can get the text from an alert box by calling the `getText()` method of the `Alert` class as follows:

```
String textOnAlert = alert.getText();
```

An alert box is closed by clicking on the **OK** button; this can be done by calling the `accept()` method as follows:

```
alert.accept();
```

There is more...

An alert box can also be accessed without creating an instance of the `Alert` class by directly calling desired methods as follows:

```
driver.switchTo().alert().accept();
```

NoAlertPresentException

The `driver.switchTo().alert()` method throws a `NoAlertPresentException` exception when it tries to access an alert box that doesn't exist. Handling this exception helps to build a robust test which will otherwise run into errors.

See also

- ▸ *Handling a confirm box alert*
- ▸ *Handling a prompt box alert*

Handling a confirm box alert

A confirm box is often used to verify or accept something from the user. When a confirm box pops up, the user will have to click either on the **OK** or the **Cancel** button to proceed, as shown in the following screenshot:

If the user clicks on the **OK** button, the box returns `true`. If the user clicks on the **Cancel** button, the box returns `false`.

In this recipe, we will handle a confirm box using the Selenium WebDriver's `Alert` class.

How to do it...

Let's create a set of tests that handle a confirm box displayed on a page as follows:

1. In the `testConfirmAccept` test, we will accept the confirm box and verify a message on the page when the confirm box is accepted, that is, when the **OK** button is clicked as follows:

```
@Test
public void testConfirmAccept()
{
    //Clicking button will show a Confirmation Alert with OK and
Cancel Button
    WebElement button = driver.findElement(By.id("confirm"));
    button.click();

    try {

        //Get the Alert
        Alert alert = driver.switchTo().alert();

        //Click OK button, by calling accept() method of Alert
        //Class
        alert.accept();

        //Verify Page displays correct message on Accept
```

```
        WebElement message = driver.findElement(By.id("demo"));
        assertEquals("You Accepted Alert!", message.getText());

    } catch (NoAlertPresentException e) {
        e.printStackTrace();
    }
}
```

2. In the `testConfirmDismiss` test, we will dismiss the confirm box by calling the `dismiss()` method; this is the same as clicking the **Cancel** button as follows:

```
@Test
public void testConfirmDismiss()
{
    //Clicking button will show a Confirmation Alert with OK and
    //Cancel Button
    WebElement button = driver.findElement(By.id("confirm"));
    button.click();

    try {

        //Get the Alert
        Alert alert = driver.switchTo().alert();

        //Click Cancel button, by calling dismiss() method of
        //Alert Class
        alert.dismiss();

        //Verify Page displays correct message on Dismiss
        WebElement message = driver.findElement(By.id("demo"));
        assertEquals("You Dismissed Alert!", message.getText());

    } catch (NoAlertPresentException e) {
        e.printStackTrace();
    }
}
```

How it works...

Handling a confirm box works in a similar way to handling a simple alert box. For cancelling a confirm box, the `dismiss()` method of the `Alert` class is used as follows:

```
//Click Cancel button, by calling dismiss() method of Alert Class
alert.dismiss();
```

▸ *Handling a simple JavaScript alert*

▸ *Handling a prompt box alert*

Handling a prompt box alert

A prompt box is often used to input a value by the user before entering a page. When a prompt box pops up, the user will have to click either on the **OK** or the **Cancel** button to proceed after entering an input value, as shown in the following screenshot:

If the user clicks on the **OK** button, the box returns the input value. If the user clicks on the **Cancel** button, the box returns `null`.

In this recipe, we will handle a prompt box using the Selenium WebDriver's `Alert` class.

How to do it...

We will create a test that handles a prompt box. We will enter text into the prompt box's input field and later verify if the same value is displayed on the page as follows:

```
@Test
public void testPrompt()
{
    //Clicking button will show a Prompt Alert asking user to enter
    //value/text with OK and Cancel Button
    WebElement button = driver.findElement(By.id("prompt"));
    button.click();

    try {

        //Get the Alert
        Alert alert = driver.switchTo().alert();
```

```
                    //Enter some value on Prompt by calling sendKeys() method of
                    //Alert Class
                    alert.sendKeys("Foo");

                    //Click OK button, by calling accept() method of Alert Class
                    alert.accept();

                    //Verify Page displays message with value entered in Prompt
                    WebElement message = driver.findElement(By.id("prompt_demo"));
                    assertEquals("Hello Foo! How are you today?", message.
            getText());

                } catch (NoAlertPresentException e) {
                    e.printStackTrace();
                }
        }
}
```

How it works...

For handling a prompt box, the `Alert` class provides an extra `sendKeys()` method to enter text in the prompt box's input field. We can enter the text and either accept or dismiss a prompt box by calling the `Alert` class's methods as follows:

```
//Enter some value on Prompt by calling sendKeys() method of Alert
Class
alert.sendKeys("Foo");

//Click OK button, by calling accept() method of Alert Class
alert.accept();
```

See also

- ▶ *Handling a simple JavaScript alert*
- ▶ *Handling a confirm box alert*

Identifying and handling frames

HTML frames allow developers to present documents in multiple views, which may be independent windows or subwindows. Multiple views offer developers a way to keep certain information visible, while other views are scrolled or replaced. For example, within the same window, one frame might display a static banner, the second a navigation menu, and the third the main document that can be scrolled through or replaced by navigating in the second frame.

A page with frames is created by using the `<frameset>` tag or the `<iframe>` tag. All frame tags are nested with a `<frameset>` tag. In the following example, a page will display three frames, each loading different HTML pages:

```html
<html>
    <frameset cols="25%,*,25%" FRAMEBORDER="NO" FRAMESPACING="0"
BORDER="0">
        <frame id="left" src="frame_a.htm" />
        <frame src="frame_b.htm" />
        <frame name="right" src="frame_c.htm" />
    </frameset>
</html>
```

Frames can be identified by an ID or through the `name` attribute. In this recipe, we will identify and work with frames by using the `driver.switchTo().frame()` method, using the `id`, `name`, instance of WebElement, and the index of a frame.

How to do it...

Let's test on a page that has three frames as follows:

1. In the `testFrameWithIdOrName()` test, the frame will be identified by the `name` and `id` attributes as follows:

```java
@Test
public void testFrameWithIdOrName()
{
    //Activate the frame on left side using it's id attribute
    driver.switchTo().frame("left");

    //Get an element from the frame on left side and verify it's
    //contents
    WebElement leftmsg = driver.findElement(By.tagName("p"));
    assertEquals("This is Left Frame", leftmsg.getText());

    //Activate the Page, this will move context from frame back to
    //the Page
    driver.switchTo().defaultContent();

    //Activate the frame on right side using it's name attribute
    driver.switchTo().frame("right");

    //Get an element from the frame on right side and verify it's
    //contents
    WebElement rightmsg = driver.findElement(By.tagName("p"));
```

```
assertEquals("This is Right Frame", rightmsg.getText());

//Activate the Page, this will move context from frame back to
//the Page
driver.switchTo().defaultContent();

}
```

2. In the second test, `testFrameByIndex()`, the index is used for identifying the frame as follows:

```
@Test
public void testFrameByIndex()
{
    //Activate the frame in middle using it's index. Index starts
    //at 0
    driver.switchTo().frame(1);

    //Get an element from the frame in the middle and verify it's
    //contents
    WebElement leftmsg = driver.findElement(By.tagName("p"));
    assertEquals("This Frame doesn't have id or name", leftmsg.
getText());

    //Activate the Page, this will move context from frame back to
    //the Page
    driver.switchTo().defaultContent();
}
```

How it works...

The Selenium WebDriver's `WebDriver` class provides the `driver.switchTo().frame()` method to activate a frame on a page and perform operations using the driver's instance. This method takes the `id`, `name` attributes, instance of a WebElement (the `<frame>` element can be located using the `driver.findElement()` method), or its index for identification. In the following example, the `id` attribute is used to identify a frame:

```
//Activate the frame on left side using it's id attribute
driver.switchTo().frame("left");
```

When frames do not have the `id` or `name` attributes defined, the index can be used to identify a frame. In the preceding example, the frame in the middle does not have the `id` or `name` attributes. The middle frame's index will be 1 as it has a frame on the left-hand side with the index as 0 and on the right-hand side with the index 2.

```
//Activate the frame in middle using it's index. Index starts at 0
driver.switchTo().frame(1);
```

Once a frame is activated, the driver's instance will allow operations on the document loaded in the frame. To return to the main document, use the `driver.switchTo().defaultContent()` method.

> Warning: While working with multiple frames, when an operation is completed on a frame and a test flow needs to move to another frame, calling the `driver.switchTo().frame()` method will not move the context to the desired frame. The test will first need to activate the main document by calling `driver.switchTo().defaultContent()` and then activating the desired frame.

See also

 ▸ *Identifying and handling frames by their content*
 ▸ *Working with IFRAME*

Identifying and handling frames by their content

While working with frames, you will find that the `id` or `name` attributes are not defined. Still frames can be identified by using their index. This may not be a reliable way when applications are dynamic and there is a need to ensure that the correct frame is activated.

In this recipe, we will identify frames by the content of the document loaded in these frames to make tests more reliable.

How to do it...

Let's create a test that will get all the `<frame>` elements in a document and then iterate through this list to find out the desired frame as follows:

```
@Test
public void testFrameByContents()
{
    //Get all frames on the Page, created with <frame> tag
    List<WebElement> frames = driver.findElements(By.
tagName("frame"));

    //In this example frame in the middle is activated by checking the
    //contents
    //Activate frame and check if it has the desired content. If found
perform the operations
```

```
        //if not, then switch back to the Page and continue checking next
        //frame
        for(WebElement frame : frames) {
                //switchTo().frame() also accepts frame elements apart from
                //id, name or index
                driver.switchTo().frame(frame);
                if(driver.getPageSource().contains("This Frame doesn't have id
or name")) {
                        assertTrue("Middle Frame Found",true);
                        break;
                }
                else
                        driver.switchTo().defaultContent();
        }

        //Activate the Page, this will move context from frame back to the
        //Page
        driver.switchTo().defaultContent();
    }
```

How it works...

In Selenium WebDriver, we can get elements of the same criteria in a list. Here we will get all the frame elements from the document using the `tagname()` method as follows:

```
//Get all frames on the Page, created with <frame> tag
List<WebElement> frames = driver.findElements(By.tagName("frame"));
```

The test will iterate through each frame element, passing this element to the `driver.switchTo().frame()` method and checking its content. If the frame has matching content, then you can continue operations on the frame and later switch back to the main document as follows:

```
for(WebElement frame : frames) {
        //switchTo().frame() also accepts frame elements apart from id,
    name or index
        driver.switchTo().frame(frame);
        if(driver.getPageSource().contains("This Frame doesn't have id or
name")) {
                assertTrue("Middle Frame Found",true);
                break;
        }
        else
                driver.switchTo().defaultContent();
}
```

You can create a utility method for switching between frames using their content.

See also

▶ *Identifying and handling frames*

▶ *Working with IFrames*

Working with IFRAME

Developers can also embed external documents or documents from another domain using the `<iframe>` tag. Various social media websites provide buttons which can be embedded in your web applications to link these websites. For example, you can add Twitter-follow button in your application as follows:

```
<iframe allowtransparency="true" frameborder="0" scrolling="no"
src="http://platform.twitter.com/widgets/follow_button.html?screen_
name=upgundecha" style="width:300px; height:20px;"></iframe>
```

Identifying and working with the `<iframe>` tag is similar to a frame created with the `<frameset>` tag. In this recipe, we will identify the `<iframe>` tag, which is nested in another frame.

How to do it...

We will create a test on a page which embeds the `<iframe>` tag within a frame. We will move to the parent frame first and then to the `<iframe>` tag. The test will click the element within the `<iframe>` tag and operate on a pop-up window displayed. Finally, it will switch back to the main document. This is implemented as follows:

```
@Test
public void testIFrame()
{
    //The frame on the right side has a nested iframe containing
    //'Twitter Follow' Button
    //Activate the frame on right side using it's name attribute
    driver.switchTo().frame("right");

    //Get the iframe element
    WebElement twitterframe = driver.findElement(By.
tagName("iframe"));
    //Activate the iframe
    driver.switchTo().frame(twitterframe);
```

```
//Get and Click the follow button from iframe
//a Popup Window will appear after click
WebElement button = driver.findElement(By.id("follow-button"));
button.click();

//Store the handle of current driver window
String currentWindow = driver.getWindowHandle();

//The Twitter Popup does not have or title.
//Script will get handles of all open windows and
//desired window will be activated by checking it's Title
Set<String> allWindows = driver.getWindowHandles();
if(!allWindows.isEmpty()) {
    for (String windowId : allWindows)
    {
        driver.switchTo().window(windowId);
        if (driver.getTitle().equals("Unmesh Gundecha (@
upgundecha) on Twitter")) {
            assertTrue("Twitter Login Popup Window Found",true);
            driver.close();
            break;
        }

    }
}
//Switch back to original driver window
driver.switchTo().window(currentWindow);
//switch back to Page from the frame
driver.switchTo().defaultContent();
}
```

How it works...

Working with IFRAME is similar to working with a normal frame. In this example, the
<iframe> element is located using the findElement() method by passing the tag:

```
WebElement twitterframe = driver.findElement(By.tagName("iframe"));
  (twitterframe);
```

To activate the frame, the driver.switchTo().frame() method is called by passing it an
instance of the WebElement as follows:

```
driver.switchTo().frame(twitterframe)
```

See also

▶ *Identifying and handling frames by their content*

▶ *Working with IFRAME*

4

Data-driven Testing

In this chapter, we will cover:

- ▶ Creating a data-driven test using JUnit
- ▶ Creating a data-driven test using TestNG
- ▶ Reading test data from a CSV file using JUnit
- ▶ Reading test data from an Excel file using JUnit and Apache POI
- ▶ Reading test data from a database using JUnit and JDBC
- ▶ Creating a data-driven test in NUnit
- ▶ Creating a data-driven test in MSTEST
- ▶ Creating a data-driven test in Ruby using Roo
- ▶ Creating a data-driven test in Python

Introduction

Testing can be very repetitive, not only because we must run the same test over and over again, but also because many of the tests are only slightly different. For example, we might want to run the same test with different test inputs or test conditions and verify that the actual output varies accordingly. Each of these tests would consist of the exact same steps; however, what differs is the test data.

We can use the data-driven approach to achieve this. The data-driven testing approach is a widely used methodology in software test automation.

We will use the BMI calculator application as an example to understand the data-driven testing approach. The **Body Mass Index** (**BMI**) is a measurement of body fat based on height and weight, which applies to both men and women between the ages of 18 and 65 years. BMI can be used to indicate whether you are overweight, obese, underweight, or normal. The following tables show the various BMI categories:

Category	BMI range
Underweight	Less than 18.5
Normal weight	18.5 to 24.9
Overweight	25 to 29.9
Obesity	Greater than or equal to 30

To test whether the BMI calculator application indicates BMI categories correctly, instead of having a separate test script for each category, we can have one script that will enter the height and weight by referring to a set of values and checking the expected values. We can use the following combinations of test conditions to test the BMI calculator application:

Height(centimeters)	Weight(kilograms)	BMI	Category
160	45	17.6	Underweight
168	70	24.8	Normal
181	89	27.2	Overweight
178	100	31.6	Obesity

In the simplest form, the tester supplies inputs from a row in the table and expected outputs, which occur in the same row.

Data-driven approach – workflow

In the data-driven-approach, we can maintain the test data in form tables in a variety of formats, such as CSV files, Excel spreadsheets, and databases.

We implement test scripts after reading input and output values from data files, row by row, then passing the values to the main test code. Then, the test code navigates through the application, executing the steps needed for the test case using the variables loaded with data values.

Data-driven tests are great for applications involving calculations for testing ranges of values, boundary values, and corner cases.

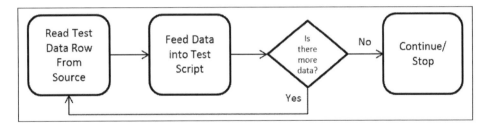

Benefits of data-driven testing

The benefits of data-driven testing are as follows:

- With data-driven tests, we can get greater test coverage while minimizing the amount of test code we need to write and maintain.
- Data-driven testing makes creating and running a lot of test conditions very easy.
- Data-driven tests require no programming skills. Even testers with limited knowledge of automation can quickly create tables on their own.
- Test data can be designed and created before the application is ready for testing.
- Data tables can also be used in manual testing.

Overall, the data-driven approach is the key for ease of use while building large-scale test automation.

Selenium WebDriver, being a pure browser automation API, does not provide built-in features to support data-driven testing. However, we can add support for data-driven testing using various options in Selenium WebDriver. In this chapter we will create some basic data-driven tests in JUnit and TestNG. Later, we will build some advanced data-driven tests using different data sources in JUnit and a data-driven test in Ruby using Roo, and Python.

We will also create data driven tests for .NET bindings using NUnit and MSTest.

Creating a data-driven test using JUnit

JUnit is a popular testing framework used to create Selenium WebDriver tests in Java. We can create data-driven Selenium WebDriver tests using the JUnit 4 parameterization feature. This can be done by using the JUnit parameterized class runner.

In this recipe, we will create a simple JUnit test case to test our BMI calculator application. We will specify the test data within our JUnit test case class. We will use various JUnit annotations to create a data-driven test.

Getting ready

▸ Set up a new project and add JUnit4 to the project's build path. You can set up the project in an IDE of your choice.

▸ Identify the set of values that need to be tested.

How to do it...

Let's create a data-driven test using JUnit, using the following steps:

1. Create a new JUnit test class that uses a parameterized runner using @ RunWith(value = Parameterized.class).

```
import org.openqa.selenium.firefox.FirefoxDriver;
import org.openqa.selenium.WebDriver;
import org.openqa.selenium.WebElement;
import org.openqa.selenium.By;

import org.junit.*;
import org.junit.runner.RunWith;
import org.junit.runners.Parameterized.Parameters;
import org.junit.runners.Parameterized;
import static org.junit.Assert.*;

import java.util.Arrays;
import java.util.Collection;

@RunWith(value = Parameterized.class)
public class SimpleDDT {
private static WebDriver driver;
private static StringBuffer verificationErrors = new
StringBuffer();
}
```

2. Declare instance variables for the parameterized values in the SimpleDDT class.

```
private String height;
private String weight;
private String bmi;
private String bmiCategory;
```

3. Define a method that will return the collection of parameters to the `SimpleDDT` class by using the `@Parameters` annotation.

```
@Parameters
public static Collection testData() {
   return Arrays.asList(
       new Object[][] {
               {"160","45","17.6","Underweight"},
               {"168","70","24.8","Normal"},
               {"181","89","27.2","Overweight"},
               {"178","100","31.6","Obesity"}
         }
       );
}
```

4. Add a constructor to the `SimpleDDT` class, which will be used by the test runner to pass the parameters to the `SimpleDDT` class instance.

```
public SimpleDDT(String height, String weight, String bmi, String
bmiCategory)
{
   this.height = height;
   this.weight = weight;
   this.bmi = bmi;
   this.bmiCategory = bmiCategory;
}
```

5. Finally, add the test case method `testBMICalculator()` that uses parameterized variables. Also, add the `setup()` and `teardown()` methods to the `SimpleDDT` class.

```
@Test
public void testBMICalculator() throws Exception {

   //Get the Height element and set the value using parameterised
   //height variable
   WebElement heightField = driver.findElement(By.
   name("heightCMS"));
   heightField.clear();
   heightField.sendKeys(height);

   //Get the Weight element and set the value using parameterised
   //Weight variable
   WebElement weightField = driver.findElement(By.
   name("weightKg"));
   weightField.clear();
   weightField.sendKeys(weight);

   //Click on Calculate Button
```

```
WebElement calculateButton = driver.findElement(By.
id("Calculate"));
calculateButton.click();

try {
  //Get the Bmi element and verify its value using parameterised
  //bmi variable
  WebElement bmiLabel = driver.findElement(By.name("bmi"));
  assertEquals(bmi, bmiLabel.getAttribute("value"));

  //Get the Bmi Category element and verify its value using
  //parameterised bmiCategory variable
  WebElement bmiCategoryLabel = driver.findElement(By.name
  ("bmi_category"));
  assertEquals(bmiCategory,bmiCategoryLabel.
  getAttribute("value"));

} catch (Error e) {
  //Capture and append Exceptions/Errors
  verificationErrors.append(e.toString());
  System.err.println("Assertion Fail "+ verificationErrors.
  toString());
  }
}
}
```

How it works...

When the test is executed, for each row in the test data collection, the test runner will instantiate the test case class, passing the test data as parameters to the `SimpleDDT` class constructor; it will then execute all the tests in the `SimpleDDT` class.

Instance variables are declared to store the test data passed by the test runner, as shown in the following code snippet:

```
private String height;
private String weight;
private String bmi;
private String bmiCategory;
```

In the test case class constructor, these variables are assigned with values at runtime by the test runner from the test data collection.

```
public SimpleDDT(String height, String weight, String bmi, String
bmiCategory)
{
   this.height = height;
```

```
    this.weight = weight;
    this.bmi = bmi;
    this.bmiCategory = bmiCategory;
}
```

In the testBMICalculator() method, we passed these variables to the Selenium WebDriver API. For example, to enter a value in the height field, we used the instance variable of the test case class as follows:

```
WebElement heightField = driver.findElement(By.name("heightCMS"));
heightField.sendKeys(this.height);
```

The expected result is also parameterized using the instance variable for BMI value.

```
WebElement bmiLabel = driver.findElement(By.name("bmi"));
assertEquals(this.bmi, bmiLabel.getAttribute("value"));
```

JUnit will display results for each set of test data along with time taken to execute it, as shown in the following screenshot:

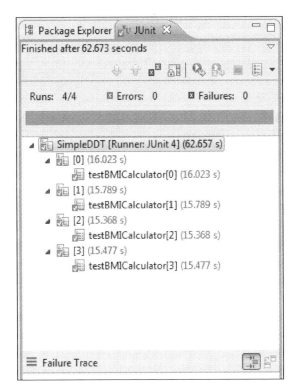

This is the simplest way to parameterize a test, however test data is hardcoded within the test case class, which could become difficult to maintain. It is always recommended that we store the test data in an external source, such as a CSV, Excel, or database file for easier maintenance.

See also

- ▶ The *Reading test data from a CSV file using JUnit* recipe
- ▶ The *Reading test data from an Excel file using JUnit and Apache POI* recipe
- ▶ The *Reading test data from a database using JUnit and JDBC* recipe

Creating a data-driven test using TestNG

TestNG is another widely used testing framework with Selenium WebDriver. It is very similar to JUnit. TestNG has rich features for testing, such as parameterization, parallel test execution, and so on.

TestNG provides the `DataProvider` feature to create data-driven tests. In this recipe, we will use the `DataProvider` feature to create a simple test. Creating data-driven tests in TestNG is fairly easy, when compared with JUnit.

Getting ready

- ▶ Download and install TestNG from `http://testng.org/doc/index.html`.
- ▶ Set up a new project and add TestNG to the project's build path. You can set up the project in an IDE of your choice.
- ▶ Identify the set of values that we need to test.

How to do it...

Let's parameterize a TestNG test with the following steps:

1. Create a new TestNG `test` class, as follows:

```
import org.openqa.selenium.WebDriver;
import org.openqa.selenium.firefox.FirefoxDriver;
import org.openqa.selenium.WebElement;
import org.openqa.selenium.By;

import org.testng.annotations.*;
import static org.testng.Assert.*;
```

```java
public class TestNGDDT {

    private WebDriver driver;
    private StringBuffer verificationErrors = new StringBuffer();
}
```

2. Define a method that will return the collection of parameters to the `TestNGDDT` class by using the `@DataProvider` annotation.

```java
@DataProvider
public Object[][] testData() {
    return new Object[][] {
        new Object[] {"160","45","17.6","Underweight"},
        new Object[] {"168","70","24.8","Normal"},
        new Object[] {"181","89","27.2","Overweight"},
        new Object[] {"178","100","31.6","Obesity"},
    };
}
```

3. Add a `@Test(dataProvider = "testData")` annotation to the test. With TestNG, we can parameterize individual tests instead of parameterizing the test case class. Pass the name of the method that will return the test data collection needed to execute this test.

```java
@BeforeTest
public void setUp() {
    // Create a new instance of the Firefox driver
    driver = new FirefoxDriver();
    driver.get("http://dl.dropbox.com/u/55228056/bmicalculator.
    html");

}

@Test(dataProvider = "testData")
public void testBMICalculator(String height, String weight, String
bmi, String category) {
    try {

        WebElement heightField = driver.findElement(By.
        name("heightCMS"));
        heightField.clear();
        heightField.sendKeys(height);

        WebElement weightField = driver.findElement(By.
        name("weightKg"));
        weightField.clear();
```

```
        weightField.sendKeys(weight);

        WebElement calculateButton = driver.findElement(By.
        id("Calculate"));
        calculateButton.click();

        WebElement bmiLabel = driver.findElement(By.name("bmi"));
        assertEquals(bmiLabel.getAttribute("value"),bmi);

        WebElement bmiCategoryLabel = driver.findElement
        (By.name("bmi_category"));
        assertEquals(bmiCategoryLabel.getAttribute("value"),category);

    } catch (Error e) {
        //Capture and append Exceptions/Errors
        verificationErrors.append(e.toString());
    }
}

@AfterTest
public void tearDown() {
    //Close the browser
    driver.quit();

    String verificationErrorString = verificationErrors.toString();
    if (!"".equals(verificationErrorString)) {
        fail(verificationErrorString);
    }
}
```

How it works...

Unlike the JUnit, where parameterization is done on a class level, TestNG supports parameterization at test level.

 In TestNG, we do not need a constructor and instance variable for the test case class to pass the parameter values. TestNG does the mapping automatically.

When a method is annotated with `@DataProvider`, it becomes a data feeder method by passing the test data to the test case. In this example, the `testData()` method will become the data feeder method and TestNG will pass the array of data rows to the test method one-by-one:

```
@DataProvider
public Object[][] testData() {
  return new Object[][] {
    new Object[] {"160","45","17.6","Underweight"},
    new Object[] {"168","70","24.8","Normal"},
    new Object[] {"181","89","27.2","Overweight"},
    new Object[] {"178","100","31.6","Obesity"},
  };
}
```

The test case method is linked to the data feeder method by passing the name of the `dataProvider` method to the `@Test` annotation.

```
@Test(dataProvider = "testData")
public void testBMICalculator(String height, String weight, String bmi, String category)
```

TestNG will execute the test four times, with different test combinations. TestNG also generates a well formatted report at the end of test execution.

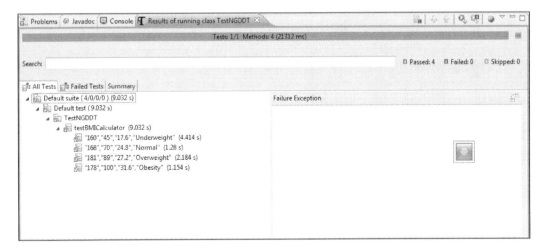

There's more...

To run Selenium tests in parallel, the TestNG parameterization feature comes in very handy. TestNG supports running Selenium tests parallel in a multithreading safe environment.

See also

▸ The *Reading test data from a CSV file using JUnit* recipe

▸ The *Reading test data from an Excel file using JUnit and Apache POI*

▸ The *Reading test data from a database using JUnit and JDBC* recipe

Reading test data from a CSV file using JUnit

We saw a simple data-driven test using JUnit and TestNG. The test data was hardcoded in test script code. This could become difficult to maintain. It is recommended that we store the test data separately from the test scripts.

Often we use data from the production environment for testing. This data can be exported in CSV format. We can read CSV files using Java IO and utility classes and can pass the data from these files to the test code.

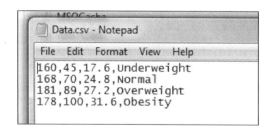

In this recipe, we will read data from a CSV file and use this data to execute the test script.

Getting ready

▸ Set up a new project and add JUnit4 to the project's build path. You can set up the project in an IDE of your choice.

▸ Create the CSV file with the required data.

How to do it...

Let's implement a parameterized test with CSV, using the following steps:

1. Create a test class with the name `CsvTestData`. Make it a parameterized class by adding the `@RunWith` attribute.

```
import org.openqa.selenium.firefox.FirefoxDriver;
import org.openqa.selenium.WebDriver;
import org.openqa.selenium.WebElement;
import org.openqa.selenium.By;

import org.junit.*;
import org.junit.runner.*;
import org.junit.runners.*;
import org.junit.runners.Parameterized.Parameters;

import static org.junit.Assert.*;

import java.io.*;
import java.util.*;

@RunWith(value = Parameterized.class)
public class CsvTestData {

   private static WebDriver driver;
   private static StringBuffer verificationErrors = new
StringBuffer();

   private String height;
   private String weight;
   private String bmi;
   private String bmiCategory;
}
```

2. Add the `testData()` method, which will return test data from the CSV file as a collection. This method internally calls the `getTestData()` method.

```
@Parameters
public static Collection testData() throws IOException {
   return  getTestData("C:\\data.csv");
}
```
Add the constructor which maps the instance variables with the test data
```
public CsvTestData(String height, String weight, String bmi,
String bmiCategory) {
```

```
        this.height = height;
        this.weight = weight;
        this.bmi = bmi;
        this.bmiCategory = bmiCategory;
    }
```

3. Add the `getTestData()` method, which reads a CSV file and returns the data in the collection.

```
public static Collection<String[]> getTestData(String fileName)
throws IOException {
    List<String[]> records = new ArrayList<String[]>();
    String record;

    BufferedReader file = new BufferedReader(new
    FileReader(fileName));
    while ((record=file.readLine())!=null) {
        String fields[] = record.split(",");
        records.add(fields);
    }
    file.close();
    return records;
}
```

4. Add the `testBMICalculator()` method along with the `setUp()` and `tearDown()` methods.

```
@BeforeClass
public static void setUp() throws Exception {
    // Create a new instance of the Firefox driver
    driver = new FirefoxDriver();
    driver.get("http://dl.dropbox.com/u/55228056/bmicalculator.
    html");
}

@Test
public void testBMICalculator() throws Exception {
    try {
        WebElement heightField = driver.findElement(By.
        name("heightCMS"));
        heightField.clear();
        heightField.sendKeys(height);

        WebElement weightField = driver.findElement(By.
        name("weightKg"));
        weightField.clear();
```

```
weightField.sendKeys(weight);

WebElement calculateButton = driver.findElement(By.
id("Calculate"));
calculateButton.click();

WebElement bmiLabel = driver.findElement(By.name("bmi"));
assertEquals(bmi, bmiLabel.getAttribute("value"));

WebElement bmiCategoryLabel = driver.findElement(By.name
("bmi_category"));
assertEquals(bmiCategory,bmiCategoryLabel.
getAttribute("value"));

} catch (Error e) {
  //Capture and append Exceptions/Errors
  verificationErrors.append(e.toString());
  System.err.println("Assertion Fail " + verificationErrors.
  toString());
  }
}

@AfterClass
public static void tearDown() throws Exception {
  //Close the browser
  driver.quit();

  String verificationErrorString = verificationErrors.toString();
  if (!"".equals(verificationErrorString)) {
    fail(verificationErrorString);
  }
}
```

How it works...

When the test is executed, the `testData()` method will call the `getTestData()` helper method by passing the path of the CSV file. Inside the `getTestData()` method, the `BufferedReader` class from the `java.io` namespace is used to read the file line-by-line. Lines are then split into an array of strings, using the comma delimiter. This array is then added to `Collection` or `ArrayList`, either of which is then returned to the `testData()` method.

For each row in the test data collection returned by the `testData()` method, the test runner will instantiate the test case class, passing the test data as parameters to the test class constructor and will then execute all the tests in the `test` class.

Changing delimiters

Sometimes, CSV files may have a separate delimiter than the comma. We can change the `getTestData()` method to handle these delimiters. For example, a tab character is used to separate records. For this, we can split the record, using the `\t` character, in the following way:

```
String fields[] = record.split("\t");
```

See also

▸ The *Creating a data-driven test using JUnit* recipe

▸ The *Reading test data from an Excel file using JUnit and Apache POI* recipe

▸ The *Reading test data from a database using JUnit and JDBC* recipe

Reading test data from an Excel file using JUnit and Apache POI

To maintain test cases and test data, Microsoft Excel is the favorite tool used by testers. Compared to the CSV file format, Excel gives numerous features and a structured way to store data. A tester can create and maintain tables of test data in an Excel spreadsheet easily.

	A	B	C	D	E
1	Height	Weight	Bmi	Category	ErrorMessage
2	160	45	17.6	Underweight	<Blank>
3	168	70	24.8	Normal	<Blank>
4	181	89	27.2	Overweight	<Blank>
5	178	100	31.6	Obesity	<Blank>
6	<Blank>	80	<Blank>	<Blank>	Please enter Height
7	181	<Blank>	<Blank>	<Blank>	Please enter Weight

In this recipe, we will use an Excel spreadsheet as your data source. We will use the Apache POI API, developed by the Apache Foundation, to manipulate the Excel spreadsheet. This recipe also implements some negative test handling.

Getting ready

▶ Set up a new project and add JUNIT4 to project's build path

▶ Download and add the following Apache POI JAR files to the project's build path, from `http://poi.apache.org/`:

  ❑ `poi-3.8.jar`

  ❑ `poi-ooxml-3.8.jar`

  ❑ `poi-ooxml-schemas-3.8.jar`

  ❑ `dom4j-1.6.1.jar`

  ❑ `stax-api-1.0.1.jar`

  ❑ `xmlbeans-2.3.0.jar`

▶ Create an Excel spreadsheet with the required data

We will also need a `SpreadsheetData` helper class to read Excel spreadsheets. This is available in the source code bundle for this book. This class supports both the old `.xls` and newer `.xlsx` formats.

How to do it...

Let's create a test that uses Excel spreadsheet test data for parameterization, using the following steps:

1. Create a `test` class with the name `ExcelTestData`. Make it a parameterized class by adding the `@RunWith` attribute:

```
import org.openqa.selenium.WebDriver;
import org.openqa.selenium.chrome.ChromeDriver;
import org.openqa.selenium.WebElement;
import org.openqa.selenium.By;

import org.junit.*;
import org.junit.runner.RunWith;
import org.junit.runners.Parameterized.Parameters;
import org.junit.runners.Parameterized;
import static org.junit.Assert.*;

import java.io.FileInputStream;
import java.io.InputStream;
import java.util.Collection;

@RunWith(value = Parameterized.class)
```

```
public class ExcelTestData {

    private static WebDriver driver;
    private static StringBuffer verificationErrors = new
    StringBuffer();

    private String height;
    private String weight;
    private String bmi;
    private String bmiCategory;
    private String error;
}
```

2. Add the `testData()` method, which will return test data from the Excel spreadsheet as a collection. This method internally calls the `SpreadsheetData` class's `getData()` method.

```
@Parameters
public static Collection testData() throws Exception {
    InputStream spreadsheet = new FileInputStream("C:\\Data.xlsx");
    return new SpreadsheetData(spreadsheet).getData();
}
```

3. Add the constructor which maps the instance variables with the test data.

```
public ExcelTestData(String height, String weight, String bmi,
String bmiCategory, String error)
{
    this.height = height;
    this.weight = weight;
    this.bmi = bmi;
    this.bmiCategory = bmiCategory;
    this.error = error;
}
```

4. Add the `test` method along with the `setUp()` and `tearDown()` methods.

```
@BeforeClass
    public static void setUp() throws Exception {

        // Create a new instance of the Chrome driver
        driver = new ChromeDriver();
        driver.get("http://dl.dropbox.com/u/55228056/bmicalculator.
        html");
    }

    @Test
```

```java
public void testBMICalculator() throws Exception {

  try {
      WebElement heightField = driver.findElement(By.
      name("heightCMS"));
      heightField.clear();
      if (!height.equals("<Blank>"))
        heightField.sendKeys(this.height);

      WebElement weightField = driver.findElement(By.
      name("weightKg"));
      weightField.clear();
      if(!weight.equals("<Blank>"))
        weightField.sendKeys(this.weight);

      WebElement calculateButton = driver.findElement(By.
      id("Calculate"));
      calculateButton.click();

      if (error.equals("<Blank>")) {
        WebElement bmiField = driver.findElement(By.
        name("bmi"));
        assertEquals(this.bmi, bmiField.getAttribute("value"));

        WebElement bmiCategoryField = driver.findElement(By.
        name("bmi_category"));
        assertEquals(this.bmiCategory,bmiCategoryField.
        getAttribute("value"));
      }
      else {
        WebElement errorLabel = driver.findElement(By.
        id("error"));
        assertEquals(this.error,errorLabel.getText());
      }
  } catch (Error e) {
    //Capture and append Exceptions/Errors
    verificationErrors.append(e.toString());
  }
}

@AfterClass
public static void tearDown() throws Exception {

  //Close the browser
```

```
        driver.quit();

        String verificationErrorString = verificationErrors.
        toString();
        if (!"".equals(verificationErrorString)) {
          fail(verificationErrorString);
        }
      }
    }
```

How it works...

When the test is executed, the `testData()` method will create an instance of the `SpreadsheetData` class. The `SpreadsheetData` class reads the contents of the Excel spreadsheet row by row in a collection and returns this collection back to the `testData()` method.

```
InputStream spreadsheet = new FileInputStream("resources//data//Data.
xls");
return new SpreadsheetData(spreadsheet).getData();
```

For each row in the test data collection returned by the `testData()` method, the test runner will instantiate the test case class, passing the test data as parameters to the test class constructor, and then execute all the tests in the `test` class.

See also

  ▸   The *Creating a data-driven test using JUnit* recipe

  ▸   The *Reading test data from a CSV file using JUnit* recipe

  ▸   The *Reading test data from a database using JUnit and JDBC* recipe

Reading test data from a database using JUnit and JDBC

In the earlier recipes, we used CSV and Excel spreadsheets to maintain the test data and read this test data in JUnit.

The test data can also be read from a database. This works similar to the previous recipes, however, we will create a helper method using JDBC to read the test data from a Microsoft Access database. This recipe can be used with any database.

Getting ready

▸ Set up a new project and add JUnit4 to the project's build path.

▸ Create a database with the required data in a test data table. This example uses a Microsoft Access database. The sample file is available with the book's sample code.

How to do it...

Let's implement a parameterized test with CSV by using the following steps:

1. Create a `test` class with name `DBTestData`. Make it a parameterized class by adding the `@RunWith` attribute.

```
import org.openqa.selenium.WebDriver;
import org.openqa.selenium.firefox.FirefoxDriver;
import org.openqa.selenium.WebElement;
import org.openqa.selenium.By;

import org.junit.*;
import org.junit.runner.*;
import org.junit.runners.*;
import org.junit.runners.Parameterized.Parameters;

import static org.junit.Assert.*;

import java.sql.*;
import java.util.*;

@RunWith(value = Parameterized.class)
public class DbTestData {

  private static WebDriver driver;
  private static StringBuffer verificationErrors = new
  StringBuffer();

  private String height;
  private String weight;
  private String bmi;
  private String bmiCategory;
}
```

2. Add the `testData()` method that will return the test data from the database as a collection of strings. This method internally calls the `getTestData()` method.

```
@Parameters
public static Collection testData() throws Exception {
    return  getTestData("C:\\BmiTesting.mdb","SELECT Height, Weight,
Bmi, Category FROM TestData");
}
```

3. Add the constructor, which maps the instance variables with the test.

```
public DbTestData(String height, String weight, String bmi, String
bmiCategory) {
    this.height = height;
    this.weight = weight;
    this.bmi = bmi;
    this.bmiCategory = bmiCategory;
}
```

4. Add the `getTestData()` method that reads a database query results and returns the data in the collection.

```
public static Collection<String[]> getTestData(String mdbFile,
String sqlQuery) throws Exception {
    ArrayList<String[]> records = new ArrayList<String[]>();

    Class.forName("sun.jdbc.odbc.JdbcOdbcDriver");
    String myDB = "jdbc:odbc:Driver={Microsoft Access Driver
(*.mdb)};DBQ=" + mdbFile;
    Connection conn = DriverManager.getConnection(myDB, "", "");

    Statement stmt = null;
    ResultSet rs = null;

    stmt = conn.createStatement(ResultSet.TYPE_SCROLL_INSENSITIVE,
       ResultSet.CONCUR_UPDATABLE);

    rs = stmt.executeQuery(sqlQuery);
    ResultSetMetaData rsMetaData = rs.getMetaData();

    int cols = rsMetaData.getColumnCount();

    while (rs.next())
    {

    String fields[] = new String[cols];
    int col = 0;
```

```
      for(int colIdx=1;colIdx<=cols;colIdx++) {
        fields[col] = rs.getString(colIdx);
        col++;
      }
      records.add(fields);
      }

      rs.close();
      stmt.close();
      conn.close();

      return records;
    }
```

5. Add the test method along with the `setUp()` and `tearDown()` methods.

```
@BeforeClass
public static void setUp() throws Exception {
  // Create a new instance of the Firefox driver
  driver = new FirefoxDriver();
  driver.get("http://dl.dropbox.com/u/55228056/bmicalculator.
  html");
}

@Test
public void testBMICalculator() {
  try {
    WebElement heightField = driver.findElement(By.
    name("heightCMS"));
    heightField.clear();
    heightField.sendKeys(this.height);

    WebElement weightField = driver.findElement(By.
    name("weightKg"));
    weightField.clear();
    weightField.sendKeys(this.weight);

    WebElement calculateButton = driver.findElement(By.
    id("Calculate"));
    calculateButton.click();

    WebElement bmiLabel = driver.findElement(By.name("bmi"));
    assertEquals(this.bmi, bmiLabel.getAttribute("value"));

    WebElement bmiCategoryLabel = driver.findElement(By.name
    ("bmi_category"));
```

```
        assertEquals(this.bmiCategory,bmiCategoryLabel.
        getAttribute("value"));

    } catch (Error e) {
        //Capture and append Exceptions/Errors
        verificationErrors.append(e.toString());
    }
}


@AfterClass
public static void tearDown() throws Exception {
    //Close the browser
    driver.quit();

    String verificationErrorString = verificationErrors.toString();
    if (!"".equals(verificationErrorString)) {

        fail(verificationErrorString);
    }
}
```

How it works...

When the test is executed, the `testData()` method will call the `getTestData()`
helper method by passing the path of the database file and the SELECT query. Inside the
`getTestData()` method, a `connection` object to the database is created by calling the
`DriverManager.getConnection()` method.

An instance of the `Statement` class is created to execute the select query specified in the
`sqlQuery` string and return the results to an instance of the `ResultSet` object. The rows
returned in the `ResultSet` object are then collected in a string array by iterating through the
result set. Finally, a collection of records is returned.

For each data row in the the test data collection returned by the `testData()` method, the
test runner will instantiate the test case class, passing the test data as parameters to the test
class constructor, and then execute all the tests in the `test` class.

Test data can also be referenced from any database other than a Microsoft Access database.
The `getTestData()` method will need a connection string as per the database used in
the project.

- ▸ The *Creating a data-driven test using JUnit* recipe
- ▸ The *Reading test data from a CSV file using JUnit* recipe
- ▸ The *Reading test data from an Excel file using JUnit and Apache POI* recipe

Creating a data-driven test in NUnit

The NUnit framework has been widely used by the Selenium WebDriver community to create test scripts with .NET bindings.

Similar to the JUnit framework, the NUnit framework also supports data-driven testing in the simplest manner. In this recipe, we will create a Selenium WebDriver test using NUnit. We will read the test data from an XML file used in the first recipe.

Getting ready

- ▸ Download and install NUnit from `http://www.nunit.org/`
- ▸ Create the test data file in the XML format as follows:

```
testdata>
<vars height="160" weight="45" bmi="17.6" bmi_
category="Underweight" />
  <vars height="168" weight="70" bmi="24.8" bmi_category="Normal"
/>
  <vars height="181" weight="89" bmi="27.2" bmi_
category="Overweight" />
  <vars height="178" weight="100" bmi="31.6" bmi_
category="Obesity" />
</testdata>
```

- ▸ Create a new C# class library project and name it `BMICalculator`
- ▸ Add a reference to NUnit, WebDriver, .NET binding, System XML, and `System.Xml.Linq`

How to do it...

Let's create a parameterized test in NUnit, with the following steps:

1. Create a new C# class item with the name `BMICalculatorNUnitTest`.

2. Copy the following code to the newly created class by replacing its contents:

```
using System;
using System.Collections.Generic;
using System.Linq;
using System.Text;
using NUnit.Framework;
using System.Collections;
using System.Xml.Linq;
using OpenQA.Selenium;
using OpenQA.Selenium.Firefox;
using OpenQA.Selenium.Support;
using OpenQA.Selenium.Support.UI;

namespace BMICalculator
{
    [TestFixture]
    public class BMICalculatorNUnitTest
    {
        IWebDriver driver;

        [SetUp]
        public void TestSetup()
        {
            // Create a instance of the Firefox driver using
IWebDriver Interface
            driver = new FirefoxDriver();
        }

        [TestCaseSource("BmiTestData")]
        public void TestBmiCalculator(string height, string weight,
        string expected_bmi, string expected_category)
        {
            driver.Navigate().GoToUrl("http://dl.dropbox.
            com/u/55228056/mobilebmicalculator.html");

            IWebElement heightElement = driver.FindElement(By.
            Name("heightCMS"));
            heightElement.SendKeys(height);

            IWebElement weightElement = driver.FindElement(By.
            Name("weightKg"));
            weightElement.SendKeys(weight);

            IWebElement calculateButton = driver.FindElement(By.
            Id("Calculate"));
```

```
        calculateButton.Click();

        IWebElement bmiElement = driver.FindElement(By.
        Name("bmi"));
        Assert.AreEqual(expected_bmi, bmiElement.
        GetAttribute("value"));

        IWebElement bmiCatElement = driver.FindElement(By.
        Name("bmi_category"));
        Assert.AreEqual(expected_category, bmiCatElement.
        GetAttribute("value"));

    }

    [TearDown]
    public void TestCleanUp()
    {
        // Close the browser
        driver.Quit();
    }

    private IEnumerable BmiTestData
    {
        get { return GetBmiTestData(); }
    }
    private IEnumerable GetBmiTestData()
    {
        var doc = XDocument.Load(@"c:\data.xml");
        return
            from vars in doc.Descendants("vars")
            let height = vars.Attribute("height").Value
            let weight = vars.Attribute("weight").Value
            let expected_bmi = vars.Attribute("bmi").Value
            let expected_category = vars.Attribute
            ("bmi_category").Value

            select new object[] { height, weight,
            expected_bmi, expected_category };
    }
  }
}
```

How it works...

While creating a data-driven test in NUnit, we use the `TestCaseSource` attribute. We will specify the name of the `IEnumerable` property that will provide test data to this test case with the `TestCaseSource` attribute shown in the following code:

```
[TestCaseSource("BmiTestData")]
public void TestBmiCalculator(string height, string weight, string
expected_bmi, string expected_category)
```

When we execute the test, NUnit framework will generate test cases by calling the `BmiTestData` property. This will return an array of arguments as `IEnumerable` by calling the `GetBmiTestData()` method. An array of arguments is created by reading an XML file using a LINQ Query in `GetBmiTestData()` method. When we open the test in the NUnit GUI, it shows the test cases for all the test data combinations provided in the input XML file:

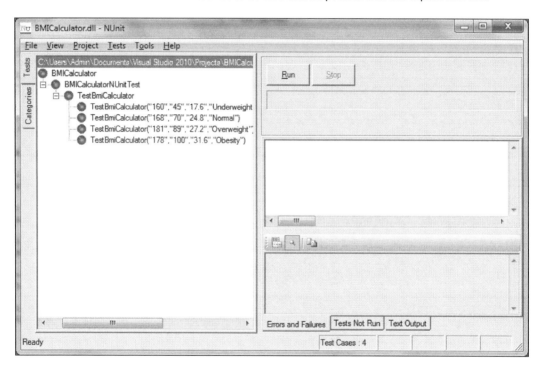

With this, we can get the test data from any source, such as CSV, Excel spreadsheet, or a database. The NUnit GUI will show the results when all the tests are executed, as seen in the following screenshot:

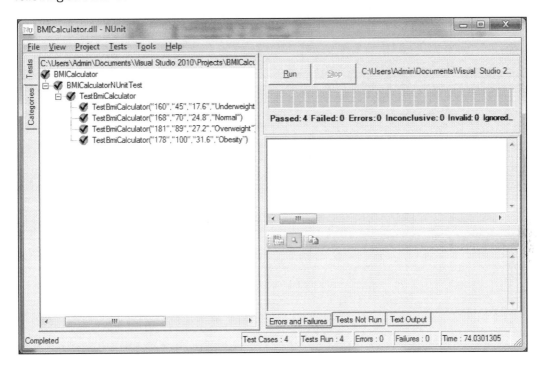

See also

▶ The *Creating a data-driven test in MSTEST* recipe

Creating a data-driven test in MSTEST

To create a data-driven test in MSTEST, the unit testing framework provided by Microsoft Visual Studio is the simplest way to parameterize the test scripts with .NET bindings.

MSTEST has in-built features to support data-driven testing, which can be configured very easily. In this recipe, we will use MSTEST to create a data-driven Selenium test by reading test data from an Excel spreadsheet.

Getting ready

▶ Create a new C# test project in Microsoft Visual Studio 2010 and name it `BMICalculator`

▶ Add a reference to the WebDriver .NET binding

How to do it...

You can parameterize a test in MSTEST by adding the Excel spreadsheet to deployment items of the test project, using the following steps:

1. Click on **Local.testsettings** under **Solution Items**, as shown in the following screenshot:

2. The **Test Settings** dialog will appear. We need to add the test data file by clicking the **Add File** button in the **Deployment** section, as shown in the following screenshot:

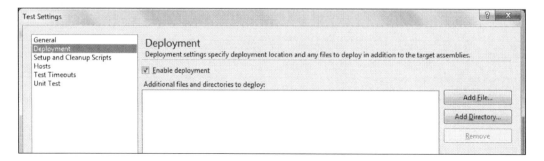

3. Once you add the file to the **Deployment** section, it will appear in the list, as shown in the following screenshot:

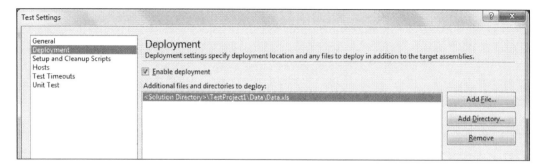

4. Create a new test class and name it `BMICalculatorTests`. Copy the following code to this class:

```csharp
using System;
using System.Text;
using System.Collections.Generic;
using System.Linq;
using Microsoft.VisualStudio.TestTools.UnitTesting;
using OpenQA.Selenium;
using OpenQA.Selenium.Firefox;
using OpenQA.Selenium.Support;
using OpenQA.Selenium.Support.UI;
using System.Data;

namespace BMICalculator
{
    [TestClass]
    public class BMICalculatorTests
    {
        IWebDriver driver;

        [TestInitialize]
        public void TestSetup()
        {

            //Create a instance of the Firefox driver using
            //IWebDriver Interface
            driver = new FirefoxDriver();
        }

        private TestContext testContextInstance;

        /// <summary>
        ///Gets or sets the test context which provides
        ///information about and functionality for the current
        //test run.
        ///</summary>
        public TestContext TestContext
        {
            get
            {
                return testContextInstance;
            }
            set
            {
                testContextInstance = value;
            }
```

```
        }

        [TestMethod]
        [DeploymentItem("Data.xls")]
        [DataSource("System.Data.OleDb", "Provider=Microsoft.
        ACE.OLEDB.12.0;Data Source=Data.xls;Persist Security
        Info=False;Extended Properties='Excel 12.0;HDR=Yes'",
        "Data$", DataAccessMethod.Sequential)]
        public void TestBMICalculator()
        {
            driver.Navigate().GoToUrl("http://dl.dropbox.
            com/u/55228056/bmicalculator.html");

            IWebElement height = driver.FindElement(By.
            Name("heightCMS"));
            height.SendKeys(TestContext.DataRow["Height"].
            ToString());

            IWebElement weight = driver.FindElement(By.
            Name("weightKg"));
            weight.SendKeys(TestContext.DataRow["Weight"].
            ToString());

            IWebElement calculateButton = driver.FindElement(By.
            Id("Calculate"));
            calculateButton.Click();

            IWebElement bmi = driver.FindElement(By.Name("bmi"));
            Assert.AreEqual(TestContext.DataRow["Bmi"].ToString(),
            bmi.GetAttribute("value"));

            IWebElement bmi_category = driver.FindElement(By.
            Name("bmi_category"));
            Assert.AreEqual(TestContext.DataRow["Category"].
            ToString(), bmi_category.GetAttribute("value"));
        }

        [TestCleanup]
        public void TestCleanUp()
        {
            // Close the browser
            driver.Quit();
        }

    }
}
```

How it works...

When we add the `DataSource` attribute to a test in MSTEST, it provides data source-specific information for data-driven testing to the framework.

```
[TestMethod]
[DeploymentItem("Data.xls")]
[DataSource("System.Data.OleDb", "Provider=Microsoft.ACE.
OLEDB.12.0;Data Source=Data.xls;Persist Security Info=False;Extended
Properties='Excel 12.0;HDR=Yes'", "Data$", DataAccessMethod.
Sequential)]
public void TestBMICalculator()
```

It reads the test data from the source. In this example, the source is an Excel spreadsheet. The framework internally creates a `DataTable` object to store the values from the source. The `TestContext` test method provides a collection of data rows for parameterization. We can access a field by specifying its name, as follows:

```
        IWebElement height = driver.FindElement(By.
Name("heightCMS"));
                height.SendKeys(TestContext.DataRow["Height"].ToString());
```

With the `DataSource` attribute, we can specify the connection string or a configuration file to read data from a variety of sources including CSV File, Excel spreadsheets, XML files, or databases.

See also

▶ The *Creating a data-driven test in NUnit* recipe

Creating a data-driven test in Ruby using Roo

In the previous recipes, we saw parameterization with Java and .NET; Ruby also has been used widely to create Selenium WebDriver tests.

Again, Ruby does not have its own way to parameterize the script. However, we can use the Roo (`http://roo.rubyforge.org/`) gem in Ruby to read spreadsheets. Roo supports multiple formats as follows:

▶ A locally stored Excel (`.xls`) file

▶ A locally stored OpenOffice (`.ods`) file

▶ An Excel file (`.xls`) stored in a Confluence wiki page with Confluence Office Connector

▶ A Google Docs spreadsheet

Roo is a great alternative to the Ruby Excel COM WIN32 API, as it does not need Excel or OpenOffice installed on the machine. It reads both these files natively.

In this recipe, we will parameterize the Selenium WebDriver test created in Ruby bindings, using an Excel spreadsheet as a test data source.

Getting ready

You need to install the Roo gem by using the following command:

```
gem install roo
```

This command will download and install all the dependencies required for Roo on your machine.

How to do it...

Let's create a simple Ruby test for parameterization, by using the following steps. This test will read test data from the Excel spreadsheet used in the *Reading test data from an Excel file using JUnit and Apache POI* recipe earlier. Create a Ruby test by importing the following modules:

```
require 'rubygems'
require 'selenium-webdriver'
require 'roo'
```

1. Create an instance of WebDriver. We will use the Firefox browser.

   ```
   #Create an instance of WebDriver for Firefox
   driver = Selenium::WebDriver.for :firefox
   ```

2. Declare the following variables to print a summary of test combinations executed from the test data source:

   ```
   #Variables for Printing Test Summary
   test_executed = 0
   test_passed = 0
   test_failed = 0
   ```

3. Create an instance of `Excel` class from Roo for reading a spreadsheet.

   ```
   #Create an instance of a Excel Spreadsheet
   data = Excel.new("C:\\Data.xls")
   data.default_sheet = data.sheets.first
   ```

4. Add the following code, which will iterate through the spreadsheet, reading each combination and then performing the operations and verifications:

```
#Iterate through the Sheet reading Rows line by line
data.first_row.upto(data.last_row) do |line|
  if data.cell(line,1) != "Height" #Ignore the first line for
  Headers
    begin
      test_status = true
      test_executed = test_executed + 1
      puts "Test " + test_executed.to_s()

      driver.get "http://dl.dropbox.com/u/55228056/bmicalculator.
      html"

      height = driver.find_element :name => "heightCMS"
      height.send_keys data.cell(line,1).to_s()

      weight = driver.find_element :name => "weightKg"
      weight.send_keys  data.cell(line,2).to_s()

      calculateButton = driver.find_element :id =>"Calculate"
      calculateButton.click

      bmi = driver.find_element :name =>"bmi"
      bmi_category = driver.find_element :name =>"bmi_category"

      if bmi.attribute("value").to_s() == data.cell(line,3).to_s()
        puts "Pass, expected value for BMI <" + data.cell(line,3).
        to_s() + ">, actual <" + bmi.attribute("value").to_s() + ">"
      else
        puts "Fail, expected value for BMI <" + data.cell(line,3).
        to_s() + ">, actual <" + bmi.attribute("value").to_s() + ">"
        test_status=false
      end

      if bmi_category.attribute("value").to_s() == data.
      cell(line,4).to_s()
        puts "Pass, expected value for BMI Category <" +
        data.cell(line,4).to_s() + ">, actual <" +  bmi_category.
        attribute("value").to_s() + ">"
      else
        puts "Fail, expected value for BMI Category <" +
        data.cell(line,4).to_s() + ">, actual <" +  bmi_category.
        attribute("value").to_s() + ">"
        test_status=false
```

```
            end

        if test_status == true
          test_passed = test_passed + 1
        else
          test_failed = test_failed + 1
        end
      rescue
        puts "An error occurred: #{$!}"
      end
    end
  end
```

5. Finally, we will print a summary of test combinations that were executed and passed, or those that failed the test using the following code:

```
puts "------------------------------------------------"
puts "Total (" + test_executed.to_s() + ") Tests Executed"
puts "Total (" + test_passed.to_s() + ") Tests Passed"
puts "Total (" + test_failed.to_s() + ") Tests Failed"

driver.quit
```

How it works...

When we execute this test, Roo will read the contents of the Excel spreadsheet into the `data` object, using the following code:

```
#Create an instance of a Excel Spreadsheet
data = Excel.new("C:\\Data.xls")
data.default_sheet = data.sheets.first
```

We can then iterate the `data` object from the first row to the last row using the following code:

```
data.first_row.upto(data.last_row) do |line|
```

This will copy the content from a row in a variable named `line`. The value from a data cell is accessed using the `data.cell()` method, by passing the line and position of the cell using the following code:

```
height = driver.find_element :name => "heightCMS"
height.send_keys data.cell(line,1).to_s()
```

We also added a custom reporting code that will generate a nicely formatted report at the end of the test execution, as shown in the following screenshot:

There's more...

We can also read the Google Docs spreadsheets from Roo. This can be done by using the `Google.new()` method, by passing the key for the Google Docs spreadsheet, as shown in the following command:

```
data = Google.new("0Al-3LZqhACsidFhlNmdnYktmTkREVEkzb3B0ZnYybHc")
```

If you want to use Google spreadsheets, you must either have set the environment variables `GOOGLE_MAIL` and `GOOGLE_PASSWORD` or passed the Google-username and password to the `Google#new` method.

Many teams maintain Excel spreadsheets on Confluence Wiki. Using Roo, you can also read a spreadsheet stored on Confluence Wiki. For more information, visit the Roo home page at `http://roo.rubyforge.org/`.

Creating a data-driven test in Python

Python is also a widely used language for building Selenium WebDriver tests. It offers various ways to parameterize tests.

In this recipe, we will parameterize a Selenium WebDriver test written in Python, using a CSV file.

How to do it...

Let's create a simple Python test for parameterization, using the following steps. This test will read test data from the CSV file used in the *Reading test data from a CSV file using JUnit* recipe earlier.

1. Create a Ruby test by importing the following modules:

```
from selenium import webdriver
import csv, sys
```

2. Declare the following variables to print a summary of the test combinations executed from the test data source:

```
#Variables for Printing Test Summary
test_executed = 0
test_passed = 0
test_failed = 0
test_status = True
```

3. Add the following code, which will iterate through the CSV data by reading each combination and then performing the operations and verifications:

```
try:
    #Create an instance of WebDriver for Firefox
    driver = webdriver.Firefox()
    driver.get("http://dl.dropbox.com/u/55228056/bmicalculator.
    html")

    #Open the CSV file
    datafile = open('c:\data.csv', "rb")
    #Create a CSV Reader from CSV file
    reader = csv.reader(datafile)

    test_executed = 0
    #Iterate through the CSV Rows line by line
    for row in reader:
        test_executed += 1
        print "Test " + str(test_executed)

        heightField = driver.find_element_by_name("heightCMS")
        heightField.clear()
        heightField.send_keys(row[0])

        weightField = driver.find_element_by_name("weightKg")
        weightField.clear()
```

```
        weightField.send_keys(row[1])

        calculateButton = driver.find_element_by_id("Calculate")
        calculateButton.click()

        bmiLabel = driver.find_element_by_name("bmi")
        bmiCategoryLabel = driver.find_element_by_name("bmi_category")

        if bmiLabel.get_attribute("value") == row[2]:
          print "Pass, expected value for BMI <" + row[2] + ">,
          actual <" + bmiLabel.get_attribute("value") + ">"
        else:
          print "Fail, expected value for BMI <" + row[2] + ">,
          actual <" + bmiLabel.get_attribute("value") + ">"
          test_status = False

        if bmiCategoryLabel.get_attribute("value") == row[3]:
          print "Pass, expected value for BMI Category <" + row[3] +
          ">, actual <" + bmiCategoryLabel.get_attribute("value") + ">"
        else:
          print "Fail, expected value for BMI Category <" + row[3] +
          ">, actual <" + bmiCategoryLabel.get_attribute("value") + ">"
          test_status = False

        if test_status == True:
          test_passed = test_passed + 1
        else:
          test_failed = test_failed + 1

except:
    print "Unexpected error:", sys.exc_info()[0]
    raise
finally:
  print "---------------------------------------------"
  print "Total (" + str(test_executed)+ ") Tests Executed"
  print "Total (" + str(test_passed)+ ") Tests Passed"
  print "Total (" + str(test_failed) + ") Tests Failed"
  driver.close()
  datafile.close()
```

How it works...

When we execute this test, Python will read the contents of the CSV file to the `reader` object.

```
#Open the CSV file
datafile  = open('c:\data.csv', "rb")
#Create a CSV Reader from CSV file
reader = csv.reader(datafile) ets.first
```

We can then iterate on the `data` object from first row to the last row, using the `for` loop, as shown in the following code:

```
for row in reader:
```

This will copy the content from `reader` into a variable named `row`. The value from a column is accessed using `row[index]`, by passing the index of the column.

```
heightField = driver.find_element_by_name("heightCMS")
heightField.clear()
heightField.send_keys(row[0])
```

We also added a custom reporting code that will generate a nicely formatted report at the end of test execution, as shown in the following screenshot:

5
Using the Page Object Model

In this chapter, we will cover the following topics:

- ▶ Using the PageFactory class for exposing the elements from a page
- ▶ Using the PageFactory class for exposing an operation on a page
- ▶ Using the LoadableComponent class
- ▶ Implementing nested Page Object instances
- ▶ Implementing the Page Object model in .NET
- ▶ Implementing the Page Object model in Python
- ▶ Implementing the Page Object model in Ruby by using the page-object gem

Introduction

Developing a maintainable automation code is one of the keys to a successful test-automation project. Test-automation code needs to be treated as production code and similar standards and patterns should to be applied while developing this code.

While developing Selenium WebDriver tests, we can use the Page Object model pattern. This pattern helps in enhancing the tests, making them highly maintainable, reducing the code duplication, building a layer of abstraction, and hiding the inner implementation from tests.

By applying object-oriented development principles, we can develop a class that serves as an interface to a web page in the application, modeling its properties and behavior. This helps in creating a layer of separation between the test code and code specific to the page, by hiding the technical implementation such as locators used to identify elements on the page, layout, and so on. The Page Object design pattern provides tests for an interface where a test can operate on that page in a manner similar to the user accessing the page, but by hiding its internals. For example, if we build a Page Object test for a login page, then it will provide a method to log in, which will accept the username and password and take the user to the home page of the application. The test need not worry about how input controls are used for the login page, their locator details, and so on.

Tests should use objects of a page at a high level, where any change in layout or attributes used for the fields in the underlying page should not break the test.

This chapter covers recipes to build tests using Page Object model and related design.

Using the PageFactory class for exposing elements from a page

For implementing the Page Object model in tests, we need to map and create a Page Object class for each page being tested. For example, to test the BMI Calculator application, a BMI Calculator page class will be defined, which will expose the internals of the BMI Calculator page to the test, as shown in following diagram. This is done by using the `PageFactory` class of Selenium WebDriver API.

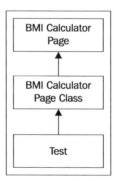

Getting ready

Before exposing the elements of a page, we need to do the following:

- Identify locators that will be needed to locate the elements uniquely
- Define the structure of the package and classes for objects of the page

How to do it...

Let's implement a Page Object test for the BMI Calculator page using the `PageFactory` class with the following steps:

1. Define and create a package for all the page's objects from the application for logical grouping. For this example, `seleniumcookbook.tests.pageobjects` is created to define all the page's objects.

2. Create a new Java class file. Give the name of the page we will be testing from the application to this class. For example, we will be creating a page object for the BMI Calculator application, so the class name could be `BmiCalcPage`. This is a single page application. The Java class file would have the following code:

    ```
    package seleniumcookbook.tests.pageobjects;

    import org.openqa.selenium.WebDriver;
    import org.openqa.selenium.WebElement;
    import org.openqa.selenium.support.PageFactory;

    public class BmiCalcPage {
    }
    ```

3. Define elements from the BMI Calculator page as instance variables in the `BmiCalcPage` class created in step 1. Use the `name` or `id` attributes to name these variables as follows:

    ```
    public WebElement heightCMS;
    public WebElement weightKg;
    public WebElement Calculate;
    public WebElement bmi;
    public WebElement bmi_category;
    ```

4. Add a constructor to the `BmiCalcPage` class, which will call the `PageFactory.initElements()` method to initialize the elements in the class. In other words, map the elements to the variables in the `BmiCalcPage` class as follows:

    ```
    public BmiCalcPage(WebDriver driver) {
        PageFactory.initElements(driver, this);
    }
    ```

5. Finally, create a test which will use the `BmiCalcPage` class for testing the BMI Calculator page as follows:

    ```
    package seleniumcookbook.tests;

    import org.openqa.selenium.WebDriver;
    ```

```
import org.openqa.selenium.chrome.ChromeDriver;

import org.junit.Test;
import static org.junit.Assert.*;

import seleniumcookbook.tests.pageobjects.*;

public class BmiCalculatorTests {

@Test
public void testBmiCalculation()
{
    //Open Chrome Browser
    //and navigate to BMI Calculator Page
    WebDriver driver = new ChromeDriver();
    driver.get("http://dl.dropbox.com/u/55228056/bmicalculator.
html");
    //Create instance of BmiCalcPage and pass the driver
    BmiCalcPage bmiCalcPage = new BmiCalcPage(driver);

    //Enter Height & Weight
    bmiCalcPage.heightCMS.sendKeys("181");
    bmiCalcPage.weightKg.sendKeys("80");

    //Click on Calculate button
    bmiCalcPage.Calculate.click();

    //Verify Bmi & Bmi Category values
    assertEquals("24.4", bmiCalcPage.bmi.getAttribute("value"));
    assertEquals("Normal", bmiCalcPage.bmi_category.
getAttribute("value"));

    //Close the Browser
    driver.close();
}
}
```

How it works...

Using the Page Object model and the PageFactory class, the BMI Calculator page's elements are exposed through the BmiCalcPage class to the test instead of the test directly accessing the internals of the page.

When we initialize the page's object using the `PageFactory` class in the `BmiCalcPage` class, the `PageFactory` class searches for the elements on the page with the `name` or `id` attributes matching the name of the `WebElement` object declared in the `BmiCalcPage` class, as follows:

```
public BmiCalcPage(WebDriver driver) {
    PageFactory.initElements(driver, this);
}
```

The `initElements()` method takes the driver object created in the test and initializes the elements declared in the `BmiCalcPage` class. We can then directly call the methods on these elements as follows:

```
bmiCalcPage.heightCMS.sendKeys("181");
bmiCalcPage.weightKg.sendKeys("80");
bmiCalcPage.Calculate.click();
```

FindBy annotations

Finding elements using the `name` or `id` attributes may not always work and we might need to use advanced locator strategies such as XPath or CSS selectors. Using the `FindBy` annotation, we can locate the elements within the `PageFactory` class as follows:

```
@FindBy(id = "heightCMS")
public WebElement heightField;
```

We declared a public member for the height element and used the `@FindBy` annotation, specifying the `id` as a locator for finding this element on the page.

CacheLookUp Attribute

One downside to using the `@FindBy` annotation is that every time we call a method on the `WebElement` object, the driver will go and find it on the current page again. This is useful in applications where elements are dynamically loaded or AJAX-heavy applications.

However, in applications where we know that the element is always going to be there and stay the same without any change, it would be handy if we could cache the element once we find it. We can use the `@CacheLookUp` annotation along with the `@FindBy` annotation as follows in order to do this:

```
@FindBy(id = "heightCMS")
@CacheLookup
public WebElement heightField;
```

This tells the `PageFactory.initElements()` method to cache the element once it's located. Tests work faster with cached elements when these elements are used repeatedly.

Using the PageFactory class for exposing an operation on a page

In the previous recipe, we created the `BmiCalcPage` class, which provides elements from the BMI Calculator page to the test. Along with elements, we define operations or behaviors on a page. In the BMI Calculator application, we are calculating the BMI by entering height and weight values. We can create an operation named `calculateBmi` and call it directly in a test, instead of calling individual elements and operations.

In this recipe, let's refine the `BmiCalcPage` class and instead of elements, provide the operations that are supported on the page and some common properties. We will also move the `WebDriver` instance of the test to the `BmiCalcPage` class to make the test generic.

Getting ready

Identify operations that will be required in a test and can be exposed from a page. This recipe uses the `BmiCalcPage` class created in the previous recipe.

How to do it...

Let's modify the `BmiCalcPage` class created in the previous recipe and refactor it a bit to provide operations and properties to the test through the following steps:

1. Make the page's elements private in the `BmiCalPage` class for better encapsulation. Also add an instance variable of the `WebDriver` class and a string variable for the URL of the page as follows:

```
package seleniumcookbook.tests.pageobjects;

import org.openqa.selenium.WebDriver;
import org.openqa.selenium.chrome.ChromeDriver;
import org.openqa.selenium.WebElement;
import org.openqa.selenium.support.PageFactory;

public class BmiCalcPage {

    private WebElement heightCMS;
    private WebElement weightKg;
    private WebElement Calculate;
    private WebElement bmi;
    private WebElement bmi_category;
    private WebDriver driver;
    private String url = "http://dl.dropbox.com/u/55228056/
bmicalculator.html";
}
```

2. Update the `BmiCalcPage` class constructor so that it initializes the WebDriver instance as follows:

```
public BmiCalcPage() {
    driver = new ChromeDriver();
    PageFactory.initElements(driver, this);
}
```

3. Add the `load()` and `close()` methods to the `BmiCalcPage` class as follows:

```
public void load() {
    this.driver.get(url);
}
public void close() {
    this.driver.close();
}
```

4. Add the `calculateBmi()` method to the `BmiCalcPage` class as follows:

```
public void calculateBmi(String height, String weight) {
    heightCMS.sendKeys(height);
    weightKg.sendKeys(weight);
    Calculate.click();
}
```

5. Add the `getBmi()` and `getBmiCategory()` methods to the `BmiCalcPage` class as follows:

```
public String getBmi() {
    return bmi.getAttribute("value");
}

public String getBmiCategory() {
    return bmi_category.getAttribute("value");
}
```

6. Finally, create a test that will use these methods defined in the `BmiCalcPage` class for testing the BMI Calculator page as follows:

```
package seleniumcookbook.tests;

import org.junit.Test;

import static org.junit.Assert.*;
import seleniumcookbook.tests.pageobjects.*;

public class BmiCalculatorTests {

@Test
```

```
public void testBmiCalculation()
{
        //Create an instance of Bmi Calculator Page class
        //and provide the driver
        BmiCalcPage bmiCalcPage = new BmiCalcPage();

        //Open the Bmi Calculator Page
        bmiCalcPage.load();

        //Calculate the Bmi by supplying Height and Weight values
        bmiCalcPage.calculateBmi("181", "80");

        //Verify Bmi & Bmi Category values
        assertEquals("24.4", bmiCalcPage.getBmi());
        assertEquals("Normal", bmiCalcPage.getBmiCategory());

        //Close the Bmi Calculator Page
        bmiCalcPage.close();
}
}
```

How it works...

In this example, the `BmiCalcPage` class defines various methods for loading, closing the page, calculation functionality, and providing access to elements as properties to the test. This simplifies the test development by creating a layer of abstraction, hiding the internals of a page, and exposing only operations and fields needed for testing from the page.

When any change happens to the structure or behavior of the page, only the `BmiCalcPage` class will be refactored while the test will remain intact.

In this example, we created the `load()` method, which navigates the application using the URL as follows:

```
public void load() {
        this.driver.get(url);
}
```

Using this approach, we can also expose the elements as properties, which provide specific attributes such as the `value` attribute instead of exposing elements fully. For example, the `getBmi()` method provides only the `value` attribute of the `bmi` label to the test as follows:

```
public String getBmi() {
        return bmi.getAttribute("value");
}
```

Selenium WebDriver provides a very neat and clean way to implement the Page Object model.

Using the LoadableComponent class

We can implement the objects of the Page Object model using the `LoadableComponent` class of Selenium WebDriver. This helps in building a robust Page Object that provides a standard way to ensure that the page is loaded and that the page load issues are easy to debug.

In this recipe, we will further refactor the `BmiCalcPage` class created in the previous recipes and extend it as a loadable component.

Getting ready

This recipe uses the `BmiCalcPage` class created in the previous recipe.

How to do it...

For implementing an object of the Page Object model as the `LoadableComponent` class, we need to extend it from the `LoadableComponent` base class by performing the following steps:

1. Add an `import` statement for `org.openqa.selenium.support.ui.LoadableComponent` and `static org.junit.Assert.*` in the `BmiCalcPage` class. Extend the `BmiCalcPage` class with `LoadableComponent<BmiCalcPage>`. Declare a new string variable `title` and assign it the title of the BMI Calculator page as follows:

   ```
   package seleniumcookbook.tests.pageobjects;

   import org.openqa.selenium.WebDriver;
   import org.openqa.selenium.chrome.ChromeDriver;
   import org.openqa.selenium.WebElement;
   import org.openqa.selenium.support.PageFactory;
   import org.openqa.selenium.support.ui.LoadableComponent;
   import static org.junit.Assert.*;

   public class BmiCalcPage extends LoadableComponent<BmiCalcPage> {

       private WebElement heightCMS;
       private WebElement weightKg;
       private WebElement Calculate;
       private WebElement bmi;
       private WebElement bmi_category;
       private WebDriver driver;
   ```

```
        private String url = "http://dl.dropbox.com/u/55228056/
    bmicalculator.html";
        private String title = "BMI Calculator";

    public BmiCalcPage() {
        driver = new ChromeDriver();
        PageFactory.initElements(driver, this);
    }
```

2. Add the @override annotation to the `load()` method and also add a new `isLoaded()` method to the `BmiCalcPage` class as follows:

```
@Override
protected void load() {
    this.driver.get(url);
}


@Override
protected void isLoaded()  {
    assertTrue(driver.getTitle().equals(title));
}
```

3. Finally, in the test, change the call of the `bmiCalcPage.load()` method to the `bmiCalcPage.get()` method as follows:

```
package seleniumcookbook.tests;

import org.junit.Test;

import static org.junit.Assert.*;
import seleniumcookbook.tests.pageobjects.*;

public class BmiCalculatorTests {

    @Test
    public void testBmiCalculation()
    {
        //Create an instance of Bmi Calculator Page class
        //and provide the driver
        BmiCalcPage bmiCalcPage = new BmiCalcPage();

        //Open the Bmi Calculator Page
        bmiCalcPage.get();

        //Calculate the Bmi by supplying Height and Weight values
        bmiCalcPage.calculateBmi("181", "80");
```

```
//Verify Bmi & Bmi Category values
assertEquals("24.4", bmiCalcPage.getBmi());
assertEquals("Normal", bmiCalcPage.getBmiCategory());

//Close the Bmi Calculator Page
bmiCalcPage.close();
    }
  }
```

How it works...

By extending the object of the Page Object model with the `LoadableComponent` base class, we overrode the `load()` and `isLoaded()` methods to the `BmiCalcPage` class.

The `load()` method will load the URL of the page we encapsulated in the Page Object and when we create the instance of this Page Object in a test, we call the `get()` method on the `BmiCalcPage` class, which will in turn call the `load()` method as follows:

```
BmiCalcPage bmiCalcPage = new BmiCalcPage();
bmiCalcPage.get();
```

The `isLoaded()` method will verify that the indented page is loaded by the `load()` method.

Implementing nested Page Object instances

So far, we explored a very simple Page Object implementation for a single page web application. We can use the Page Object model to implement the objects of a page in a complex web application to simplify the testing.

In this recipe, we will create the objects of the Page Object model for the search functionality in an e-commerce application found at `http://demo.magentocommerce.com/`. We can implement a Page Object model even if the specific functionality is not a page of its own. In the sample application, the search feature is available throughout the application. However, let's find out how it's been used from the application's home page.

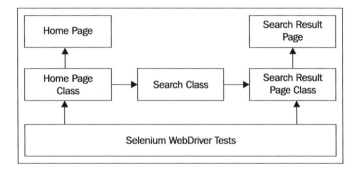

Each page of the application provides the user with the ability to search products from the site by entering a query and hitting the search button. When a search query is submitted, the application returns a new page with a list of products matching the search query. Using the approach described in this recipe, we can build a more modular framework.

In this recipe, we will create this nested hierarchy where the HomePage class implements the Search class, which in turn returns an object of the SearchResults class to the test.

Getting ready

Identify the page and logical relationship between these pages to build a nested component set.

How to do it...

For implementing nested Page Object instances, perform the following steps:

1. Create the Browser class which will provide a static and shared WebDriver instance for all the pages as follows:

```
package demo.magentocommerce.pages;

import org.openqa.selenium.WebDriver;
import org.openqa.selenium.chrome.*;

public class Browser {

    private static WebDriver driver = new ChromeDriver();

    public static WebDriver driver() {
        return driver;
    }

    public static void open(String url) {
        driver.get(url);
    }

    public static void close() {
        driver.close();
    }
}
```

2. Create the HomePage class, which allows the test to navigate to the home page of the application. It also provides access to the Search class, which is shared among the various pages of the application, as follows:

```
package demo.magentocommerce.pages;

import org.openqa.selenium.support.PageFactory;
import org.openqa.selenium.support.ui.LoadableComponent;
import static org.junit.Assert.*;

public class HomePage extends LoadableComponent<HomePage> {

    static String url = "http://demo.magentocommerce.com/";
    private static String title = "Home page - Magento Commerce
Demo Store";

    public HomePage() {
        PageFactory.initElements(Browser.driver(), this);
    }

    @Override
    public void load() {
        Browser.open(url);
    }

    @Override
    public void isLoaded() {
        assertTrue(Browser.driver().getTitle().equals(title));
    }

    public void close() {
        Browser.close();
    }

    public Search Search() {
        Search search = new Search();
        return search;
    }
}
```

3. Create the Search class. This class provides all the objects of the Page Object model to search for products in the application as follows:

```
package demo.magentocommerce.pages;

import org.openqa.selenium.WebElement;
```

```
import org.openqa.selenium.support.FindBy;
import org.openqa.selenium.support.PageFactory;

public class Search {

    private WebElement search;
    @FindBy(css = "button.button")
    private WebElement searchButton;

    public Search() {
        PageFactory.initElements(Browser.driver(), this);
    }

    public SearchResults searchInStore(String query) {
        search.sendKeys(query);
        searchButton.click();
        return new SearchResults(query);
    }
}
```

4. Create the `SearchResult` class, which is nested in the `Search` class. The `SearchResult` class represents the results page when the user submits a search query. As discussed previously, the `SearchResult` class also provides access to the `Search` class so that users can search again for a different query. This is done as follows:

```
package demo.magentocommerce.pages;

import java.util.ArrayList;
import java.util.List;

import org.openqa.selenium.By;
import org.openqa.selenium.WebElement;
import org.openqa.selenium.support.PageFactory;
import org.openqa.selenium.support.ui.LoadableComponent;
import static org.junit.Assert.assertTrue;

public class SearchResults extends LoadableComponent<SearchResul
ts> {

    private String query;

    public SearchResults(String query){
        PageFactory.initElements(Browser.driver(),this);
```

```
    }

    @Override
    public void isLoaded() {
        assertTrue(Browser.driver().getTitle().equals("Search
results for: '" + this.query
                    + "' - Magento1 Commerce Demo Store"));
    }

    @Override
    protected void load() {
        // TODO Auto-generated method stub
    }

    public List<String> getProducts() {
        List<String> products = new ArrayList<String>();
        List<WebElement> productList = Browser.driver().
findElements(By.cssSelector("ul.products-grid > li"));
        for(WebElement item : productList)
            products.add(item.findElement(By.cssSelector("h2 >
a")).getText());
        return products;
    }

    public void close() {
        Browser.close();
    }

    public Search Search() {
            Search search = new Search();
            return search;
    }
}
```

5. Finally, create a test which tests the search functionality from the home page of the application as follows:

```
package demo.magentocommerce.test;

import org.junit.Test;
import static org.junit.Assert.*;

import demo.magentocommerce.pages.*;
```

```
public class SearchTest {

    @Test
    public void testProductSearch()
    {
        //Create an instance of Home page
        HomePage homePage = new HomePage();

        //Navigate to the Home page
        homePage.get();

        //Search for 'sony', the searchInStore method will return
        //SearchResults class
        SearchResults searchResult = homePage.Search().
searchInStore("sony");

        //Verify there are 2 products available with this search
        assertEquals(2, searchResult.getProducts().size());
        assertTrue(searchResult.getProducts().contains("Sony
Ericsson W810i"));

        //Close the Search result page
        searchResult.close();
    }
}
```

How it works...

The test starts with creating an instance of the `HomePage` class. As you can see, the application home page provides the user with the ability to search the site; in a similar way, the `HomePage` class provides the ability to search by using the `Search` class as follows:

```
HomePage homePage = new HomePage();
homePage.get();
SearchResults searchResult = homePage.Search().searchInStore("sony")
```

The `searchInStore()` method of the `Search` class takes the query string as arguments and interacts with the search form to send the query. It returns the `SearchResults` class as a page. The `SearchResults` class provides a list of products that match the query back to the test using the `getProducts()` method as follows:

```
public List<String> getProducts() {
    List<String> products = new ArrayList<String>();
    List<WebElement> productList = Browser.driver().findElements(By.
cssSelector("ul.products-grid > li"));
```

```
    for(WebElement item : productList)
        products.add(item.findElement(By.cssSelector("h2 > a")).
getText());
    return products;
}
```

The test can verify the number of products as well as the names of the products by checking the return value of the getProducts() method as follows:

```
assertEquals(2, searchResult.getProducts().size());
assertTrue(searchResult.getProducts().contains("Sony Ericsson
W810i"));
```

Using the nested objects of the Page Object model, we can build a logical chain of pages within an application and build a robust and maintainable test automation framework.

See also

▶ Using the LoadableComponent class

Implementing the Page Object model in .NET

Similar to Java bindings, Selenium WebDriver provides the PageFactory class in .NET bindings for implementing the Page Object model.

However, the PageFactory class is implemented a little differently with .NET bindings where it needs the FindsBy annotation while locating the elements. It does not support locating elements using the name or id attributes specified as the name of the element variable is similar to Java.

In this recipe, we will implement the Page Object model for the BMI Calculator page using the PageFactory class in C#.

Getting ready

We need to identify the locators that will be needed to locate the elements uniquely.

How to do it...

For implementing Page Object model .NET, perform the follow steps:

1. Define a class for the Page Object model by creating a new C# class with the name of the page. In this example, we will create the page's object for the BMI Calculator application:

```
using System;
using OpenQA.Selenium;
using OpenQA.Selenium.Chrome;
using OpenQA.Selenium.Support.PageObjects;

namespace PageFactoryTests
{
    public class BmiCalcPage
    {
        static string Url = "http://dl.dropbox.com/u/55228056/
bmicalculator.html";
        private static string Title = "BMI Calculator";

        [FindsBy(How = How.Id, Using = "heightCMS")]
        [CacheLookup]
        private IWebElement HeightField;

        [FindsBy(How = How.Id, Using = "weightKg")]
        private IWebElement WeightField;

        [FindsBy(How = How.Id, Using = "Calculate")]
        private IWebElement CalculateButton;

        [FindsBy(How = How.Name, Using = "bmi")]
        private IWebElement BmiField;

        [FindsBy(How = How.Name, Using = "bmi_category")]
        private IWebElement BmiCategoryField;

        private IWebDriver driver;

        public BmiCalcPage() {
            driver = new ChromeDriver(@"C:\ChromeDriver");
            PageFactory.InitElements(driver, this);
        }

        public void Load()
```

```
        {
            driver.Navigate().GoToUrl(Url);
        }

        public void Close()
        {
            driver.Close();
        }

        public bool IsLoaded
        {
            get { return driver.Title.Equals(Title); }
        }

        public void CalculateBmi(String height, String weight)
        {
            HeightField.SendKeys(height);
            WeightField.SendKeys(weight);
            CalculateButton.Click();
        }

        public String Bmi
        {
            get { return BmiField.GetAttribute("value"); }
        }

        public String BmiCategory
        {
            get { return BmiCategoryField.GetAttribute("value"); }
        }
    }
}
```

2. Using the BmiCalcPage class, let's create a test for the calculation feature, as follows:

```
using NUnit.Framework;

namespace PageFactoryTests
{
    public class BmiCalcTests
    {
        [TestCase]
        public void TestBmiCalculator()
        {
            BmiCalcPage bmiCalcPage = new BmiCalcPage();
```

```
bmiCalcPage.Load();
    Assert.IsTrue(bmiCalcPage.IsLoaded);
bmiCalcPage.CalculateBmi("181", "80");
Assert.AreEqual("24.4", bmiCalcPage.Bmi);
Assert.AreEqual("Normal", bmiCalcPage.BmiCategory);
bmiCalcPage.Close();
        }
    }
}
```

How it works...

In this example, the `BmiCalcPage` class provides various operations and properties from the BMI Calculator page to the test. The elements on the page are defined as instances of the `IWebDriver` interface with a `FindsBy` annotation as follows:

```
[FindsBy(How = How.Id, Using = "heightCMS")]
private IWebElement HeightField;
```

When the page is initialized by the `PageFactory.InitElements()` method, these annotations are used to search the elements on the page.

The `BmiCalcPage` class implements methods for opening and closing the BMI Calculator page. This will provide a high level of abstraction to the test.

The `BmiCalcPage` class also implements the `IsLoaded` property, which will tell a test if the BMI Calculator page is loaded into the browser. This class also defined properties for the `Bmi` and `BmiCategory` fields, which provide values from these fields to test, rather than complete access to the underlying elements as follows:

```
public bool IsLoaded
{
    get { return driver.Title.Equals(Title); }
}

public String Bmi
{
    get { return BmiField.GetAttribute("value"); }
}

public String BmiCategory
{
    get { return BmiCategoryField.GetAttribute("value"); }
}
```

It also provides a `CalculateBmi()` method which takes the height and weight as an argument and interacts with underlying elements to perform actions.

Implementing the Page Object model in Python

Implementing the Page Object model in Python is similar to what we have done previously in Java and C#. The Selenium WebDriver Python bindings provide support for objects of the Page Object model.

In this recipe, we will implement the Page Object model using Python bindings.

Getting ready

Before implementing the Page Object model for Python bindings, we must do the following:

▶ Identify pages and the elements from the application that will be required in the tests

▶ Define locators that will be needed to identify the elements uniquely

How to do it...

To implement the Page Object model in Python, follow these steps:

1. Define a class for the Page Object model by creating a Python script with the name of the page. In this example, we we will be creating a Page Object model for the main page of the BMI Calculator application as follows:

```python
class bmicalcpage(object):
    def __init__(self, driver):
        self._driver = driver
        self._url = 'http://dl.dropbox.com/u/55228056/
bmicalculator.html'
        self._title = 'BMI Calculator'

    @property
    def is_loaded(self):
        return self._driver.title == self._title

    @property
    def bmi(self):
        bmi_field = self._driver.find_element_by_id('bmi')
        return bmi_field.get_attribute('value')

    @property
```

```python
    def bmi_category(self):
        bmi_category_field = self._driver.find_element_by_id('bmi_
category')
        return bmi_category_field.get_attribute('value')

    def open(self):
        self._driver.get(self._url)

    def calculate(self, height, weight):
        height_field = self._driver.find_element_by_
id('heightCMS')
        weight_field = self._driver.find_element_by_id('weightKg')
        calc_button = self._driver.find_element_by_id('Calculate')

        height_field.send_keys(height)
        weight_field.send_keys(weight)
        calc_button.click()

    def close(self):
        self._driver.close()
```

2. Using the `BmiCalcPage` object, let's create a test for the calculation feature as follows:

```python
import unittest
from selenium.webdriver.chrome.webdriver import WebDriver
from bmi_calc_page import bmicalcpage

class BmiCalcTest(unittest.TestCase):
    def testCalc(self):
        driver = WebDriver()
        bmi_calc = bmicalcpage(driver)
        bmi_calc.open()
        self.assertEqual(True,bmi_calc.is_loaded)
        bmi_calc.calculate('181','80')
        self.assertEqual('24.4', bmi_calc.bmi)
        self.assertEqual('Normal', bmi_calc.bmi_category)
        bmi_calc.close()

if __name__ == '__main__':
    unittest.main()
```

How it works...

Implementing the Page Object model in Python is relatively simple. The Page Object model can be implemented by creating classes, defining methods and properties, and only exposing the functionality from the application page that needed it for testing.

In this example, the `bmicalcpage` class is defined to represent the BMI Calculator application's main page. This class needs an instance of WebDriver through which it will interact with the main page as follows:

```
class bmicalcpage(object):
    def __init__(self, driver):
        self._driver = driver
```

The `bmicalcpage` class implements the `is_loaded` property, which will tell tests if the BMI Calculator page is loaded into the browser. This class also defined properties for the `bmi` and `bmi_category` fields, which provide values from these fields to test, rather than a complete access to the underlying elements:

```
@property
def is_loaded(self):
    return self._driver.title == self._title


@property
def bmi(self):
    bmi_field = self._driver.find_element_by_id('bmi')
    return bmi_field.get_attribute('value')


@property
def bmi_category(self):
    bmi_category_field = self._driver.find_element_by_id('bmi_category')
    return bmi_category_field.get_attribute('value')
```

It provides the `calculate()` method which takes the height and weight as an argument and interacts with underlying elements to perform actions.

The `bmicalcpage` class also implements methods for opening and closing the BMI Calculator page. This will provide a high level of abstraction to the test, hiding the underlying details of page and elements. This makes writing tests, in a kind of domain-specific language, easier and faster.

Implementing the Page Object model in Ruby by using the page-object gem

While developing tests in Ruby, we can use the page-object gem for implementing the Page Object model within the tests. The page-object gem provides simple features for building the objects of a Page Object along with Watir-WebDriver.

In this recipe, we will see how to use the page-object gem for implementing the Page Object model for the BMI Calculator's main page.

Getting ready

You need to download and install the page-object gem with the help of the following command:

```
gem install page-object
```

How to do it...

For implementing the Page Object model in Ruby using the page-object gem, perform the following steps:

1. Define a class for the Page Object model by creating a Ruby script with the name of the page. In this example, we will be creating a Page Object model for the main page of the BMI Calculator application and including the page-object module:

```ruby
require 'page-object'
class BmiCalcPage
    include PageObject

    text_field(:height, :id => 'heightCMS')
    text_field(:weight, :id => 'weightKg')
    button(:calculate, :value => 'Calculate')

    text_field(:bmi, :id => 'bmi')
    text_field(:bmi_category, :id => 'bmi_category')

    def calculate_bmi(height, weight)
        self.height = height
        self.weight = weight
        calculate
    end

    def open()
```

```
        @browser.get 'http://dl.dropbox.com/u/55228056/
bmicalculator.html'
    end

    def close()
        @browser.close()
    end
end
```

2. Using the object of the `BmiCalcPage` class, create a test for the calculation feature as follows:

```
require 'rubygems'
require 'watir-webdriver'
require 'test/unit'
require_relative 'bmicalcpage.rb'

class BmiCalcTest < Test::Unit::TestCase
    def test_bmi_calculation
        @driver = Selenium::WebDriver.for :chrome
        bmi_calc = BmiCalcPage.new(@driver)
        bmi_calc.open()
        bmi_calc.calculate_bmi('181','80')
        assert_equal '24.4', bmi_calc.bmi
        assert_equal 'Normal', bmi_calc.bmi_category
        bmi_calc.close()
    end
end
```

How it works...

We can use the Page Object model implemented with the page-object gem by creating an instance of the `BmiCalcPage` class and passing the browser as an argument to the constructor. The rest of the magic is performed by the page-object gem.

While defining the elements, we need to specify the type of element and the locator as follows:

```
text_field(:Height, :id => 'heightCMS')
```

The page-object gem adds a few more methods automatically to these objects at runtime. For example, we created an element for the `Calculate` button in the Page Object model as follows:

```
button(:Calculate, :value => 'Calculate')
```

The page-object gem creates a method called `calculate`, which will click the `Calculate` button when called from the `calculate_bmi()` method as follows:

```
def calculate_bmi(height, weight)
        self.height = height
        self.weight = weight
        calculate
    end
```

You can find more information about the page-object gem API at the following URL:

```
http://rubydoc.info/github/cheezy/page-object/master/PageObject/
Accessors
```

6
Extending Selenium

In this chapter, we will cover:

- ▶ Creating an extension class for web tables
- ▶ Creating an extension for the jQueryUI Tab widget
- ▶ Implementing an extension for the WebElement object to set the element attribute values
- ▶ Implementing an extension for the WebElement object to highlight elements
- ▶ Creating an object map for Selenium tests
- ▶ Capturing screenshots of elements in the Selenium WebDriver
- ▶ Comparing images in Selenium

Introduction

Selenium WebDriver provides a highly flexible and robust API to extend the features and commands and add customization for building a scalable test automation framework. This chapter covers some of the important recipes for extending Selenium WebDriver for various practical scenarios.

In this chapter we will write Selenium WebDriver extensions that support web tables, object maps, and image comparison features.

We will also build an extension for jQuery UI control. You can use this pattern for implementing support for third party or custom controls used in your application by hiding technical details from the tests. This makes test development a lot easier.

Creating an extension class for web tables

Selenium WebDriver provides a generic `WebElement` class to work with various types of HTML elements. It also provides helper classes to work with the `Select` element. However, there is no built-in class to support the web tables or `<table>` elements.

In this recipe, we will implement a helper class for web tables. Using this class, we will retrieve properties and perform some basic operations on a web table element.

Getting ready

Create a new Java class `WebTable.java`, which we will use to implement the support for table elements.

How to do it...

Let's implement the web table extension code with `WebTable.java` using the following steps:

1. Add a constructor for the `WebTable` class and for the setter and getter property methods as well. The `WebTable` constructor will accept the `WebElement` object.

    ```java
    import org.openqa.selenium.WebElement;
    import org.openqa.selenium.By;

    import java.util.List;

    public class WebTable {

      private WebElement _webTable;

      public WebTable(WebElement webTable)
      {
        set_webTable(webTable);
      }

      public WebElement get_webTable() {
        return _webTable;
      }

      public void set_webTable(WebElement _webTable) {
        this._webTable = _webTable;
      }
    }
    ```

2. Now add methods to retrieve rows and columns from a table, as shown in following code:

```
public int getRowCount() {
      List<WebElement> tableRows = _webTable.findElements(By.
tagName("tr"));
      return tableRows.size();
   }


public int getColumnCount() {
    List<WebElement> tableRows = _webTable.findElements(By.
    tagName("tr"));
    WebElement headerRow = tableRows.get(0);
    List<WebElement> tableCols = headerRow.findElements(By.
    tagName("td"));
    return tableCols.size();
   }
```

3. Add a method to retrieve data from a specific cell of the table.

```
public WebElement getCellEditor(int rowIdx, int colIdx, int
editorIdx) throws NoSuchElementException {
   try {

      List<WebElement> tableRows = _webTable.findElements(By.
      tagName("tr"));
      WebElement currentRow = tableRows.get(rowIdx-1);
      List<WebElement> tableCols = currentRow.findElements(By.
      tagName("td"));
      WebElement cell = tableCols.get(colIdx-1);
      WebElement cellEditor = cell.findElements(By.
      tagName("input")).get(editorIdx);
      return cellEditor;

   } catch (NoSuchElementException e) {
      throw new NoSuchElementException("Failed to get cell editor");
   }
}
```

4. Add a method to retrieve the cell editor element; this is useful while working with editable cells.

```
public WebElement getCellEditor(int rowIdx, int colIdx, int
editorIdx) {
   List<WebElement> tableRows = _webTable.findElements(By.
   tagName("tr"));
   WebElement currentRow = tableRows.get(rowIdx-1);
```

```
    List<WebElement> tableCols = currentRow.findElements(By.
    tagName("td"));
    WebElement cell = tableCols.get(colIdx-1);
    WebElement cellEditor = cell.findElements(By.tagName("input")).
get(0);
    return cellEditor;
  }
```

5. Let's create a test on a shopping cart Page, using a newly created `WebTable` class.

```
import org.openqa.selenium.WebDriver;
import org.openqa.selenium.firefox.FirefoxDriver;
import org.openqa.selenium.WebElement;
import org.openqa.selenium.By;

import static org.junit.Assert.*;

import org.junit.After;
import org.junit.Before;
import org.junit.Test;

public class WebTableTests {

  private WebDriver driver;
  private StringBuffer verificationErrors = new StringBuffer();

  @Before
  public void setUp() {
    // Create a new instance of the Firefox driver
    driver = new FirefoxDriver();
    driver.get("http://dl.dropbox.com/u/55228056/Locators.html");
  }

  @Test
  public void testWebTableTests() {
    try {

      //Get the table element as WebTable instance using CSS
      //Selector
      WebTable table = new WebTable(driver.findElement(By.
      cssSelector("div.cart-info table")));

      //Verify that it has three rows
      assertEquals(3,table.getRowCount());
      //Verify that it has six columns
      assertEquals(5,table.getColumnCount());
```

```
        //Verify that specified value exists in second cell of
        //third row
        assertEquals("iPhone",table.getCellData(3,1));

        //Get in cell editor and enter some value
        WebElement cellEdit = table.getCellEditor(3,3,0);
        cellEdit.clear();
        cellEdit.sendKeys("2");

    } catch (Error e) {
        //Capture and append Exceptions/Errors
        verificationErrors.append(e.toString());
    }
}

    @After
    public void tearDown() {

        //Close the browser
        driver.quit();

        String verificationErrorString = verificationErrors.
        toString();
        if (!"".equals(verificationErrorString)) {
            fail(verificationErrorString);
        }
    }
}
```

How it works...

The `WebTable` class accepts a `WebElement` object and extends it to provide table-specific properties and operations.

To retrieve the number of rows from a table, we locate `<tr>` elements from the `_webTable` object. We used the `tagName()` method of the `By` class and collected all the `<tr>` elements as a list of `WebElement` objects. Using the `size()` method, we can find out how may rows are available in the table element.

```
List<WebElement> tableRows = _webTable.findElements(By.tagName("tr"));
```

Similarly, we inspected a number of `<td>` elements in the first row of the table (normally the header), to retrieve the number of columns available in the table element, as shown in the following code:

```
List<WebElement> tableRows = _webTable.findElements(By.tagName("tr"));
    WebElement headerRow = tableRows.get(0);
List<WebElement> tableCols = headerRow.findElements(By.tagName("td"));
```

To retrieve data from a specific cell, the `getCellData()` function accepts row and column number arguments. First, it gets the `<tr>` element from the list by using the row argument as an index, as shown in the following code:

```
List<WebElement> tableRows = _webTable.findElements(By.tagName("tr"));
WebElement currentRow = tableRows.get(rowIdx-1);
```

Then, it retrieves the `<td>` elements from `currentRow`, using column argument as an index, as shown in following code:

```
List<WebElement> tableCols = currentRow.findElements(By.
tagName("td"));
    WebElement cell = tableCols.get(colIdx-1);
```

To retrieve the text, it calls the `cell` object's `getText()` method, as shown in following code:

```
    return cell.getText();
```

Often, we need to test tables with editable cells. These could be dynamic tables based on database values. The `getCellEditor()` method of the `WebTable` object provides access to the first input element of the cell. We can then use this input element and perform actions such as `Click()` or `SendKeys()`. The `getCellEditor()` method uses a similar method to reach the desired cell and then finds the first input element inside a cell, that is, a `<td>` element using the `ByTagName` locator strategy, as shown in the following code:

```
WebElement cellEditor = cell.findElements(By.tagName("input")).get(0);
```

Creating an extension for the jQueryUI Tab widget

jQuery UI is a jQuery user-interface library. It provides interactions, widgets, effects, and theming for building rich Internet applications. jQuery UI provides a number of UI widgets, such as Accordion, Datepicker, Slider, Dialog, and Tabs.

These widgets are built using a number of low-level HTML elements, such as DIVs, unordered lists, and input tags. While Selenium can recognize these elements individually, we can build support for Selenium to recognize these controls as native jQuery UI widgets. We can then perform native operations supported by jQuery framework.

In this recipe, we will implement support for the jQuery UI Tab widget.

Getting ready

Visit `http://jqueryui.com/demos/tabs/` to understand more about the jQuery UI tabs widget. Explore how they are implemented and various options, methods and events related to this widget.

How to do it...

Similar to the `WebTable` extension class we created earlier, we will create a `JQueryUITab` class to represent the Tab widget in Selenium, by following the ensuing steps:

1. First, create a `JQueryUITab` class with setter and getter properties.

```java
import org.openqa.selenium.By;
import org.openqa.selenium.JavascriptExecutor;
import org.openqa.selenium.WebElement;
import org.openqa.selenium.internal.WrapsDriver;

import java.util.Iterator;
import java.util.List;

public class JQueryUITab {

    private WebElement _jQueryUITab;

    public JQueryUITab(WebElement jQueryUITab)
    {
        set_jQueryUITab(jQueryUITab);
    }

    public WebElement get_jQueryUITab() {
        return _jQueryUITab;
    }

    public void set_jQueryUITab(WebElement _jQueryUITab) {
        this._jQueryUITab = _jQueryUITab;
    }
}
```

2. Add a method to retrieve the count of tabs available on tab widget. We can use this to verify that the tab widget is displaying the expected number of tabs.

```
public int getTabCount() {
    List<WebElement> tabs = _jQueryUITab.findElements(By.
cssSelector(".ui-tabs-nav > li"));
    return tabs.size();
}
```

3. Add a method to get the name of the selected tab, using the following code:

```
public String getSelectedTab() {
    WebElement tab = _jQueryUITab.findElement(By.cssSelector(".ui-
tabs-nav > li[class*='ui-tabs-selected']"));
    return tab.getText();
}
```

4. Add a method to select a tab. We will pass the name of the tab that we want to select, to this method, by using the following code:

```
public void selectTab(String tabName) throws Exception
{
    int idx=0;
    boolean found=false;
    List<WebElement> tabs = _jQueryUITab.findElements(By.
cssSelector(".ui-tabs-nav > li"));

    for(WebElement tab : tabs) {
        if(tabName.equals(tab.getText().toString())) {
            WrapsDriver wrappedElement = (WrapsDriver) _jQueryUITab;
            JavascriptExecutor driver = (JavascriptExecutor)
            wrappedElement.getWrappedDriver();
            driver.executeScript("jQuery(arguments[0]).tabs().
            tabs('select',arguments[1]);",_jQueryUITab,idx);
            found = true;
            break;
        }
        idx++;
    }
    //Throw an exception if specified tab is not found
    if (found==false)
        throw new Exception("Could not find tab '" + tabName + "'");
}
```

5. Let's implement the `JQueryUITab` class in a sample test, with the following code:

```java
import org.openqa.selenium.WebDriver;
import org.openqa.selenium.firefox.FirefoxDriver;

import org.openqa.selenium.By;
import static org.junit.Assert.*;

import org.junit.After;
import org.junit.Before;
import org.junit.Test;

public class JQueryUITabWidgetTest {

  private WebDriver driver;
  private StringBuffer verificationErrors = new StringBuffer();

  @Before
  public void setUp() {
    driver = new FirefoxDriver();
    driver.get("http://dl.dropbox.com/u/55228056/jQueryUITabDemo.
    html");
  }

  @Test
  public void testjQueryUITabWidget() {
    try {

      JQueryUITab tab = new JQueryUITab(driver.findElement(By.
      cssSelector("div[id=MyTab][class^=ui-tabs]")));

      //Verify Tab Widget has 3 Tabs
      assertEquals(3,tab.getTabCount());

      //Verify Home Tab is selected
      assertEquals("Home",tab.getSelectedTab());

      //Select Options Tab and verify it is selected
      tab.selectTab("Options");
      assertEquals("Options",tab.getSelectedTab());

      //Select Admin Tab and verify it is selected
      tab.selectTab("Admin");
      assertEquals("Admin",tab.getSelectedTab());
```

```
            //Select Home Tab
            tab.selectTab("Home");

        } catch (Exception e) {
            //Capture and append Exceptions/Errors
            verificationErrors.append(e.toString());
        }
    }

    @After
    public void tearDown() {
      //Close the browser
      driver.quit();

      String verificationErrorString = verificationErrors.
      toString();
      if (!"".equals(verificationErrorString)) {
        fail(verificationErrorString);
      }
    }
}
```

How it works...

The `JQueryUITab` class is ready for use in testing the Tab widget. The `JQueryUITab` class accepts a `WebElement` object passed to its constructor. To retrieve the number of tabs in a Tab widget, we pass the tab element. Internally, the Tab widget defines an unordered list for tab headers. We can locate these headers by using the `cssSelector()` method of the `By` class in a list of WebElements using the `findElements()` method. We can get the count of the tabs by looking at the list size.

```
List<WebElement> tabs = _jQueryUITab.findElements(By.cssSelector(".ui-
tabs-nav > li"));
    return tabs.size();
```

To retrieve the selected tab name, we will use a similar `cssSelector()` method with a filter to locate the `<li>` element whose class is `ui-tabs-selected`. When we select a tab in the Tab widget, jQuery framework adds all these class attributes to the `<li>` element internally, as shown in the following code:

```
        WebElement tab = _jQueryUITab.findElement(By.cssSelector
        (".ui-tabs-nav > li[class*='ui-tabs-selected']"));
        return tab.getText();
```

Finally, to select a tab in the Tab widget, we need to execute the jQuery native API functions. The Tab widget has a method to select a tab by its index. However, selecting a tab by its index may not be user-friendly. Therefore, we will accept the name of the tab and then find out its index internally, using the following code:

```
int idx=0;
List<WebElement> tabs = _jQueryUITab.findElements(By.cssSelector(".ui-
tabs-nav > li"));
Iterator<WebElement> itr = tabs.iterator();
while(itr.hasNext()) {
    WebElement element = itr.next();
    if(tabName.equals(element.getText().toString()))
        break;
    idx++;
}
```

Now, we will call the native jQuery API by using `JavaScriptExecutor` and pass the index to the `select` method of the Tab widget, using the following code:

```
WrapsDriver wrappedElement = (WrapsDriver) _jQueryUITab;
JavascriptExecutor driver = (JavascriptExecutor) wrappedElement.
getWrappedDriver();
    driver.executeScript("jQuery(arguments[0]).tabs().
tabs('select',arguments[1]);",_jQueryUITab,idx);
}
```

There's more...

Using a similar approach, we can also build support for other widgets in jQuery UI or other UI frameworks such as Yahoo UI, Doojo, and GWT. This provides a neat and clean way to work with custom widgets and UI controls.

Implementing an extension for the WebElement object to set the element attribute values

Setting an element's attribute can be useful in various situations where the test needs to manipulate properties of an element. For example, for a masked textbox, the `sendKeys()` method may not work well, and setting the value of the textbox will help to overcome these issues. The `WebElement` object does not have a method that supports setting all types of attributes.

In this recipe, we will create an extension for `WebElement` and provide a method to set the attribute value of an element at runtime.

Create a new Java class file for the `WebElementExtender.java` class. We will use this class to host all the extension methods for the `WebElement` objects.

How to do it...

Add the `setAttribute()` method to the `WebElementExtender` class, as follows:

```
import org.openqa.selenium.JavascriptExecutor;
import org.openqa.selenium.WebElement;
import org.openqa.selenium.internal.WrapsDriver;

public class WebElementExtender {

    public static void setAttribute(WebElement element, String
    attributeName, String value)
    {
        WrapsDriver wrappedElement = (WrapsDriver) element;

        JavascriptExecutor driver = (JavascriptExecutor)
        wrappedElement.getWrappedDriver();
        driver.executeScript("arguments[0].setAttribute(arguments[1],
        arguments[2])", element, attributeName, value);
    }

}
```

How it works...

In the `setAttribute()` method, we created an object of `JavaScriptExecutor` and retrieved `WrappedDriver` of the `WebElement` object on which we want to call the `setAttribute()` method.

Using `JavaScriptExecutor`, we called the JavaScript `setAttribute()` method to set the attribute value of an element. In this example, the contents of a input element are cleared before calling the `SendKeys()` method. This can also be done by calling the `clear()` method of the `WebElement` class.

```
WebElement email = driver.findElement(By.id("email"));
WebElementExtender.setAttribute(userName, "value", "");
userName.sendKeys("test@test.com");
```

See also

▶ The *Implementing an extension for the WebElement object to highlight elements* recipe

Implementing an extension for the WebElement object to highlight elements

During test execution, there is no way to highlight an element. This will help us to see what is actually going on in the browser. This method will slow down the tests a bit, but sometimes it's a useful way to debug tests.

In this recipe, we will create an extension for `WebElement` and provide the `highlight Elements()` method at runtime.

Getting ready

Create a new Java class file for the `WebElementExtender.java` class, or you can use the class created in the previous recipe.

How to do it...

Add the `highlightElement()` method to the `WebElementExtender` class, as follows:

```
import org.openqa.selenium.JavascriptExecutor;
import org.openqa.selenium.WebElement;
import org.openqa.selenium.internal.WrapsDriver;

public class WebElementExtender {

    public static void highlightElement(WebElement element) {
        for (int i = 0; i < 5; i++) {
            WrapsDriver wrappedElement = (WrapsDriver) element;
            JavascriptExecutor driver = (JavascriptExecutor)
            wrappedElement.getWrappedDriver();
            driver.executeScript("arguments[0].setAttribute('style',
            arguments[1]);",
                    element, "color: green; border: 2px solid yellow;");
            driver.executeScript("arguments[0].setAttribute('style',
            arguments[1]);",
                    element, "");
        }
    }
}
```

How it works...

In the `highlightElement()` method, we created an instance of the `JavaScriptExecutor` class and got an instance of the `WrappedDriver` class from the element, on which we want to call the `highlightElement()` method.

Using the `JavaScriptExecutor` class, we called the JavaScript `setAttribute()` method to set the `style` attribute value to green and then back to original. We do this a few times using a loop. During execution, the element is highlighted with a green flash. Here is an example on using the `highlightElement()` method:

```
WebElement userName = driver.findElement(By.id("username"));
WebElementExtender.highlightElement(userName);
userName.sendKeys("test_user");
```

This comes in very handy while debugging or visualizing the test progress.

See also

▶ The *Implementing an extension for the WebElement object to set the element attribute values* recipe

Creating an object map for Selenium tests

So far, we have seen how the Selenium WebDriver API needs locator information to find the elements on the page. When a large suite of tests is created, a lot of locator information is duplicated in the test code. It becomes difficult to manage locator details when the number of tests increases. If any changes happen in the element locator, we need to find all the tests that use this locator and update these tests. This becomes a maintenance nightmare.

One way to overcome this problem is to use page objects and create a repository of pages as reusable classes.

There is another way to overcome this problem — by using object map. An object or a UI map is a mechanism that stores all the locators for a test suite in one place for easy modification when identifiers or paths to GUI elements change in the application under test. The test script then uses the object map to locate the elements to be tested.

Object maps help in making test script management much easier. When a locator needs to be edited, there is a central location for easily finding that object, rather than having to search through the test script code. Also, it allows changing the identifier in a single place, rather than having to make the change in multiple places within a test script, or for that matter, in multiple test scripts. The object map files can also be version-controlled.

In this recipe, we will implement the `ObjectMap` class for maintaining locator details obtained from the tests.

Getting ready

Set up a new Java Project for the `ObjectMap` class. This class will be used by Selenium tests as an extension for reading the `ObjectMap` file.

How to do it...

Let's implement object map to store the locators used in a test with the following steps:

1. We will create a properties file named `objectmap.properties`. We will add the locators in a key/value pair. The part before the equal-to sign will be the key or the logical name of the element, and the part after will be the locator details, in the following format:

    ```
    [logical_name]=[locator_type]>[locator_value]
    ```

    The following code is an example of the object map for the BMI calculator page:

    ```
    height_field=name>heightCMS
    weight_field=id>weightKg
    calculate_button=id>Calculate
    bmi_field=id>bmi
    ```

2. Implement the `ObjectMap` class to read the property file and provide the locator information to the test.

    ```java
    import java.io.FileInputStream;
    import java.io.IOException;
    import java.util.Properties;

    public class ObjectMap {

        Properties properties;

        public ObjectMap(String mapFile)
        {
            properties = new Properties();
            try {
                FileInputStream in = new FileInputStream(mapFile);
                properties.load(in);
                in.close();
            }catch (IOException e) {
                System.out.println(e.getMessage());
            }

        }

    }
    ```

3. Add a method to the `ObjectMap` class, which will read the locator details from the properties file and create and return the locator using the `By` class, as shown in following code:

```
public By getLocator(String logicalElementName) throws Exception
{
    //Read value using the logical name as Key
    String locator = properties.getProperty(logicalElementName);

    //Split the value which contains locator type and locator value
    String locatorType = locator.split(">")[0];
    String locatorValue = locator.split(">")[1];

    //Return a instance of By class based on type of locator
    if (locatorType.toLowerCase().equals("id"))
        return By.id(locatorValue);
    else if (locatorType.toLowerCase().equals("name"))
        return By.name(locatorValue);
    else if ((locatorType.toLowerCase().equals("classname")) ||
    (locatorType.toLowerCase().equals("class")))
        return By.className(locatorValue);
    else if ((locatorType.toLowerCase().equals("tagname")) ||
    (locatorType.toLowerCase().equals("tag")))
        return By.className(locatorValue);
    else if ((locatorType.toLowerCase().equals("linktext")) ||
    (locatorType.toLowerCase().equals("link")))
        return By.linkText(locatorValue);
    else if (locatorType.toLowerCase().equals("partiallinktext"))
        return By.partialLinkText(locatorValue);
    else if ((locatorType.toLowerCase().equals("cssselector")) ||
    (locatorType.toLowerCase().equals("css")))
        return By.cssSelector(locatorValue);
    else if (locatorType.toLowerCase().equals("xpath"))
        return By.xpath(locatorValue);
    else
        throw new Exception("Locator type '" + locatorType + "' not
        defined!!");
}
```

4. Finally, create a test that uses the property file to store the locator information, using the following code:

```
import org.openqa.selenium.WebDriver;
import org.openqa.selenium.firefox.FirefoxDriver;
import org.openqa.selenium.WebElement;
```

```
import org.openqa.selenium.By;

import org.junit.*;
import static org.junit.Assert.assertEquals;
import static org.junit.Assert.fail;

public class ObjectMapDemo {

  private WebDriver driver;
  private StringBuffer verificationErrors = new StringBuffer();
  private ObjectMap map;

  @Before
  public void setUp() throws Exception {
    // Create a new instance of the Firefox driver
    driver = new FirefoxDriver();
    driver.get("http://dl.dropbox.com/u/55228056/bmicalculator.
    html");
  }

  @Test
  public void testBmiCalculator() {
    try {
      //Get the Object Map File
      map = new ObjectMap("C:\\Users\\Admin\\workspace\\
      SeCookBook\\src\\objectmap.properties");

      //Get the Height element
      WebElement height = driver.findElement
      (map.getLocator("height_field"));;
      height.sendKeys("181");

      //Get the Weight element
      WebElement weight = driver.findElement
      (map.getLocator("weight_field"));
      weight.sendKeys("80");

      //Click on the Calculate button
      WebElement calculateButton = driver.findElement
      (map.getLocator("calculate_button"));
      calculateButton.click();

      //Verify the Bmi
      WebElement bmi = driver.findElement(map.getLocator
      ("bmi_field"));
```

```
        assertEquals("24.4", bmi.getAttribute("value"));

    } catch (Exception e) {
        //Capture and append Exceptions/Errors
        verificationErrors.append(e.toString());
    }
}

@After
public void tearDown() throws Exception {

    //Close the browser
    driver.quit();

    String verificationErrorString = verificationErrors.
    toString();
    if (!"".equals(verificationErrorString)) {
        fail(verificationErrorString);
    }
}
}
```

How it works...

First, we created a Java properties file with the key/value pair, storing a logical name for an element and locator value. The properties files are flat text files, and the `java.util.Properties` namespace provides the `Properties` class to access a property file.

```
properties = new Properties();
```

By passing a logical name or key to the `getProperty()` method of the `Properties` class, we can retrieve a value from the pair.

The `getLocator()` method uses the value returned by the `getProperty()` method and returns a matching `By` locator method, along with the value, to the test.

In the test, we created an instance of object map and then passed the location of the property file, as shown in the following code:

```
map = new ObjectMap("C:\\Users\\Admin\\workspace\\SeCookBook\\src\\
objectmap.properties");
```

We passed the locator value to the `findElement()` method by passing the logical name or key of the element to the `getLocator()` method of the `ObjectMap` class.

```
WebElement height = driver.findElement(map.getLocator("height_
field"));
```

We can have a single object map file for storing all the locators and can use the same locators in multiple tests.

There's more...

Object maps can also be created in XML files. The following code is an example of an XML-based object map:

```xml
<elements>
  <element name="HeightField" locator_type="name" locator_value="heightCMS"/>
  <element name="WeightField" locator_type="id" locator_value="weightKg"/>
  <element name="CalculateButton" locator_type="xpath" locator_value="//input[@value='Calculate']"/>
  <element name="BmiField" locator_type="id" locator_value="bmi"/>
  <element name="BmiCategoryField" locator_type="css" locator_value="#bmi_category"/>
</elements>
```

The following code is the C# implementation of the `getLocator()` method:

```csharp
public By GetLocator(string locatorName)
{
  var element = from elements in _root.Elements("element")
          where elements.Attributes("name").First().Value ==
          locatorName
          select elements;
  try
  {
    string locatorType = element.Attributes("locator_type").First().
    Value.ToString();
    string locatorValue = element.Attributes("locator_value").First().
    Value.ToString();

    switch (locatorType.ToLower())
    {
      case "id":
        return By.Id(locatorValue);
      case "name":
        return By.Name(locatorValue);
      case "classname":
        return By.ClassName(locatorValue);
      case "linktext":
        return By.LinkText(locatorValue);
      case "partiallinktext":
```

```
            return By.PartialLinkText(locatorValue);
         case "css":
            return By.CssSelector(locatorValue);
         case "xpath":
            return By.XPath(locatorValue);
         case "tagname":
            return By.TagName(locatorValue);
         default:
            throw new Exception("Locator Type '" + locatorType + "'
            not supported!!");
      }
   }
   catch (Exception)
   {
      throw new Exception("Failed to generate locator for '" +
      locatorName + "'");
   }
}
```

A similar approach can be taken with other Selenium WebDriver language bindings, such as Java, Python, or Ruby.

Capturing screenshots of elements in the Selenium WebDriver

The `TakesScreenshot` interface captures the screenshot of the entire page, current window, visible portion of the page, or of the complete desktop window in their respective order as supported by the browser. It does not provide a way to capture an image of the specific element.

We can extend the screen capture functionality to capture images of `WebElement` using the Java Image API in addition to the `TakesScreenshot` interface.

In this recipe, we will implement a helper method for capturing images of elements.

How to do it...

Let's implement the `captureElementBitmap()` method to capture an image of `WebElement`. We will pass an instance `WebElement` to this method.

```
public static File captureElementBitmap(WebElement element) throws
Exception {
   //Get the WrapsDriver of the WebElement
```

```
WrapsDriver wrapsDriver = (WrapsDriver) element;

//Get the entire Screenshot from the driver of passed WebElement
File screen = ((TakesScreenshot)  wrapsDriver.getWrappedDriver()).
getScreenshotAs(OutputType.FILE);

//Create an instance of Buffered Image from captured screenshot
BufferedImage img = ImageIO.read(screen);

// Get the Width and Height of the WebElement using
int width = element.getSize().getWidth();
int height = element.getSize().getHeight();

//Create a rectangle using Width and Height
Rectangle rect = new Rectangle(width, height);

//Get the Location of WebElement in a Point.
//This will provide X & Y co-ordinates of the WebElement
Point p = element.getLocation();

//Create image by for element using its location and size.
//This will give image data specific to the WebElement
BufferedImage dest = img.getSubimage(p.getX(), p.getY(), rect.width,
rect.height);

//Write back the image data for element in File object
ImageIO.write(dest, "png", screen);

//Return the File object containing image data
return screen;
}
```

How it works...

When the `captureElementBitmap()` method is called with `WebElement` as an argument, it gets the underlying `driver` instance of the element using the `WrapsDriver` class. Then it captures the screenshot of the page displayed in the driver using the `getScreenShotAs()` method of the `TakesScreenshot` interface using the location and size of the element, we will crop the image of the element from the image of the entire page.

In the following example, the `captureElementBitmap()` method is used to capture the image of a `<div>` element.

```java
@Test
public void testElementScreenshot(){

    WebElement pmoabsdiv = driver.findElement(By.className("pmoabs"));

    try {
            FileUtils.copyFile(WebElementExtender.captureElementBitmap
            (pmoabsdiv), new File("c:\\tmp\\div.png"));
    } catch (Exception e) {
      e.printStackTrace();
    }
}
```

See also

 ▸ The *Capturing Screenshots with Selenium WebDriver* recipe in *Chapter 2, Working with Selenium API*

Comparing images in Selenium

Many a time, our tests need image-based comparison. For example, verifying whether correct icons are displayed, whether correct images are displayed in web pages, or comparing baseline screen layout with the actual layout.

Selenium WebDriver does have features to capture screenshots or images from the application under test, however, it does not have the feature to compare the images.

In this recipe, we will create an extension class for comparing images and use it in our Selenium tests.

Getting ready

Set up a new Java project for the `CompareUtil` class. This class will be used by Selenium tests as an extension for comparing images.

How to do it...

Let's implement the `CompareUtil` class with a method to compare two image files, as shown in the following code:

```java
import java.awt.Image;
import java.awt.Toolkit;
import java.awt.image.PixelGrabber;

public class CompareUtil {

    public enum Result { Matched, SizeMismatch, PixelMismatch };

    static Result CompareImage(String baseFile, String actualFile) {

        Result compareResult = Result.PixelMismatch;
        Image baseImage = Toolkit.getDefaultToolkit().getImage(baseFile);
        Image actualImage = Toolkit.getDefaultToolkit().
        getImage(actualFile);
        try {
            PixelGrabber baseImageGrab = new PixelGrabber(baseImage, 0, 0,
            -1, -1, false);
            PixelGrabber actualImageGrab = new PixelGrabber(actualImage,
            0, 0, -1, -1, false);

            int[] baseImageData = null;
            int[] actualImageData = null;

            if(baseImageGrab.grabPixels()) {
                int width = baseImageGrab.getWidth();
                int height = baseImageGrab.getHeight();
                baseImageData = new int[width * height];
                baseImageData = (int[])baseImageGrab.getPixels();
            }

            if(actualImageGrab.grabPixels()) {
                int width = actualImageGrab.getWidth();
                int height = actualImageGrab.getHeight();
                actualImageData = new int[width * height];
                actualImageData = (int[])actualImageGrab.getPixels();
            }


            System.out.println(baseImageGrab.getHeight() +  "<>" +
            actualImageGrab.getHeight());
```

```
        System.out.println(baseImageGrab.getWidth() +  "<>" +
        actualImageGrab.getWidth());

        if ((baseImageGrab.getHeight() != actualImageGrab.getHeight())
        || (baseImageGrab.getWidth() != actualImageGrab.getWidth()))
          compareResult = Result.SizeMismatch;
        else if(java.util.Arrays.equals(baseImageData,
        actualImageData))
          compareResult = Result.Matched;

    } catch (Exception e) {
      e.printStackTrace();
    }
    return compareResult;
  }
}
```

How it works...

The `CompareUtil` class uses the `java.awt.Image` namespace to work with images. The `CompareImage()` method takes the path of the base file and the actual file as an argument. It then retrieves these images to the `Image` class.

```
Image baseImage = Toolkit.getDefaultToolkit().getImage(baseFile);
Image actualImage = Toolkit.getDefaultToolkit().getImage(actualFile);
```

Finally, it uses the `PixelGrabber` class to get the pixels from these images to an array, as shown in the following code:

```
PixelGrabber baseImageGrab = new PixelGrabber(baseImage, 0, 0, -1, -1,
false);
PixelGrabber actualImageGrab = new PixelGrabber(actualImage, 0, 0, -1,
-1, false);

int[] baseImageData = null;
int[] actualImageData = null;

if(baseImageGrab.grabPixels()) {
    int width = baseImageGrab.getWidth();
    int height = baseImageGrab.getHeight();
    baseImageData = new int[width * height];
    baseImageData = (int[])baseImageGrab.getPixels();
}

if(actualImageGrab.grabPixels()) {
    int width = actualImageGrab.getWidth();
```

```
        int height = actualImageGrab.getHeight();
        actualImageData = new int[width * height];
        actualImageData = (int[])actualImageGrab.getPixels();
    }
```

The images are first tested for size mismatch, and then for pixel mismatch, using the following code:

```
if ((baseImageGrab.getHeight() != actualImageGrab.getHeight()) ||
(baseImageGrab.getWidth() != actualImageGrab.getWidth()))
    compareResult = Result.SizeMismatch;
else if(java.util.Arrays.equals(baseImageData, actualImageData))
    compareResult = Result.Matched;
```

The following code is a sample test, comparing the layout of application being tested with a base layout captured from an earlier release:

```java
import org.openqa.selenium.firefox.FirefoxDriver;
import org.openqa.selenium.*;
import org.apache.commons.io.FileUtils;
import org.junit.*;
import static org.junit.Assert.*;
import java.io.File;

public class BmiCalculatorTest {

    public WebDriver driver;
    private StringBuffer verificationErrors = new StringBuffer();

    @Before
    public void setUp() throws Exception {
        // Create a new instance of the Firefox driver
        driver = new FirefoxDriver();
    }

    @Test
    public void testBmiCalculatorLayout() throws Exception {

        String scrFile = "c:\\screenshot.png";
        String baseScrFile = "c:\\baseScreenshot.png";

        //Open the BMI Calculator Page and get a Screen Shot of Page into
        a File
        driver.get("http://dl.dropbox.com/u/55228056/bmicalculator.html");
        File screenshotFile = ((TakesScreenshot) driver).
        getScreenshotAs(OutputType.FILE);
```

```
      FileUtils.copyFile(screenshotFile, new File(scrFile));

      try {
        //Verify baseline image with actual image
        assertEquals(CompareUtil.Result.Matched,
        CompareUtil.CompareImage(baseScrFile,scrFile));
      } catch (Error e) {
        //Capture and append Exceptions/Errors
        verificationErrors.append(e.toString());
      }
    }


    @After
    public void tearDown() throws Exception {
      //Close the browser
      driver.quit();

      String verificationErrorString = verificationErrors.toString();
      if (!"".equals(verificationErrorString)) {
        fail(verificationErrorString);
      }
    }
  }
```

There's more...

The following code is the C# implementation of CompareUtil. You can use this class for
Selenium tests created with .NET bindings.

```
using System;
using System.Collections.Generic;
using System.Linq;
using System.Text;
using System.Drawing;
using System.Drawing.Imaging;

namespace CompareUtil
{
    public class CompareUtil
    {
        public enum Result { Matched, SizeMismatch, PixelMismatch };

        public static Result CompareImage(string baseFile,
        string actualFile)
```

```
    {
        Result result = Result.Matched;

        Bitmap baseBmp = (Bitmap)Image.FromFile(baseFile);
        Bitmap actBmp = (Bitmap)Image.FromFile(actualFile);

        if (baseBmp.Size != actBmp.Size)
            result = Result.SizeMismatch;
        else
        {
            int height = Math.Min(baseBmp.Height, actBmp.Height);
            int width = Math.Min(baseBmp.Width, actBmp.Width);

            bool are_identical = true;
            for (int x = 0; x <= width - 1; x++)
            {
                for (int y = 0; y <= height - 1; y++)
                {
                    if (baseBmp.GetPixel(x, y).Equals(actBmp.
                    GetPixel(x, y)))
                    {
                    }
                    else
                    {
                        are_identical = false;
                    }
                }
            }
            if (are_identical == true)
                result = Result.Matched;
            else
                result = Result.PixelMismatch;
        }

        return result;
    }
  }
}
```

See also

- ▸ The *Capturing screenshots with Selenium WebDriver* recipe in *Chapter 2, Working with Selenium API*

- ▸ The *Capturing screenshots with RemoteWebDriver/Grid* recipe in *Chapter 2, Working with Selenium API*

- ▸ The *Capturing screenshots of elements in the Selenium WebDriver* recipe

7
Testing on Mobile Browsers

In this chapter, we will cover:

- ▶ Setting up the iWebDriver App for the iPhone/iPad simulator
- ▶ Setting up the iWebDriver App for an iPhone/iPad device
- ▶ Running tests on iOS using the iWebDriver App and iPhone driver
- ▶ Setting up the Android emulator for Selenium
- ▶ Setting up the Android device for Selenium
- ▶ Running tests using AndroidDriver

Introduction

With the increasing adoption of Smartphones and tablets, mobile applications have taken a center stage. Everyone is talking about iPhone, iPad, and Android. It has become essential to build/migrate and test applications for these platforms.

Selenium supports testing web applications in mobile web browsers. In this chapter, we will cover recipes for configuring and using Selenium for testing applications on iOS and Android-based phones and tablets.

We can run automated tests on a simulator/emulator or on a real device using iOS and Android drivers. These drivers implement the RemoteWebDriver for enabling testing through the WebDriver. Both these drivers provide an application that implements RemoteWebDriver server and a lightweight HTTP server. These applications can be installed on a simulator/emulator or on a device for testing.

We will test a mobile web application developed using jQuery mobile on these platforms.

IPhoneDriver architecture

The IPhoneDriver allows running automated tests, ensuring your web application works correctly on an iOS Safari browser in a simulator or on a real device for various versions of the iOS platform. It provides the core WebDriver API along with HTML 5 APIs.

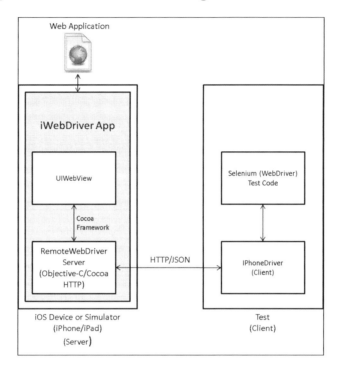

As shown in the previous diagram, IPhoneDriver requires an iWebDriver application installed on the simulator or on the device. The iWebDriver application implements the RemoteWebDriver server functionality. It uses a UIWebView (the rendering component used in iOS Safari browser) to execute the tests using the Cocoa framework. The iWebDriver application is implemented in the Objective-C and Cocoa HTTP framework.

Once the iWebDriver is set up on the simulator or on a device, the test code connects to the iWebDriver application using the HTTP/JSON protocol to execute the tests in a way similar to a client/server application.

AndroidDriver architecture

Similar to the IPhoneDriver, the AndroidDriver allows running the automated tests and ensuring your web application works correctly on an Android browser for various versions of Android. The AndroidDriver supports user interactions such as taps, flicks, and scrolls. It can also rotate the display and interact with HTML 5 features such as local and session storage and application cache.

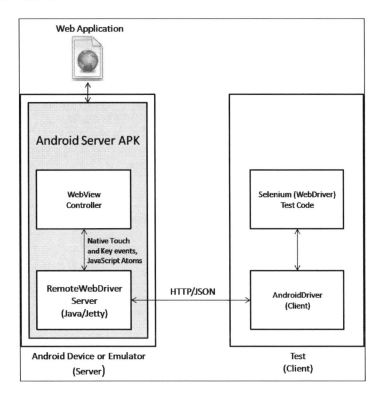

The AndroidDriver requires the Android server APK to be installed on the emulator or device. The Android Server APK implements the RemoteWebDriver server functionality. It uses a WebView (the rendering component used in Android browser) to execute the tests using the native touch and key events. It uses JavaScript Atom libraries to interact with the DOM. Android server APK is implemented as an Android application developed using Java. It uses Jetty for web server functionality.

Once the Android server APK is set up on the emulator or device, the test code connects to the Android server APK using the HTTP/JSON protocol to execute the tests similar to a client/server application. We also need to enable port-forwarding from the host machine to the Android emulator or device.

Setting up the iWebDriver App for the iPhone/iPad simulator

The iOS simulator enables you to test your web applications without using an actual device, whether it's an iPhone or any other iOS device, such as iPad or iPod Touch. The iOS simulator also has the capability of simulating different versions of the iOS, and this becomes extremely useful if your application needs to be installed on different iOS versions.

You need to set up the iWebDriver application for Selenium to test web applications on iOS Platform.

The iWebDriver application is developed using the Objective-C and Cocoa framework. The iWebDriver application implements the RemoteWebDriver server for the test code to run on the iOS platform. It is supported on both, the simulator and the real device. In this recipe, we will see how to download and configure the iWebDriver Xcode project from the Selenium code base to run against a simulator.

Getting ready

We need to download and compile the iWebDriver application using the Xcode IDE on Mac OS X. You can download and install the Xcode IDE from Mac App Store or from the Apple Developer Resources website at `https://developer.apple.com/xcode/index.php` (this is available for registered developers under Apple iOS Developer Program).

How to do it...

We will perform the following steps for setting up the iWebDriver App for iPhone/iPad simulator:

1. First, download the `iWebDriver.xcodeproj` file by using the following command in the terminal window:

    ```
    svn checkout http://selenium.googlecode.com/svn/trunk/ selenium-read-only
    ```

    It will take a while to download the code repository. A new directory named `selenium-read-only` will be created with the complete Selenium source code from the trunk. In the next step, we will set up the **iWebDriver Project** in the Xcode IDE.

2. Navigate to the `selenium-read-only` directory using Finder and open the `iphone` subdirectory.

3. Click on the **iWebDriver.xcodeproj** icon. This will launch the **Xcode IDE** window with the **iWebDriver project**.

4. Set your build configuration to **iWebDriver > iPhone 5.0 Simulator** in the **Scheme** drop-down box on the top left-hand side of the `Navigator` pane in Xcode IDE. Apple releases newer iOS versions and you might see a latest version for selection in the build configuration. Please select the appropriate or latest iOS version in the build configuration.

A warning will be displayed in Xcode as **Validate Project Settings** in the `Navigator` pane, as shown in the following screenshot:

5. Click on **Validate Project Settings**. This will launch the **Build Settings** dialog box.

6. Click on the **Perform Changes** button in the **Build Settings** dialog box.

7. Optionally, the `Xcode` IDE may show a dialog box asking for creating a snapshot of the project. Click on the **Enable** button if asked.

8. Project will be ready with no issues.

9. To build and run the iWebDriver application, click on the **Run** button to build the project and run the application.

10. Xcode IDE will build the **iWebDriver project** and launch the **iPhone simulator** with the iWebDriver application running on http://localhost:3001/wd/hub as shown in the following screenshot:

How it works...

The iWebDriver application is not available in the Apple App Store and we need to build it for installing it on the simulator using the Xcode IDE.

For building the iWebDriver application, we downloaded the iWebDriver.xcodeproj file and its dependencies from the Selenium code base.

We changed the build settings to deploy the iWebDriver application on the simulator. When we click on the **Run** button in Xcode IDE, it compiles the iWebDriver application along with its dependencies. Xcode IDE launches the iOS simulator automatically with the target device selected in the build configuration. Xcode IDE then installs the iWebDriver application on the simulator automatically. Finally, the iWebDriver application is launched as a web server running on port 3001 on the simulator.

There's more...

We saw how to configure the iWebDriver application for the iPhone simulator. You can also run the iWebDriver application with the iPad simulator. To configure the iWebDriver application for iPad, change the scheme to **iWebDriver > iPad 5.0 Simulator** and click on the **Run** button.

This will launch the iPad simulator with the iWebDriver application, as shown in the following screenshot:

▶ The *Running tests on iOS using the iWebDriver App and iPhone driver* recipe

Setting up the iWebDriver App for an iPhone/iPad device

While the iOS simulator acts as a good test bed for your testing needs, it is recommended that you test your web application on an actual device, rather than relying on the iOS simulator for testing.

Setting up the iWebDriver application on a real device is similar to installing it on the simulator with the only difference in installing and configuring the provisioning profile from Apple. You can install an application on an iOS device only from the App Store. However, if you want to install an application for testing purposes, you need to procure a provisioning profile from Apple by enrolling in the iOS Developer Program, which costs $99 annually. For more information visit `https://developer.apple.com/programs/ios/`.

Getting ready

We need to download and compile the iWebDriver application using the Xcode IDE on Mac OS X. You can download and install the Xcode IDE from Mac App Store or from Apple Developer Resources website at (this is available for registered developers under the Apple iOS Developer Program) `https://developer.apple.com/xcode/index.php`.

How to do it...

Let's perform the following steps for setting up the iWebDriver App for the iPhone/iPad device:

1. If you haven't downloaded the `iWebDriver.xcodeproj` file in the earlier recipe, you can download this by using the following command in the terminal window:

    ```
    svn checkout http://selenium.googlecode.com/svn/trunk/ selenium-
    read-only
    ```

    This will take a while to download. A new directory named `selenium-read-only` will be created with complete Selenium source code from the trunk. In the next steps, we will set up the **iWebDriver project** in **Xcode IDE**.

2. Navigate to the `selenium-read-only` directory using Finder. Open the `iphone` subdirectory and click on the **iWebDriver.xcodeproj** icon. This will launch the **Xcode IDE** window with the iWebDriver project.

3. Set your build configuration to **iWebDriver > iOS Device** in the **Scheme** drop-down box on the top left-hand side of the `Navigator` pane in **Xcode IDE**, as shown in the following screenshot:

4. You will also need a provisioning profile from Apple to be installed and configured for your device.

   Open `info.plist` and edit the **Bundle identifier** to com.NAME.$ {PRODUCT_ NAME:identifier} where NAME is the name you registered your provisioning profile to be an authority. In the example shown in the following screenshot, **com.google** has been provided. Replace **google** with your profile name.

Icon file		String	selenium–icon.png
Bundle identifier	⇅ ⊕ ⊖	String	⇅ com.google.${PRODUCT_NAME:identifier}
InfoDictionary version		String	6.0

 If you use the default provisioning profile, which may simply use a wildcard for all domains, you don't need to edit the **NAME** field in the **Bundle identifier**.

A warning will be displayed in Xcode to validate the `Project Settings` in the `Navigator` pane.

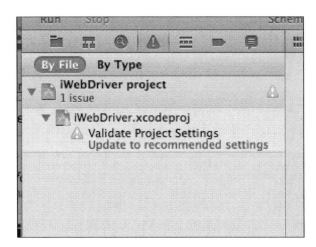

5. Click on **Validate Project Settings**. This will launch the **Build Settings** dialog box.

6. Click on the **Perform Changes** button in the **Build Settings** dialog box.

7. Optionally, Xcode IDE may show a dialog box asking for creating a snapshot of the project. Click on the **Enable** button if asked.

8. Project will be ready with no issues.

9. Make sure your device is connected to your computer. Your device must also be routable from your computer. The easiest way to do this is to configure a Wi-Fi network and connect your device to it.

10. Click on the **Run (Play)** button to build the project and run the application.

11. Xcode IDE will build the **iWebDriver project** and automatically install and launch the iWebDriver application in the connected iOS device on `http://localhost:3001/wd/hub`.

How it works...

As the iWebDriver application is not available in Apple App Store, we need to build it for installation on the device using the Xcode IDE.

For building the iWebDriver application, we downloaded the `iWebDriver.xcodeproj` file and its dependencies from the Selenium code base.

We changed the build settings to deploy the iWebDriver application on a real device. When we click on the **Run** button in Xcode IDE, it compiles the iWebDriver application along with its dependencies. Then the Xcode IDE installs the iWebDriver application on the device automatically using the provisioning profile. Finally, the iWebDriver application is launched as a web server running on port 3001 on the device.

See also

► The *Running tests on iOS using the iWebDriver App and iPhone driver* recipe

Running tests on iOS using the iWebDriver App and iPhone driver

Once we have the iOS simulator or the device set up with the iWebDriver application, you can create and run the tests using the `IPhoneDriver` class.

In this recipe, we will test a simple mobile BMI calculator web application, developed using jQuery Mobile on the iOS platform.

Getting ready

Before we start running the test with the iPhone driver, set up the iOS simulator or device with the iWebDriver application.

If you are testing on a real device, then make sure it is connected to the machine running the tests using the iPhone driver over the network.

- ▶ Set up the iOS simulator or a real device with the iWebDriver application
- ▶ Set up a new Java project
- ▶ Add the WebDriver JARs to the project's build-path
- ▶ Add the JUnit library to the project

How to do it...

Execute the following test with iWebDriver:

1. Create a new JUnit test named `IPhoneDriverTest`.
2. Copy the following code to the newly created `IPhoneDriverTest` class:

```java
import org.openqa.selenium.WebDriver;
import org.openqa.selenium.iphone.IPhoneDriver;
import org.openqa.selenium.WebElement;
import org.openqa.selenium.By;
import org.junit.*;
import static org.junit.Assert.*;

public class IPhoneDriverTest {

  private WebDriver driver;
  private StringBuffer verificationErrors = new StringBuffer();

  @Before
  public void setUp() throws Exception {
    // Create a new instance of the iPhone driver
    driver = new IPhoneDriver();
    // Open the BMI Calculator Mobile Application
    driver.get("http://dl.dropbox.com/u/55228056/
    mobilebmicalculator.html");
  }

  @Test
  public void testBMICalculator() throws Exception {
    try {
```

```
        WebElement height = driver.findElement(By.
        name("heightCMS"));
        height.sendKeys("181");

        WebElement weight = driver.findElement(By.name("weightKg"));
        weight.sendKeys("80");

        WebElement calculateButton = driver.findElement(By.
        id("Calculate"));
        calculateButton.click();


        WebElement bmi = driver.findElement(By.name("bmi"));
        assertEquals("24.4", bmi.getAttribute("value"));

        WebElement bmi_category = driver.findElement
        (By.name("bmi_category"));
        assertEquals("Normal",bmi_category.getAttribute("value"));

      } catch (Error e) {
      //Capture and append Exceptions/Errors
      verificationErrors.append(e.toString());
      }
    }


  @After
  public void tearDown() throws Exception {
    // Close the browser
    driver.quit();

    String verificationErrorString = verificationErrors.
    toString();
    if (!"".equals(verificationErrorString)) {
      fail(verificationErrorString);
    }
  }
}
```

3. Run this test as a JUnit test.

How it works...

For this test, we created an object of the `IPhoneDriver` class by calling the constructor. This internally creates an instance of the `RemoteWebDriver` class.

```
driver = new IPhoneDriver();
```

If you are running this test on a local machine where the simulator is running, it will connect to the local instance of the iWebDriver on port 3001.

If you are running the simulator on a different machine and testing it on any other machine, you can pass the remote host details as an argument to the `IPhoneDriver` constructor by using the following code:

```
driver = new IPhoneDriver("http://192.168.1.100:3001/wd/hub");
```

When we run the test, it connects to the iWebDriver, which is running as the RemoteWebDriver server and starts the test execution.

The following screenshot shows the **Mobile BMI Calculator** application being tested on the iPhone:

As you can see in the code, it uses the pure WebDriver API to execute the test on a mobile application.

There's more...

Instead of using the `IPhoneDriver` class, you can also use the `RemoteWebDriver` class with the desired capabilities to execute the tests on the iOS in the following way:

```
//Create a new instance of DesiredCapabilities
DesiredCapabilities caps = new DesiredCapabilities();

// Create a new instance of the RemoteWebDriver using RemoteWebDriver
// Server URL & Desired Capabilities
driver = new RemoteWebDriver(new URL("http://192.168.1.100:3001/wd/
hub"), caps.iphone());
```

Setting up the Android emulator for Selenium

Similar to the iOS simulator, the Android emulator enables you to test your applications without using an actual Android device, whether it is any Android-based phone or tablet. The Android emulator also has the capability of simulating different versions of Android, and this becomes extremely useful if your application needs to be installed on different Android versions.

We need to set up the Android server APK for Selenium to test web applications on the Android platform.

The Android server APK is developed as an Android application using Java/Jetty. The Android server APK application implements the RemoteWebDriver server for the test code to run on the Android platform. It is supported on both the emulator and the real device. In this recipe, we will see how to download and configure the Android server APK on the Android emulator.

Getting ready

Before setting up the Android emulator for Selenium to run tests, we need to set up the Android development environment. Use the following steps:

▸ Install the SDK starter package (if you are using Windows, download the installer for help with the initial setup) from `http://developer.android.com/sdk/index.html`

▸ Add Android platforms and other components to your SDK by using the SDK Manager

How to do it...

You can use the command line or the graphical interface provided by the Android SDK to create and set up a new Android emulator. Use the following steps on a command line to create a new **Android Virtual Device** (**AVD**), and use this AVD in the emulator for Android:

We will create a new AVD using the command line.

1. Navigate to the `tools` directory in the `android-sdk` directory.

2. We will create a new AVD using the following command:

   ```
   android create avd -n my_android -t 14 -c 512M
   ```

   This command uses the following parameters:

Parameter	Description
-n	It specifies the name of the AVD.
-t	It specifies the platform target. Use the android list targets command to get the list of platforms available with the SDK.
-c	It specifies the SD card storage space.

   When you are prompted **Do you wish to create a custom hardware profile [no]**, enter **no** in the field.

3. Start the emulator by using the following command:

   ```
   emulator -avd my_android &
   ```

It will take a while to start the emulator. Once the Android boots up in the emulator, you will see a screen as shown in the following screenshot:

We can also use the AVD Manager GUI to create a new AVD and launch the AVD in the emulator. Use the following steps to create and launch a new AVD using the AVD Manager:

1. Launch the AVD Manager. A window as shown in the following screenshot will be displayed:

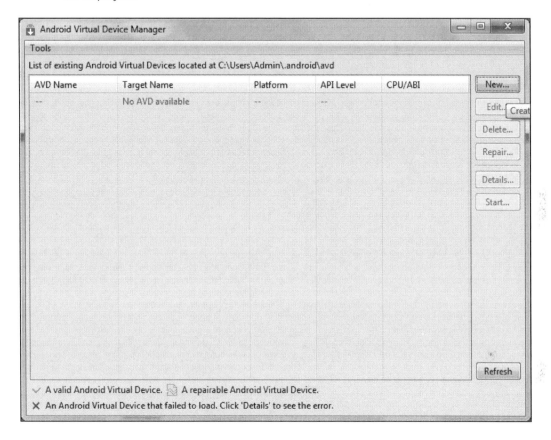

2. Click on the **New...** button in the **Android Virtual Device Manager** and a **Create new Android Virtual Device (AVD)** window will be displayed:

   ❑ Specify the **Name** for the new AVD.

   ❑ Select the Android version in the **Target** field. In the following example **Android 4.0 - API Level 14** is specified.

   ❑ Specify the **Size** in the **SD Card** field. In the following example **512 MiB** is specified.

❏ Keep the rest of the values as default, unless you need to change anything.

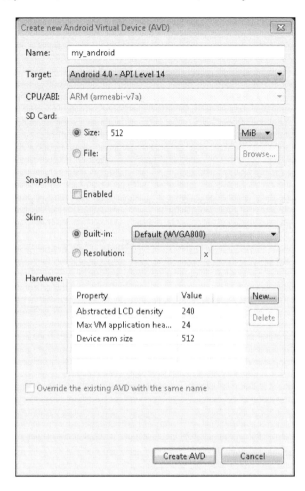

3. Click on the **Create AVD** button. The message shown in the following screenshot will be displayed on success:

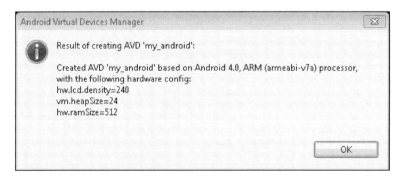

4. To launch the newly created AVD, select the newly created AVD in the AVD Manager and click on the **Start...** button as shown in the following screenshot:

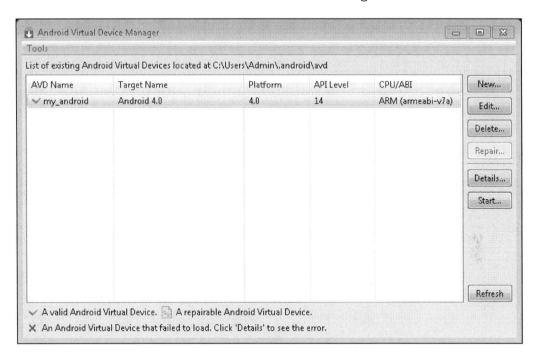

5. The **Launch Options** dialog box will be displayed. Keep all the options as default and click on the **Launch** button to start the AVD, as shown in the following screenshot:

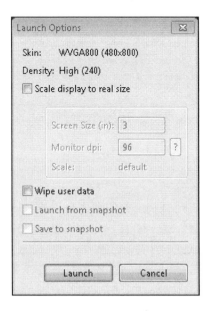

Now we will install the WebDriver APK as follows:

1. Navigate to the `platform-tools` directory in the `android-sdk` directory.

2. Every device or emulator has a serial ID. Run the following command to get the serial ID of the device or emulator:

   adb devices

   In the previous example the serial ID will be `emulator-5554`.

3. Next, download the Android server APK from `http://code.google.com/p/selenium/downloads/list`.

4. Copy the Android server APK file to the `platform-tools` directory in the `android-sdk` directory.

5. Now install the Android server APK on the emulator by using the following command:

   adb -s emulator-5554 -e install -r <android-server.apk>

6. After installing the Android server APK, launch the WebDriver application by using the following command:

   adb -s emulator-5554 shell am start -a android.intent.action.MAIN -n org.openqa.selenium.android.app/.MainActivity

   The emulator will start the WebDriver application. A **WebDriver Ready** message will be displayed on the emulator screen.

    You can also launch the WebDriver application by clicking on the **WebDriver Application** icon in the **Application** menu on an Android device or emulator.

7. Finally, we need to set up the port forwarding in order to forward the traffic from the host machine to the emulator by using the following command:

   adb emulator-5554 forward tcp:8080 tcp:8080

   The Android server will be available at `http://localhost:8080/wd/hub` from the host machine. Now the emulator is ready to run the tests.

How it works...

For executing the tests on an Android emulator, we created a virtual Android device using the Android SDK and AVD Manager. Then, we installed the Android server APK on the virtual device.

When Android server APK is launched, a RemoteWebDriver enabled client can interact with it for executing the tests using the HTTP/JSON protocol. Android server APK processes the HTTP requests using the `http://localhost:8080/wd/hub` URL.

See also

▸ The *Running tests using AndroidDriver* recipe

Setting up the Android device for Selenium

Testing your web application on the Android emulator will definitely help; however, it is also essential to test the application on a real Android device. While the iOS platform and devices such as iPhone and iPad are limited to Apple, Android on the other hand is an open source platform. Android has been widely adopted by mobile phone and tablet manufacturers, such as Samsung, Motorola, LG, and so on, with up to 56 percent market share (September 2011). There are a number of devices available that are running on Android with multiple form factors.

Setting up the Android server APK on a real device is similar to installing it on a simulator. In this recipe, you will see how to configure and install Android server APK on a real Android device. I have used a Samsung Galaxy Smartphone running on Android 2.3 (Gingerbread) for the following example.

Getting ready

Before setting up the Android device for Selenium to run tests, we need to set up the Android development environment. Perform the following steps for the setup:

▸ Install the SDK starter package (if you are using Windows, download the installer for help with the initial setup) from `http://developer.android.com/sdk/index.html`

▸ Add Android platforms and other components to your SDK by using the SDK Manager

▸ Install the correct USB drivers for your device

How to do it...

First connect the Android device to the computer using a USB cable. Make sure the device is connected to the host machine by using the following command:

```
adb devices
```

Note the serial ID of the device. We will need the serial ID for installing the WebDriver APK in the next step.

Now let's install the WebDriver APK on the connected Android device as follows:

1. Download the Android Server APK from `http://code.google.com/p/selenium/downloads/list`.

2. Copy the Android server APK file to the `platform-tools` directory in the `android-sdk` directory.

3. Now install the Android server APK on the device using the following command:

   ```
   adb -s <serial_id> -e install -r <android-server.apk>
   ```

4. After installing the Android server APK, launch the WebDriver application using the following command:

   ```
   adb -s <serial_id> shell am start -a android.intent.action.MAIN -n
   org.openqa.selenium.android.app/.MainActivity
   ```

   The WebDriver application will be launched on the device. Now we need to set up the port forwarding in order to forward traffic from the host machine to the device. Enter the following command in the terminal:

   ```
   adb -s <serial_id> forward tcp:8080 tcp:8080
   ```

   The Android server will be available at `http://localhost:8080/wd/hub` from the host machine. Now the device is ready to run the tests.

How it works...

For executing tests on the Android emulator, we created a virtual Android device using the Android SDK and AVD Manager. Then we installed the Android server APK on the virtual device.

When Android server APK is launched, a RemoteWebDriver enabled client can interact with it for executing the tests using the HTTP/JSON protocol. A **WebDriver Ready** message will be displayed on the device screen, as shown in the following screenshot:

The Android server APK processes the HTTP requests using the address
`http://localhost:8080/wd/hub` URL.

There's more...

Android SDK provides the Android Test framework for testing the Android Native applications. Lately, Google has added the WebDriver implementation to the Android Test framework. You can use this as an alternative to set up and execute tests on the Android emulator or device. A lot of the above tasks are automatically performed by the Android Test framework instead of using commands or GUI to set up the test environment. For more information on the Android Test framework, visit `http://developer.android.com/guide/topics/testing/testing_android.html`.

You can set up the Android Test framework with Eclipse by installing the **Android Development Tools** (**ADT**) plugin.

See also

> ▸ The *Running tests using AndroidDriver* recipe

Running tests using AndroidDriver

Once we have the Android server APK installed and configured on the Android emulator or device, we can create and run the tests using the `AndroidDriver` class.

In this recipe, we will test a simple mobile BMI calculator web application developed using jQuery Mobile on the iOS platform.

Getting ready

Before we start running the test with `AndroidDriver`, set up the Android emulator or device with the following steps:

> ▸ Set up the Android emulator or a real device with the Android server APK
> ▸ Set up the port-forwarding by using the following command:
>
>   **adb -s <serial_id> forward tcp:8080 tcp:8080**
>
> ▸ Set up a new Java project
> ▸ Add the WebDriver JARS to the project's build path
> ▸ Add the JUnit library to the project

How to do it...

To execute the test with iWebDriver follow these steps:

1. Create a new JUnit test. Name it AndroidDriverTest.

2. Copy the following code to the newly created AndroidDriverTest class:

```java
import org.openqa.selenium.WebDriver;
import org.openqa.selenium.android.AndroidDriver;
import org.openqa.selenium.WebElement;
import org.openqa.selenium.By;
import org.junit.*;
import static org.junit.Assert.*;

public class AndroidDriverTest {

private WebDriver driver;
private StringBuffer verificationErrors = new StringBuffer();

@Before
public void setUp() throws Exception {
  // Create a new instance of the Android driver
  driver = new AndroidDriver();
  driver.get("http://dl.dropbox.com/u/55228056/
mobilebmicalculator.html");
}

@Test
public void testBMICalculator() throws Exception {
  try {
    WebElement height = driver.findElement(By.name("heightCMS"));
    height.sendKeys("181");

    WebElement weight = driver.findElement(By.name("weightKg"));
    weight.sendKeys("80");

    WebElement calculateButton = driver.findElement(By.
    id("Calculate"));
```

```
        calculateButton.click();

        WebElement bmi = driver.findElement(By.name("bmi"));
        assertEquals("24.4", bmi.getAttribute("value"));

        WebElement bmi_category = driver.findElement
        (By.name("bmi_category"));
        assertEquals("Normal",bmi_category.getAttribute("value"));

    } catch (Error e) {
        //Capture and append Exceptions/Errors
        verificationErrors.append(e.toString());
    }
}


@After
public void tearDown() throws Exception {
    // Close the browser
    driver.quit();

    String verificationErrorString = verificationErrors.toString();
    if (!"".equals(verificationErrorString)) {
        fail(verificationErrorString);
    }
}
}
```

3. Run this test as a JUnit test.

How it works...

For this test, we created an object of the `AndroidDriver` class by calling the constructor. This internally creates an instance of the `RemoteWebDriver` class.

```
driver = new AndroidDriver();
```

If you are running this test on a local machine where the simulator is running, it will connect to the local instance of the Android server APK automatically. Otherwise, you can pass the host details as an argument to the `AndroidDriver` constructor by using the following command:

```
driver = new AndroidDriver("http://192.168.1.100/wd/hub");
```

When we run the test, it connects to the Android server APK that is running as the RemoteWebDriver server and starts the test execution. The following screenshot shows the **Mobile BMI Calculator** application being tested:

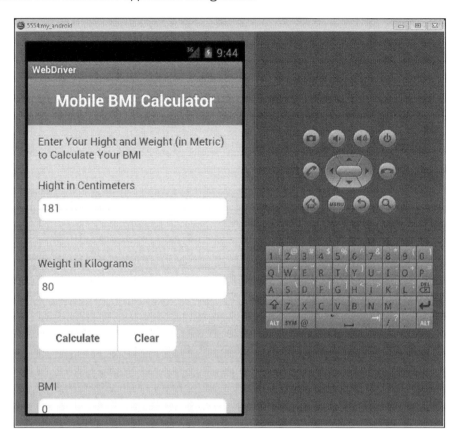

As you can see in the previous code, it uses a pure WebDriver API to execute the test on the mobile application.

There's more...

Android driver also allows us to interact with mobile functionalities, such as Screen Rotation, Tap, Flick, and so on using the mobile API. In the previous example, we are rotating the screen to the landscape mode then back to the portrait mode by using the following code:

```
((Rotatable) driver).rotate(ScreenOrientation.LANDSCAPE);

WebElement height = driver.findElement(By.name("heightCMS"));
height.sendKeys("181");
```

```
WebElement weight = driver.findElement(By.name("weightKg"));
weight.sendKeys("80");

WebElement calculateButton = driver.findElement
(By.id("Calculate"));
calculateButton.click();
```

```
((Rotatable) driver).rotate(ScreenOrientation.PORTRAIT);
```

Running the test with RemoteWebDriver

Instead of using the `AndroidDriver` class, you can also use the `RemoteWebDriver` class with the desired capabilities to execute the tests on iOS in the following way:

```
//Create a new instance of DesiredCapabilities
DesiredCapabilities caps = new DesiredCapabilities();

// Create a new instance of the RemoteWebDriver using RemoteWebDriver
// Server URL & Desired Capabilities
driver = new RemoteWebDriver(new URL("http://192.168.1.100/wd/hub"),
caps.android());
```

This will be useful when we run the tests in parallel and we need to parameterize the target environments.

8
Client-side Performance Testing

In this chapter, we will cover:

- ► Measuring the response time using a timer
- ► Measuring performance with the Navigation Timing API
- ► Using the BrowserMob proxy for measuring performance
- ► Using dynaTrace for measuring the performance
- ► Using HttpWatch for measuring performance
- ► Client-side performance testing with Watir-WebDriver-Performance in Ruby

Introduction

Measuring and optimizing the client-side performance is essential for a seamless user experience and this is critical for web 2.0 applications using AJAX.

Capturing vital information, such as the time taken for page load, rendering of the elements, and the JavaScript code execution, helps in identifying the areas where performance is slow and optimizes the overall client-side performance.

Sometimes, third-party controls, images, and media content also cause degradation in the performance. Using Selenium WebDriver and various other tools together, we can measure the performance and eliminate the weaker content.

There are various APIs and tools that we can integrate with the Selenium WebDriver for measuring the performance of the client-side user interaction and script code. This chapter contains recipes to use the Selenium WebDriver for testing the client-side performance.

Measuring the response time using a timer

Measuring page load or response time is one of the basic metrics that we can capture in the Selenium WebDriver tests. We can use timers in the test code to capture the time taken for page load, rendering of the elements, JavaScript code execution, and so on. This approach can be implemented using the `Date/Time` classes in programming languages.

We can also use the `Stopwatch` class to measure the time taken for an activity of interest. The only downside of this approach will be testing with a lot of timers added.

In this recipe, we will see how to calculate the timespan between two events in various ways.

Getting ready

We need to identify the areas where we we need to evaluate the response time. We will measure the response time by adding a timer.

How to do it...

We can use various strategies to use timers in our code to measure the response time or the load time. For example, if we want to measure the time for a page load based on a particular element that is being rendered on the page, we can use two variables, namely, capturing start time, which is the time when the page is requested, and the end time, which is the time after the element is rendered on that page. We will use the `System.currentTimeMillis()` method to get the current time as follows:

```
// Get the Start Time
long startTime = System.currentTimeMillis();

// Open the BMI Calculator Mobile Application
driver.get("http://dl.dropbox.com/u/55228056/bmicalculator.html");

// Wait for the Calculate Button
new WebDriverWait(driver, 10).until(ExpectedConditions.
presenceOfElementLocated(By.id("Calculate")));

// Get the End Time
long endTime = System.currentTimeMillis();

// Measure total time
long totalTime = endTime - startTime;
System.out.println("Total Page Load Time: " + totalTime + "
milliseconds");
```

Refer to the TimerDemo.java section in the book's sample code for a complete test.

How it works...

When this test will be executed, before we start requesting the page, the startTime variable will be assigned with the current time in milliseconds using the System. currentTimeMillis() method. We then wait for the Calculate button to be loaded in the DOM using the ExpectedConditions.presenceOfElementLocated() method. This will delay the script until the expected element is present in the DOM.

```
// Wait for the Calculate Button
new WebDriverWait(driver, 10).until(ExpectedConditions.
presenceOfElementLocated(By.id("Calculate")));
```

After the element is available in the DOM, we will again collect the current time in milliseconds in the endTime variable. We will calculate the difference between the startTime and endTime variables to find out how many milliseconds it took to load the page as follows:

```
// Measure total time
long totalTime = endTime - startTime
```

Though this is not a perfect approach, it will give us a good measure of the page load time.

There's more...

Instead of using the variables and the System.currentTimeMillis() method, we can use an easier approach by creating an instance of the StopWatch class from the org. apache.commons.lang.time namespace as follows:

```
// Get the StopWatch Object and start the StopWatch
StopWatch pageLoad = new StopWatch();
pageLoad.start();

// Open the BMI Calculator Mobile Application
driver.get("http://dl.dropbox.com/u/55228056/bmicalculator.html");

// Wait for the Calculate Button
new WebDriverWait(driver, 10).until(ExpectedConditions.
presenceOfElementLocated(By.id("Calculate")));

// Stop the StopWatch
pageLoad.stop();
System.out.println("Total Page Load Time: " + pageLoad.getTime() + "
milliseconds");
```

Refer to the `StopWatchDemo.java` section in the book's sample code for a complete test.

The `StopWatch` class provides a neat way to calculate the elapsed time between the events. It also provides a method to suspend and resume the `Stopwatch` class.

StopWatch in .NET bindings

For .NET users, the `System.Diagnostics` namespace provides a similar `StopWatch` class that you can use in the Selenium WebDriver test developed in .NET languages. For detailed information, please visit `http://msdn.microsoft.com/en-us/library/system.diagnostics.stopwatch.aspx`.

See also

▶ The *Measuring performance with the Navigation Timing API* recipe

Measuring performance with the Navigation Timing API

Navigation Timing is a W3C Standard JavaScript API for measuring performance on the Web. The API provides a simple way to get accurate and detailed timing statistics natively for page navigation and load events. It is available on Internet Explorer 9, Google Chrome, Firefox, and WebKit-based browsers.

The API is accessed via the properties of the timing interface of the `window.performance` object using JavaScript.

Each `performance.timing` attribute shows the time of a navigation event when the page was requested or when the page load event was measured in milliseconds since midnight of January 1, 1970 (UTC). A zero value means that an event did not occur.

The order of the `performance.timing` events is shown in the following diagram from the Navigation Timing draft:

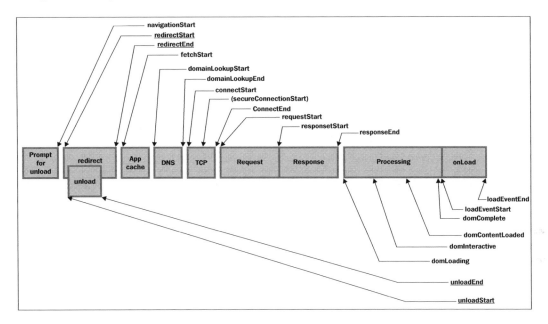

Identify a test where you want to measure the performance as well as decide what performance counters you want to measure.

We need to access the `window.performance` object by using `JavascriptExecutor` to collect the timing metric.

```
// Open the BMI Calculator Mobile Application
driver.get("http://dl.dropbox.com/u/55228056/bmicalculator.html");

JavascriptExecutor js = (JavascriptExecutor) driver;

// Get the Load Event End
long loadEventEnd = (Long) js.executeScript("return window.
performance.timing.loadEventEnd;");

// Get the Navigation Event Start
```

```
long navigationStart = (Long) js.executeScript("return window.
performance.timing.navigationStart;");

// Difference between Load Event End and Navigation Event Start is
// Page Load Time
System.out.println("Page Load Time is " + (loadEventEnd -
navigationStart)/1000 + " seconds.");
```

 Refer to the `NavTimingDemo.java` section in the book's sample code for a complete test.

How it works...

As discussed in the previous code, the `window.performance` object provides us with the performance metric that is available within the Browser Window object. We need to use JavaScript to retrieve this metric using the following code:

```
JavascriptExecutor js = (JavascriptExecutor) driver;

// Get the Load Event End
long loadEventEnd = (Long) js.executeScript("return window.
performance.timing.loadEventEnd;");
```

Here we are collecting the `loadEventEnd` time and the `navigationEventStart` time and calculating the difference between them, which will give us the page load time.

Using the BrowserMob proxy for measuring performance

BrowserMob proxy is a free tool that supports monitoring and manipulating the network traffic from web applications. It can capture the performance data from a web application in an **HTML Archive (HAR)** format, as well as manipulate the browser behavior and traffic, such as whitelisting and blacklisting content, simulating network traffic and latency, and rewriting HTTP requests and responses.

BrowserMob proxy helps in automating client-side performance data collection for a web application using the Selenium WebDriver.

In this recipe, we will set up a BrowserMob proxy for the Selenium WebDriver test to collect the performance data in an HAR format.

Getting ready

Download the BrowserMob proxy from `https://github.com/webmetrics/browsermob-proxy/downloads`.

Reference the BrowserMob proxy JARs from the `lib` folder in the `BrowserMob` proxy folder to your existing Selenium WebDriver test project.

How to do it...

Let's create a test that uses BrowserMob for performance monitoring by carrying out the following steps:

1. The test first needs to launch a BrowserMob proxy server, which is done as follows:

```
// Start the BrowserMob Proxy
ProxyServer server = new ProxyServer(9090);
server.start();
```

2. Create an object of `SeleniumProxy` and `DesiredCapabilities` to use the BrowserMob proxy as follows:

```
// Get the Selenium proxy object
Proxy proxy = server.seleniumProxy();

// Configure Desired capability for using Proxy Server
DesiredCapabilities capabilities = new DesiredCapabilities();
capabilities.setCapability(CapabilityType.PROXY, proxy);
```

3. Create and launch a browser instance with the proxy as follows:

```
// Start the Browser up
WebDriver driver = new FirefoxDriver(capabilities);
```

4. Create a new HAR file and navigate to the URL, as shown in the following code:

```
// Create a new HAR with the label "bmiCalculator"
server.newHar("bmiCalculator");
```

5. Implement the test steps that will interact with the application as follows:

```
// Open the BMI Calculator Application
driver.get("http://dl.dropbox.com/u/55228056/bmicalculator.html");

WebElement height = driver.findElement(By.name("heightCMS"));
height.sendKeys("181");

WebElement weight = driver.findElement(By.name("weightKg"));
```

```
weight.sendKeys("80");

WebElement calculateButton = driver.findElement(By.
id("Calculate"));
calculateButton.click();

Thread.sleep(5000);
```

6. Finally, the test needs to collect the performance data from the BrowserMob proxy server in the following code:

```
// Get the HAR data
Har har = server.getHar();

// Write the HAR Data in a File
File harFile = new File("C:\\bmiCalculator.har");
har.writeTo(harFile);

// Stop the BrowserMob Proxy Server
server.stop();

// Close the browser
driver.quit();
```

How it works...

The BrowserMob proxy server works like a normal proxy server between the application and the browser. However, it can monitor the traffic and collect the performance data that can be used for analysis. We can also manipulate the BrowserMob proxy to create a low-latency network to observe the performance of the application.

The BrowserMob proxy collects the performance data in the HAR format and we can access this data by using the getHar() method. We can save this data in an HAR file, using the writeTo() method of the Har class available in the BrowserMob proxy API. We can open the HAR file for analysis using a HAR viewer. The following screenshot is a HAR representation using an online HAR viewer available at http://www.softwareishard.com/har/viewer/.

▸ The *Using dynaTrace for measuring the performance* recipe

▸ The *Using HttpWatch for measuring performance* recipe

Using dynaTrace for measuring the performance

The dynaTrace AJAX Edition is a widely used tool for building optimized and faster web 2.0 applications. dynaTrace helps in analyzing problems in JavaScript, network requests, page load performance, and so on. dynaTrace provides support for Internet Explorer and Firefox web browsers.

When you monitor an application with dynaTrace, it analyzes the application and finds problems while providing detail metrics about the application's performance on various levels. It also provides optimization recommendations automatically. dynaTrace provides support for various testing tools including the Selenium WebDriver, where we can combine dynaTrace with tests.

In this recipe, we will set up dynaTrace to capture the various performance metrics using a Selenium WebDriver test.

Getting ready

For this recipe, we will need to download and install dynaTrace AJAX Edition from `http://ajax.dynatrace.com/ajax/en/`.

You may also download and install the premium edition for more features.

During installation, the dynaTrace AJAX Edition will automatically install Agents (add-on) in Internet Explorer and Firefox. After completing the installation, please make sure that these Agents (add-on) are enabled in the browser.

How to do it...

For using dynaTrace with the Selenium WebDriver, we have to set up some environment variables. These variables will enable dynaTrace to monitor the browser instance launched from the Selenium WebDriver test and capture the performance metrics.

You can set these variables either in the command line or in Eclipse. If you are setting the variables from command line, you can either create a batch file or enter the following command before starting the test run:

```
SET DT_AE_AGENTACTIVE=true
SET DT_AE-AGENTNAME=Firefox
```

For configuring the environment variables in Eclipse and running the test with dynaTrace, perform the following steps:

1. Start the dynaTrace AJAX Edition (You need to launch the dynaTrace AJAX Edition before running your test).
2. Select the project from **Project Explorer** in Eclipse.
3. Right-click on the selected project and select **Run As | Run Configurations...** from the **context** menu.
4. Select the test that you want to run along with dynaTrace from the right-hand side pane in the **Run Configurations** dialog box.
5. Select the **Environment** tab on the **Run Configurations** dialog box.
6. On the **Environment** tab, click on the **New...** button to add a new environment variable.
7. Enter the values in the **Name** and **Value** fields for a new environment variable on the **New Environment Variable** dialog box and click on the **OK** button, as shown in the following screenshot:

    Add the following environment variables:

Name	Value
DT_AE_AGENTACTIVE	true
DT_AE_AGENTNAME	Firefox

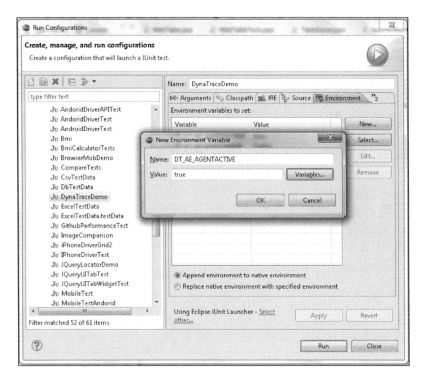

8. Click on the **Run** button in Eclipse to start the test run.

    After completing the test, dynaTrace will display results, as shown in the following screenshot:

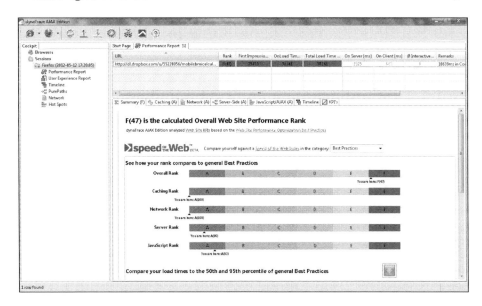

How it works...

When the Selenium WebDriver test launches a browser with predefined environment variables, the dynaTrace Agents installed as add-ons in the browser get activated, monitor the browser for various events, and collect the performance metrics. This data is passed to the dynaTrace AJAX Edition for further analysis and reporting.

You can view the results in the **dynaTrace AJAX Edition** window under the **Sessions** option. dynaTrace will show the performance data and recommendations, which can help you to optimize the application.

There's more...

When we use `FirefoxDriver()` in a test, it launches Firefox without the add-on. However, for the dynaTrace Agent, we need to use the default Firefox profile. When we launch Firefox with the default profile, it loads all the installed add-ons.

We can launch Firefox along with a profile using the following code:

```
@Before
public void setUp() throws Exception
{
  // Create a Profile Object and get Default Profile
  ProfilesIni profile = new ProfilesIni();
  FirefoxProfile ffprofile = profile.getProfile("default");

  // Create a new instance of the Firefox Driver, pass the default
  // profile
  driver = new FirefoxDriver(ffprofile);
}
```

See also

▶ The *Using the BrowserMob proxy for measuring performance* recipe
▶ The *Using HttpWatch for measuring performance* recipe

Using HttpWatch for measuring performance

HttpWatch is another famous tool for watching the client-side performance of a web application with Internet Explorer and Firefox. Similar to dynaTrace, HttpWatch provides various metrics to analyze problems in JavaScript, network requests, page resources, and page load performance. It offers API support for monitoring and capturing the log files in C#, Ruby, JavaScript, and so on.

In this recipe, we will set up HttpWatch to capture the various performance metrics using a Selenium WebDriver test.

Getting ready

For this recipe, we will need to download and install HttpWatch Basic Edition from `http://www.httpwatch.com/`.

You may also download and install the Professional edition for more features.

During installation, the dynaTrace AJAX Edition will automatically install the plugins in Internet Explorer and Firefox. After completing the installation, please make sure that these plugins are enabled in the browser.

How to do it...

Before using HttpWatch in a test, we have to set up an option to capture the metric when the HttpWatch plugin is launched in the browser in the following way:

1. Open the browser.
2. Open the HttpWatch plugin and select **Tools | Options**.

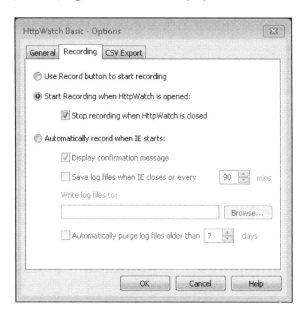

3. On the **HttpWatch Basic - Options** dialog box, select the **Recording tab.**
4. Then select the **Start Recording when HttpWatch is opened:** radio button and select the **Stop recording when HttpWatch is closed** checkbox.

5. Click on **OK** to close the **HttpWatch Basic - Options** dialog box.

6. Close the browser.

7. Let's create a sample C# Script using Selenium WebDriver .NET bindings.

    i.   Create a new C# Console application project in Visual Studio. You may also create a class library project for NUnit or MSTest project instead.

    ii. Add a reference to `WebDriver.dll` and `WebDriver.Support dll`.

    iii. Also add a reference to `HttpWatch.dll`, located in `C:\Program Files\HttpWatch`.

    iv. Add `using` directives for the following types:

    ```
    using HttpWatch;
    using OpenQA.Selenium;
    using OpenQA.Selenium.Support;
    using OpenQA.Selenium.Firefox;
    using OpenQA.Selenium.IE;
    ```

    v.   Add the following code in the `main()` method:

    ```
    //Create an instance of HTTPWatch Controller
    Controller control = new Controller();

    //Start IE Driver. IE Driver Server is located in C:\\
    IWebDriver driver = new InternetExplorerDriver("C:\\");

    // Set a unique initial page title so that HttpWatch can
    // attach to it
    string uniqueTitle = Guid.NewGuid().ToString();
    IJavaScriptExecutor js = driver as IJavaScriptExecutor;
    js.ExecuteScript("document.title = '" + uniqueTitle + "';");

    // Attach HttpWatch to the instance of Internet Explorer
    // created through WebDriver
    Plugin plugin = control.AttachByTitle(uniqueTitle);

    //Open the HTTPWatch Window
    plugin.OpenWindow(false);

    //Navigate to the BMI Application Page
    driver.Navigate().GoToUrl("http://dl.dropbox.com/u/55228056/
    bmicalculator.html");

    //Perform some steps
    driver.FindElement(By.Id("heightCMS")).SendKeys("181");
    driver.FindElement(By.Id("weightKg")).SendKeys("80");
    ```

```
driver.FindElement(By.Id("Calculate")).Click();

//Export the HttpWatch Log generated to a file
plugin.Log.Save("C:\\bmicalc.hwl");

//Close the Internet Explorer
driver.Close();
```

How it works...

When the test is executed, it first creates an instance of the `HttpWatch Controller` class. This class provides API access to the test through the plugin interface.

```
//Create an instance of HTTPWatch Controller
Controller control = new Controller();
```

The HttpWatch plugin needs a unique title, so that it can access the HTTP requests from the browser. In this test, a unique GUID is created and assigned as a title to the browser window.

```
// Set a unique initial page title so that HttpWatch can attach to it
string uniqueTitle = Guid.NewGuid().ToString();
IJavaScriptExecutor js = driver as IJavaScriptExecutor;
js.ExecuteScript("document.title = '" + uniqueTitle + "';");
```

The test creates an instance of the plugin interface by calling the `AttachByTitle()` method of the controller. This method takes the `uniqueTitle` assigned to the browser window as an argument.

```
// Attach HttpWatch to the instance of Internet Explorer created
// through WebDriver
Plugin plugin = control.AttachByTitle(uniqueTitle);
```

Once the HttpWatch plugin is attached to the browser window, the test can open the plugin window by calling the `OpenWIndow()` method. This will display the HttpWatch GUI along with the application page in the browser window.

```
//Open the HTTPWatch Window
plugin.OpenWindow(false);
```

HttpWatch starts the recording of the HTTP traffic once the plugin window is displayed. The test navigates to the test application and performs some operation to capture the HTTP metric. The captured data can be saved in the HttpWatch log file format as a `.hwl` file by calling the `Log.Save()` method and specifying the path where the log file will be saved.

```
//Export the HttpWatch Log generated to a file
plugin.Log.Save(@"C:\bmicalc.hwl");
```

Once the test is executed, the log generated by the HttpWatch plugin can be analyzed using HttpWatch Studio that is installed along with HttpWatch. The HttpWatch Studio displays all the metrics and performance data, as shown in the following screenshot:

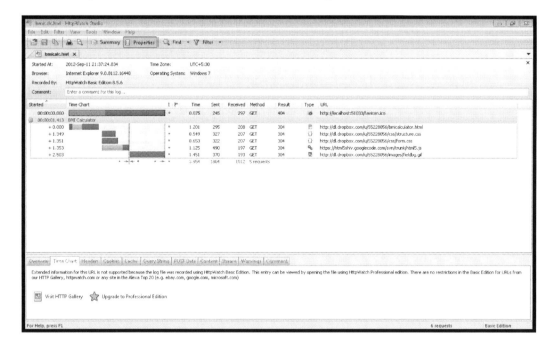

See also

▶ The *Using the BrowserMob proxy for measuring performance* recipe

▶ The *Using HttpWatch for measuring performance* recipe

Client-side performance testing with Watir-WebDriver-Performance in Ruby

The Watir-WebDriver-Performance gem provides a set of timing metrics using the W3C Page Performance standard in the Watir-WebDriver.

The Watir-WebDriver-Performance gem is the perfect solution to capture the response time metrics, and it's very straightforward to set up.

One way of effectively measuring performance testing is by conducting a response time test every time the application is built. If there is a huge degradation in the performance, break the build!

In this recipe, we will set up the Watir-WebDriver-Performance gem and collect various performance metrics in our test.

Getting ready

You will need a Ruby environment. You will need the Watir-WebDriver gem along with the Watir-WebDriver-Performance gem.

First, install the Watir-WebDriver gem by the using the following command:

```
gem install watir-webdriver
```

Then, install the Watir-WebDriver-Performance gem by using the following command:

```
gem install watir-webdriver-performance
```

How to do it...

Let's try a simple example using the **Interactive Ruby Shell** (**IRB**).

1. Load `watir-webdriver` and `watir-webdriver-performance` in Ruby as follows:

   ```
   irb(main):001:0> require 'watir-webdriver'
   irb(main):002:0> require 'watir-webdriver-performance'
   ```

2. Create an instance of Firefox by using the `Watir::Browser.new` method and launch the `unmesh.me` website as follows:

   ```
   irb(main):003:0> browser = Watir::Browser.new :firefox
   irb(main):004:0> browser.goto "unmesh.me"
   => http://unmesh.me/
   ```

3. Once the website is loaded in the browser, we can find out the `End User Response Time` by using the following command. In the following example, it took 17 seconds:

   ```
   irb(main):005:0> # End User Response Time
   irb(main):006:0* browser.performance.summary[:response_time]/1000
   => 17
   irb(main):007:0> #seconds...
   ```

4. You can find other important metrics from `browser.performance.summary` by using the following code:

   ```
   irb(main):008:0* browser.performance.summary
   => {:app_cache=>-492, :dns=>2017, :tcp_connection=>-2067,
   :request=>2753, :respo
   nse=>724, :dom_processing=>6403, :time_to_first_byte=>5088, :time_
   to_last_byte=>
   5812, :response_time=>17743}
   irb(main):009:0>
   ```

You can see the output for the previous commands in the following screenshot:

We will create a test that will launch the unmesh.me website and measure the response time. If the response time is more than 15 seconds, the test will fail:

```ruby
require 'rubygems'
require 'watir-webdriver'
require 'watir-webdriver-performance'
require "test/unit"

class BmiCalcTest < Test::Unit::TestCase
  def setup
    @browser = Watir::Browser.new :firefox
    @verification_errors = []
  end

  def test_responseTime
    @browser.goto 'unmesh.me'
    @load_secs  = @browser.performance.summary[:response_time]/1000
    puts "Response Time: " + @load_secs.to_s()
    assert_equal true, @load_secs < 15
  end

  def teardown
    @browser.close
    assert_equal [], @verification_errors
  end
```

How it works...

The Watir-WebDriver-Performance gem provides the ability to capture the response time metrics from the test created with the Watir-WebDriver. By instrumenting the Watir-WebDriver automated tests that run regularly, we can capture and measure the web application performance over time, and be alerted to the possibility of a change being introduced with adverse performance effects.

The Watir-WebDriver-Performance gem collects all the available metrics from the browser using the `PerformanceTiming` interface and summarizes them. The `PerformanceTiming` interface allows JavaScript mechanisms to provide a client-side latency metric within the application.

In the previous examples, the `@browser` object provides us with an additional performance object through which we can retrieve the performance metrics collected from the browser. For example, we can retrieve the overall response time in our test by using the following code snippet:

```
@browser.performance.summary[:response_time]
```

There's more...

The Watir-WebDriver-Performance gem provides various timing metrics in the following format:

```
timing={
    :navigation_start=>1336668835275,
    :unload_event_start=>0,
    :unload_event_end=>0,
    :redirect_start=>0,
    :redirect_end=>0,
    :fetch_start=>1336668835545,
    :domain_lookup_start=>1336668835275,
    :domain_lookup_end=>1336668835615,
    :connect_start=>1336668835930,
    :connect_end=>1336668836226,
    :request_start=>1336668835936,
    :response_start=>1336668836812,
    :response_end=>1336668837125,
    :dom_loading=>1336668836813,
    :dom_interactive=>1336668839215,
    :dom_content_loaded_event_start=>1336668839385,
    :dom_content_loaded_event_end=>1336668839419,
    :dom_complete=>1336668842077,
    :load_event_start=>1336668842077,
    :load_event_end=>1336668842278},
```

```
navigation={
  :type=>0,
  :redirect_count=>0,
  :type_navigate=>0,
  :type_reload=>1,
  :type_back_forward=>2,
  :type_reserved=>255},
summary={
  :app_cache=>-270,
  :dns=>340,
  :tcp_connection=>296,
  :request=>876,
  :response=>313,
  :dom_processing=>2572,
  :time_to_first_byte=>1537,
  :time_to_last_byte=>1850,
  :response_time=>7003}
```

9
Testing HTML5 Web Applications

In this chapter, we will cover:

- ▶ Automating the HTML5 video player
- ▶ Automating interaction on the HTML5 canvas element
- ▶ Web storage – testing local storage
- ▶ Web storage – testing session storage
- ▶ Cleaning local and session storage

Introduction

As HTML5 is gaining popularity, major browsers are now equipped to support HTML5, extending the scope of the HTML combined with JavaScript and CSS3 into powerful, rich Internet applications. There are many applications being developed using new HTML5 elements such as canvas, video, and so on, and features such as web storage giving users a rich Internet experience. For many web developers adopting these standards, it is essential that we test these features automatically.

Selenium WebDriver supports testing HTML5 web applications on certain browsers out of the box. However, we can also use JavaScript to test these features, which will work on all the browsers supported by Selenium WebDriver.

In this chapter, we will focus on the most important features of HTML5 and see how to test them using Selenium WebDriver.

Automating the HTML5 video player

Up till now, there has not been a standard for showing a video on web pages. Most of the browsers depend on a plugin such as Flash to playback a video. However, different browsers have different plugins.

HTML5 defines a new element that specifies a standard way to embed a video or movie clips on a web page by using the `<video>` element. Internet Explorer 9+, Firefox, Opera, Chrome, and Safari support the `<video>` element.

In this recipe, we will explore how we can automate testing of the `<video>` element, which provides a JavaScript interface with various methods and properties for automation.

How to do it...

We will create a new test named `testHTML5VideoPlayer` for testing the `<video>` element. We will use the `JavaScriptExecutor` class from Selenium WebDriver to interact with the `<video>` element. We will control the video from our test code and also verify some properties of the video in the following way:

```java
@Test
public void testHTML5VideoPlayer() throws Exception {

    File scrFile = null;

    //Get the HTML5 Video Element
    WebElement videoPlayer = driver.findElement(By.id("vplayer"));

    //We will need a JavaScript Executor for interacting
    //with Video Element's
    //methods and properties for automation
    JavascriptExecutor jsExecutor = (JavascriptExecutor) driver;

    //Get the Source of Video that will be played in Video Player
    String source = (String) jsExecutor.executeScript("return
        arguments[0].currentSrc;", videoPlayer);
    //Get the Duration of Video
    long duration = (Long) jsExecutor.executeScript("return
        arguments[0].duration", videoPlayer);
    System.out.println(duration);

    //Verify Correct Video is loaded and duration
    assertEquals("http://html5demos.com/assets/dizzy.mp4", source);
```

```
assertEquals(25, duration);

//Play the Video
jsExecutor.executeScript("return arguments[0].play()",
    videoPlayer);

Thread.sleep(5000);

//Pause the video
jsExecutor.executeScript("arguments[0].pause()", videoPlayer);

//Take a screen-shot for later verification
scrFile = ((TakesScreenshot)driver).getScreenshotAs
    (OutputType.FILE);
FileUtils.copyFile(scrFile, new File("c:\\tmp\\pause_play.png"));
}
```

How it works...

Firstly, we locate the `<video>` element so we can call its associated methods in JavaScript as well as the retrieve/set properties. We can locate the `<video>` element similar to another HTML element by using the `findElement()` method as follows:

```
//Get the HTML5 Video Element
WebElement videoPlayer = driver.findElement(By.id("vplayer"));
```

We can verify which video file is being used with video player for playback and duration of the video by looking at the `currentSrc` and `duration` properties. We are retrieving these properties by accessing the `<video>` element through JavaScript. For this, we created an instance of the `JavaScriptExecutor` class as follows:

```
JavascriptExecutor jsExecutor = (JavascriptExecutor) driver;
```

Using the `executeScript()` method of the `JavaScriptExecutor` class of Selenium WebDriver, we can execute the JavaScript code within the browser window. We can return a value from the JavaScript code by assigning the value to a variable. However, we need to cast this value appropriately based on the type of value being returned. In this case, the `currentSrc` property will return a URL of the video file as a `String`:

```
String source = (String) jsExecutor.executeScript("return
arguments[0].currentSrc;", videoPlayer);
```

In the previous example, `arguments[0]` was replaced by the `videoPlayer` WebElement using the `executeScript()` method.

Video playback

As discussed earlier, we can also control the playback of a video using the methods of the `<video>` element such as `play()` and `pause()`. We can call these methods by using the `executeScript()` method in the following way:

```
//Play the Video
jsExecutor.executeScript("return arguments[0].play()", videoPlayer);
```

See also

> ▶ The *Executing JavaScript code* recipe in *Chapter 2, Working with Selenium API*

Automating interaction on the HTML5 canvas element

Web developers can now create cool drawing applications within web browsers using the new HTML5 `<canvas>` element. This element is used to build drawing and charting applications by using JavaScript. Canvas has several methods for drawing paths, boxes, circles, characters, and adding images.

In this recipe, we will automate a simple drawing application through the Selenium WebDriver action class for mouse movements. We will also implement an image comparison feature to test the drawing on a canvas.

Internet Explorer 9+, Firefox, Opera, Chrome, and Safari support the `<canvas>` element.

How to do it...

Create a new test named `testHTML5CanvasDrawing` for testing the `<canvas>` element. We draw a shape by using a sequence of mouse movements on the `<canvas>` element. We will verify the canvas with a previously captured image and check the shape has been redrawn as follows:

```
@Test
public void testHTML5CanvasDrawing() throws Exception {

    //Get the HTML5 Canvas Element
    WebElement canvas = driver.findElement(By.id("imageTemp"));
    //Select the Pencil Tool
    Select drawtool = new Select(driver.findElement(By.id("dtool")));
    drawtool.selectByValue("pencil");

    //Create a Action Chain for Draw a shape on Canvas
```

```
Actions builder = new Actions(driver);
builder.clickAndHold(canvas).moveByOffset(10, 50).
                moveByOffset(50,10).
                moveByOffset(-10,-50).
                moveByOffset(-50,-10).release().perform();

//Get a screenshot of Canvas element after Drawing and
//compare it to the base version
//to verify if the Drawing is performed
FileUtils.copyFile(WebElementExtender.captureElementBitmap(canvas),
  new File("c:\\tmp\\post.png"));
assertEquals(CompareUtil.Result.Matched,
  CompareUtil.CompareImage("c:\\tmp\\base_post.png",
  "c:\\tmp\\post.png"));
}
```

How it works...

To draw on the canvas, we will first select a drawing tool by selecting the `pencil` option from the **Drawing Tool** drop-down. Selenium WebDriver provides a `Select` class for working with drop-downs and lists. In the test, the `selectByValue()` method is called for selecting the `pencil` tool:

```
Select drawtool = new Select(driver.findElement(By.id("dtool")));
drawtool.selectByValue("pencil");
```

We will draw a shape on the canvas by using the Selenium WebDriver actions generator. Selenium WebDriver will perform a sequence of mouse movements by calling the `moveByOffset()` method while holding the mouse button to draw the shape, releasing the mouse button at the end:

```
builder.clickAndHold(canvas).moveByOffset(10, 50).
                moveByOffset(50,10).
                moveByOffset(-10,-50).
                moveByOffset(-50,-10).release().perform();
```

The Selenium actions generator mimics the mouse operations exactly like an end user drawing a shape on the canvas.

Finally, we will capture an image of the canvas using the `captureElementBitmap()` method of the `WebElementExtender` class. This image will be compared with a baseline image to verify that the drawing operation works on the canvas as expected using the Selenium WebDriver.

See also

▶ The *Executing JavaScript code* recipe in *Chapter 2, Working with Selenium API*

▶ The *Comparing images in Selenium* recipe in *Chapter 6, Extending Selenium*

Web storage – testing local storage

HTML5 introduced a more secure and faster way of storing data locally within the user's browser from the Web application. Earlier, this was done with cookies. This data is not included with every server request, but used ONLY when asked for. It is also possible to store large amounts of data without affecting the website's performance. The data is stored in key/value pairs, and a web application can only access data stored by itself.

HTML5 provides a `localStorage` interface through JavaScript that stores the data with no expiration date. The data will not be deleted when the browser is closed, and will be available all the time. You can view this data in Google Chrome by clicking on **Inspect Element** | **Resources** tab.

Internet Explorer 8+, Firefox, Opera, Chrome, and Safari support web storage.

In this recipe, we will verify that a web page stores data in local storage as expected.

How to do it...

We will create a test that will verify the web page has created an entry in local storage and stored a value. We will use the Selenium WebDriver `JavaScriptExecutor` class to access the `localStorage` interface as follows:

```
@Test
public void testHTML5LocalStorage() throws Exception {

  String lastName;

  JavascriptExecutor jsExecutor = (JavascriptExecutor) driver;

  //Get the current value of localStorage.lastname, this should be
  //Smith
  lastName = (String) jsExecutor.executeScript("return localStorage.
    lastname;");
  assertEquals("Smith", lastName);

}
```

How it works...

While executing this test, Selenium WebDriver will load a page that will access the local storage and create a new key/value pair as `lastName = Smith`. We can validate this by accessing the `lastName` key from the `localStorage` interface using the `executeScript()` method of the `JavaScriptExecutor` class. This will return the value of the `lastName` key as a `String`:

```
lastName = (String) jsExecutor.executeScript("return localStorage.
lastname;");
```

There's more...

During testing, there might be a need to directly set the value of the key in local storage. We can assign a new value to an existing key by directly assigning the value in the following way, using JavaScript:

```
//Set the value of localStorage.lastname to Dustin
jsExecutor.executeScript("localStorage.lastname = 'Dustin';");
```

See also

▸   The *Cleaning local and session storage* recipe

Web storage – testing session storage

Similar to local storage, the **session storage** stores the data for only one session. The data is deleted when the user closes the browser window. We can access the session storage using the `sessionStorage` interface through JavaScript.

In this recipe, we will verify that a web page stores data in session storage as expected.

How to do it...

Let's create a test case that will load a web page which implements a counter and stores the value of the counter every time a button is clicked in session storage. We will verify that a new counter value is stored in session storage:

```
@Test
public void testHTML5SessionStorage() throws Exception {

    String clickcount=null;

    WebElement clickButton = driver.findElement(By.id("click"));
```

```
    WebElement clicksField = driver.findElement(By.id("clicks"));

    JavascriptExecutor jsExecutor = (JavascriptExecutor) driver;

    //Get current value of sessionStorage.clickcount, should be null
    clickcount = (String) jsExecutor.executeScript("return
      sessionStorage.clickcount;");
    assertEquals(null, clickcount);
    assertEquals("0", clicksField.getAttribute("value"));

    //Click the Button, this will increase the
    //sessionStorage.clickcount value by 1
    clickButton.click();

    //Get current value of sessionStorage.clickcount, should be 1
    clickcount = (String) jsExecutor.executeScript("return
      sessionStorage.clickcount;");
    assertEquals("1", clickcount);
    assertEquals("1", clicksField.getAttribute("value"));
}
```

How it works...

While executing this test, whenever a button is clicked by Selenium WebDriver, a new session storage key will be created for the first time in session storage. For subsequent clicks, this value will be incremented by the web page.

Similar to local storage, we can validate this by accessing the clickcount key from the sessionStorage interface using the executeScript() method of the JavaScriptExecutor class. This will return the value of the clickcount key as a String:

```
    //Click the Button, this will increase the sessionStorage.clickcount
    //value by 1
    clickButton.click();

    //Get current value of sessionStorage.clickcount, should be 1
    clickcount = (String) jsExecutor.executeScript("return
      sessionStorage.clickcount;");
```

When the browser is closed and the test has ended, the clickcount key will be removed from session storage.

See also

▸ The *Cleaning local and session storage* recipe

Cleaning local and session storage

When tests are run on HTML5 applications using local or session storage, lots of local and session storage entries will be created. When running tests in batch on an already used environment, cleaning the local and session storage is a good idea before you begin your tests.

In this recipe, we will briefly see how to remove local or session storage items and clean the values.

How it works...

To remove a specific item from local or session storage, you can use the `removeItem()` method in the following way:

```
//To Remove a specific Key along with it's value
JavascriptExecutor jsExecutor = (JavascriptExecutor) driver;
jsExecutor.executeScript("localStorage.removeItem(lastname);");
```

For session storage, the following code snippet will be used:

```
//To Remove a specific Key along with it's value
JavascriptExecutor jsExecutor = (JavascriptExecutor) driver;
jsExecutor.executeScript("sessionStorage.removeItem(lastname);");
```

To clear all items, local or session storage, you can use the `clear()` method in the following way:

```
//To Clear Storage values
JavascriptExecutor jsExecutor = (JavascriptExecutor) driver;
jsExecutor.executeScript("localStorage.clear();");
```

For session storage, the following code snippet will be used:

```
//To Clear Storage values
JavascriptExecutor jsExecutor = (JavascriptExecutor) driver;
jsExecutor.executeScript("sessionStorage.Clear();");
```

See also

- ▶ The *Web storage – testing session storage* recipe
- ▶ The *Web storage – testing local storage* recipe

10
Recording Videos of Tests

In this chapter, we will cover:

 ▸ Recording videos of tests using Monte Media Library in Java
 ▸ Recording videos of tests using Microsoft Expression Encoder 4 SDK in .NET
 ▸ Recording videos of tests using Castro in Python

Introduction

Capturing a video showing test execution becomes useful when tests are run. While tests are executed unattended, recording a video will help in understanding how things went during the test run, capturing application, or script errors or successes.

Whether you are a developer or a tester, these videos can be useful in analyzing test results and reproducing the defects recorded during test execution.

It also helps in capturing the evidence for adhering to processes. These videos can also be used in demoing features to customers or as a training aid.

Selenium WebDriver does not have in-built features to record videos of test runs. However, Selenium WebDriver scripts can be extended using open source or free-to-use tools to support recording videos.

This chapter will cover various recipes to record videos of tests in Selenium WebDriver using tools like Monte Media Library for Java, Microsoft Expression Encoder SDK for .NET, and Castro for Python.

Recording videos of tests using Monte Media Library in Java

In Java, we can extend Selenium WebDriver test scripts to record videos by using an open source tool named **Monte Media Library**. The Monte Media Library developed by Werner Randelshofer is an open source tool available under Creative Commons Attribution License.

In this recipe, we will explore how to configure and use the Monte Media Library's `ScreenRecorder` class with Selenium to record movies of tests.

`ScreenRecoder` supports the AVI and QuickTime formats for recording movies. For playing movies in AVI format, you will need to install **Techsmith Screen Capture Codec (TSCC Codec)** while QuickTime format is supported by Apple's QuickTime player. `ScreenRecorder` provides multiple configurations for colors, mouse cursor, screen rate, mouse rate, audio, and so on.

Getting ready

1. Go to Monte Media Library's home page `http://www.randelshofer.ch/monte/index.html` and download the `ScreenRecorder.jar` file. In this recipe, version 0.7 is used.

2. Add the `ScreenRecorder.jar` file to the project's build path.

How to do it...

Monte Media Library is integrated with the Selenium WebDriver test for recording videos with the following steps:

1. Create a new test class `GoogleSearch` with the following imports and instances of WebDriver and the `ScreenRecorder` class:

```java
import org.openqa.selenium.firefox.FirefoxDriver;
import org.openqa.selenium.WebDriver;
import org.openqa.selenium.WebElement;
import org.openqa.selenium.By;
import org.openqa.selenium.support.ui.ExpectedCondition;
import org.openqa.selenium.support.ui.WebDriverWait;
import org.monte.media.math.Rational;
import org.monte.media.Format;
import org.monte.screenrecorder.ScreenRecorder;
import static org.monte.media.AudioFormatKeys.*;
import static org.monte.media.VideoFormatKeys.*;
import org.junit.*;
import static org.junit.Assert.*;
```

```
import java.awt.*;

public class GoogleSearch {

    private WebDriver driver;
    private StringBuffer verificationErrors = new StringBuffer();
    private ScreenRecorder screenRecorder;
}
```

2. Add a `setUp()` method, which will create a new instance of the `ScreenRecorder` class by getting the graphics configuration of the machine in the `GoogleSearch` class. This method also creates an instance of `FirefoxDriver()`, as shown in the following code:

```
@Before
public void setUp() throws Exception {

    // Create an instance of GraphicsConfiguration to get the
    // Graphics configuration
    // of the Screen. This is needed for ScreenRecorder class.
      GraphicsConfiguration gc = GraphicsEnvironment
          .getLocalGraphicsEnvironment()
          .getDefaultScreenDevice()
          .getDefaultConfiguration();

    // Create a instance of ScreenRecorder with the required
    // configurations
    screenRecorder = new ScreenRecorder(gc,
        new Format(MediaTypeKey, MediaType.FILE, MimeTypeKey,
          MIME_AVI),
        new Format(MediaTypeKey, MediaType.VIDEO, EncodingKey,
          ENCODING_AVI_TECHSMITH_SCREEN_CAPTURE,
           CompressorNameKey, ENCODING_AVI_TECHSMITH_SCREEN_CAPTURE,
           DepthKey, (int)24, FrameRateKey, Rational.valueOf(15),
           QualityKey, 1.0f,
           KeyFrameIntervalKey, (int) (15 * 60)),
        new Format(MediaTypeKey, MediaType.VIDEO,
          EncodingKey,"black",
           FrameRateKey, Rational.valueOf(30)),
             null);

    // Create a new instance of the Firefox driver
```

```
driver = new FirefoxDriver();

//Call the start method of ScreenRecorder to begin recording
screenRecorder.start();
}
```

3. Add a test method `testGoogleSearch()` in the `GoogleSearch` class. This method will test the search functionality by calling the Selenium WebDriver API. In the background, `ScreenRecorder` will capture this interaction in a video file:

```java
@Test
public void testGoogleSearch() throws Exception {

    // And now use this to visit Google
    driver.get("http://www.google.com");

    // Find the text input element by its name
    WebElement element = driver.findElement(By.name("q"));
    // Enter something to search for
    element.sendKeys("Cheese!");
    // Now submit the form. WebDriver will find the form for us
    // from the element
    element.submit();

    try {

        // Google's search is rendered dynamically with JavaScript.
        // Wait for the page to load, timeout after 10 seconds
        (new WebDriverWait(driver, 10)).until(new
          ExpectedCondition<Boolean>() {
            public Boolean apply(WebDriver d) {
             return d.getTitle().toLowerCase().startsWith("cheese!");
            }});

        // Should see: "cheese! - Google Search"
        assertEquals("cheese! - Google Search", driver.getTitle());

    } catch (Error e) {
        //Capture and append Exceptions/Errors
        verificationErrors.append(e.toString());
    }
}
```

4. Finally, add a `tearDown()` method in the `GoogleSearch` class which will call the `stop()` method of the `ScreenRecorder` class to finish the video recording:

```
@After
public void tearDown() throws Exception {
    //Close the browser
    driver.quit();

    // Call the stop method of ScreenRecorder to end the recording
    screenRecorder.stop();

    String verificationErrorString = verificationErrors.toString();
    if (!"".equals(verificationErrorString)) {
        fail(verificationErrorString);
    }
}
```

How it works...

While recording the video of the desktop, the `ScreenRecorder` class needs the graphics configuration of the display screen on which tests are executed. Java's AWT package has a class named `GraphicsConfiguration` through which we can pass this information to the `ScreenRecorder` class.

We can collect the graphics configuration details from the `GraphicsEnvironment` class of AWT in the following way:

```
GraphicsConfiguration gc = GraphicsEnvironment
    .getLocalGraphicsEnvironment()
    .getDefaultScreenDevice()
    .getDefaultConfiguration();
```

This will get the graphics configuration of the default display screen of the system in an instance of `GraphicsConfiguration`.

An instance of the `ScreenRecorder` class is created by calling the constructor and passing the video recording settings. This will provide us with the necessary methods to start and stop the recording:

```
// Create a instance of ScreenRecorder with the required
// configurations
screenRecorder = new ScreenRecorder(gc,
    new Format(MediaTypeKey, MediaType.FILE, MimeTypeKey, MIME_AVI),
    new Format(MediaTypeKey, MediaType.VIDEO, EncodingKey,
      ENCODING_AVI_TECHSMITH_SCREEN_CAPTURE,
      CompressorNameKey, ENCODING_AVI_TECHSMITH_SCREEN_CAPTURE,
      DepthKey, (int)24, FrameRateKey, Rational.valueOf(15),
```

```
        QualityKey, 1.0f,
        KeyFrameIntervalKey, (int) (15 * 60)),
        new Format(MediaTypeKey, MediaType.VIDEO, EncodingKey,"black",
        FrameRateKey, Rational.valueOf(30)),
    null);
```

The `ScreenRecorder` constructor is supplied with the following parameters:

Parameter	Passed valued	Description
GraphicsConfiguration	gc	Provides display screen information such as size, resolution, and so on.
Video and compression format	video/avi, tscc	The output format of the movie, encoding mechanism, color depth, frames per second, keyframe interval.
		ScreenRecorder supports AVI and QuickTime movie formats.
Color of the mouse cursor and refresh rate	black, 30	The color of the mouse cursor and refresh rate.
Audio format	null	No audio will be recorded.

Video recording is invoked by calling the ScreenRecorder's `start()` method and completed by calling the ScreenRecorder's `stop()` method.

When a recording is finished, `ScreenRecorder` stores the output file in the user's `Home` directory. On Windows, it will save the recorded file in the `C:\Users\<username>\Videos` folder and on Mac it will save in the `~/Movies` folder.

Recorded videos can be viewed with QuickTime or open source video players like VLC. Video recorded in AVI format needs a media player that supports Techsmith Screen Capture Codec (TSCC). This Codec is available for download and use at `http://www.techsmith.com/download.html`.

There's more...

Often we use dual monitor setups to develop or test the code. `ScreenRecorder` allows recording across dual monitors as well. This can be done by tweaking the `GraphicsConfiguration` class to get the array of screen devices attached to the system using `getScreenDevices()[index]` as follows:

```
GraphicsConfiguration gc = GraphicsEnvironment//
    .getLocalGraphicsEnvironment()//
    .getScreenDevices()[1]
    .getDefaultConfiguration();
```

In the previous example, `ScreenRecorder` will record the videos from the secondary display screen attached to the system.

Tip/Warning Monte Media Library does not support recording videos of tests with Selenium WebDriver Remote Server where tests are executed on remote machines.

Recording videos of tests using Microsoft Expression Encoder 4 SDK in .NET

Unfortunately, Monte Media Library cannot be used with Selenium WebDriver .NET bindings. However, there is a very simple and interesting solution available from Microsoft named **Microsoft Expression Encoder**.

The Expression Encoder tool is available as a part of Microsoft Expression Toolset. This tool provides a very simple and neat API to record videos of the screen interaction. It also provides a GUI to edit the recorded videos.

There are two versions available. The Basic version supports a proprietary/limited codec from Microsoft and comes free to use. The Pro version supports a number of other codecs and provides additional features. However, you need to buy the Pro version from Microsoft.

In this recipe, we will use the Basic Microsoft Expression Encoder version to record a video of a test in C# using Selenium WebDriver .NET bindings.

Getting ready

Download and install Microsoft Expression Encoder 4 with SP 2 from `http://www.microsoft.com/expression/try-it/Default.aspx`.

How to do it...

Recording a video of a test run with Selenium WebDriver .NET bindings can be done with the following steps. In this recipe, Microsoft Visual Studio 2012 is used along with NUnit:

1. Add a Microsoft Expression Encoder assembly (`Microsoft.Expression.Encoder.dll`) reference to your project in Microsoft Visual Studio. This file is located in the `C:\Program Files\Microsoft Expression\Encoder 4\SDK` folder.

2. Create a new C# class `GoogleSearch` with the NUnit `TestFixture` attribute with the following imports and instance variables for the `IWebDriver` interface and the `ScreenCaptureJob` class:

   ```
   using System;
   using System.Text;
   using System.Collections.Generic;
   ```

```
using System.Linq;

using NUnit.Framework;
using OpenQA.Selenium;
using OpenQA.Selenium.Firefox;
using OpenQA.Selenium.Support;
using OpenQA.Selenium.Support.UI;
using Microsoft.Expression.Encoder.ScreenCapture;

namespace SeVideoRecording
{
    [TestFixture]
    public class GoogleSearch
    {
        IWebDriver driver;
        ScreenCaptureJob scj;
    }
}
```

3. Add a `TestSetup()` method to the `GoogleSearch` class created earlier. This method will instantiate the `ScreenCaptureJob` object and set the file path where a video recording will be saved. This method will also instantiate `FirefoxDriver`:

```
[SetUp]
public void TestSetup()
{
    // Create a instance of ScreenCaptureJob from Expression
    // Encoder
    scj = new ScreenCaptureJob();

    // Specify the path & name of the file to which Encoder will
    // store the recording.
    // Name of Test is passed to create individual recordings of
    // each test
    scj.OutputScreenCaptureFileName = @"C:\Results\TestGooleSearch.
        wmv";

    // Start the Screen Capture Job
    scj.Start();

    driver = new FirefoxDriver();
}
```

4. Add the test case method `TestGoogleSearch()` to the `GoogleSearch` class. This method will call the Selenium WebDriver API for testing the search functionality while `ScreenCaptureJob` will record the video in the background:

```
[TestCase]
public void TestGoogleSearch()
{
    driver.Navigate().GoToUrl("http://www.google.com/");

    IWebElement query = driver.FindElement(By.Name("q"));
    query.SendKeys("Cheese");

    WebDriverWait wait = new WebDriverWait(driver,
      TimeSpan.FromSeconds(10));
    Boolean titleMatched = wait.Until<Boolean>((d) =>
    {
        return d.Title.ToLower().StartsWith("cheese");
    });

    Assert.AreEqual("cheese - Google Search", driver.Title);
}
```

5. Finally, add a `TestCleanUp()` method in the `GoogleSearch` class which will call the `stop()` method of the `ScreenCaptureJob` class to stop and complete the video recording:

```
[TearDown]
public void TestCleanUp()
{
    //Close the Browser
    driver.Close();

    //Stop the Screen Capture Job
    scj.Stop();
}
```

How it works...

The `ScreenCapture` namespace in Microsoft Expression Encoder SDK provides the `ScreenCaptureJob` class through which we can record the videos. In the sample script, we created an instance of `ScreenCaptureJob` and assigned a path and filename to its `OutputScreenCaptureFileName` property in the `TestSetup()` method to store the output file. Adding this code to the `TestSetup()` method will create individual recording sessions for all the tests that are part of this test class:

```
scj = new ScreenCaptureJob();
scj.OutputScreenCaptureFileName = @"C:\Results\TestGooleSearch.wmv";
scj.Start();
```

The `start()` method of `ScreenCaptureJob` called in the `TestSetup()` method will start the recording of video. And the `stop()` method called in the `TestCleanUp()` method will stop the recording session.

There's more...

The `ScreenCaptureJob` class provides various methods and properties to control the recording sessions. For more information, visit `http://msdn.microsoft.com/en-us/library/ff726642(v=expression.40).aspx`.

You can also edit the recorded videos in Encoder GUI and add captions, thumbnails, and so on, to the recorded video.

Recording videos of tests using Castro in Python

Castro is a widely used tool in the Selenium community to record videos of test runs in Python. This tool works differently than `ScreenRecorder` or Microsoft Expression Encoder.

Castro is based on a cross-platform screen recording tool named **Pyvnc2swf** (`http://www.unixuser.org/~euske/vnc2swf/pyvnc2swf.html`). It captures a screen using the VNC protocol and generates a **Shockwave Flash** (**SWF**) movie file.

With VNC protocol support, we can record a video from a remote machine with Castro. It needs a VNC program installed on the machine to record the videos, though.

Getting ready

1. Install Castro using `easy_install` or the pip tool from the command line:

   ❑ `easy_install Castro` or

   ❑ `pip install Castro`

2. Install/enable VNC:

   ❑ On Windows, you need to install the VNC program. TightVNC (`http://www.tightvnc.com/`) will be a good choice. Install the TightVNC server and viewer on Windows.

   ❑ On Ubuntu, go to **Settings | Preference | Remote Desktop** and check the **Allow other users to view your desktop** checkbox.

   ❑ On Mac, you can install the Vine VNC server from `http://www.testplant.com/products/vine/` or enable **Remote Desktop** from **System Preferences**.

How to do it...

Create a Selenium WebDriver test in python calling Castro as follows:

```python
from selenium import webdriver
from selenium.webdriver.support.ui import WebDriverWait
from castro import Castro
import time, unittest

class VideoRecordingTests (unittest.TestCase) :
    def setUp(self)    :
        # Create an instance of Castro and provide name for the output
          file
        self.screenCapture = Castro(filename="testGoogleSearch.swf")
        # Start the recording of movie
        self.screenCapture.start()
        self.driver = webdriver.Firefox()

    def testGoogleSearch(self) :
        driver = self.driver
        driver.get("http://www.google.com")
        inputElement = driver.find_element_by_name("q")
        inputElement.send_keys("Cheese!")
        inputElement.submit()
        WebDriverWait(driver, 20).until(lambda driver :
          driver.title.lower().startswith("cheese!"))
```

```
        self.assertEqual("cheese! - Google Search",driver.title)

    def tearDown(self) :
        self.driver.quit()
        # Stop the recording
        self.screenCapture.stop();

if __name__ == "__main__":
    unittest.main()
```

How it works...

In the `setUp()` method, we created an instance of Castro, passing the name of the output file as follows:

```
    self.screenCapture = Castro(filename="testGoogleSearch.swf")
```

We called the `start()` method to start recording the video. In the `tearDown()` method, we called the `stop()` method to complete the recording. Castro will create two files, namely, `testGoogleSearch.swf` and `testGoogleSearch.html` in the user's `temp` directory. The recorded video can be viewed by opening the `testGoogleSearch.html` file in a browser window.

There's more...

We can use Castro to record video on a remote host. This will be useful when we run tests in a distributed environment with `RemoteWebDriver`. This can be achieved by passing `host` and `passwd` parameters while creating an instance of Castro in the following way:

```
    screenCapture = Castro(host     = 'hostname_or_ip',
                           display  = 1,
                           filename = "testname.swf",
                           passwd   = "/home/me/.vnc/passwd")
```

11
Behavior-driven Development

In this chapter, we will cover:

- ► Using Cucumber-JVM and Selenium WebDriver in Java for BDD
- ► Using SpecFlow.NET and Selenium WebDriver in .NET for BDD
- ► Using JBehave and Selenium WebDriver in Java
- ► Using Capybara, Cucumber, and Selenium WebDriver in Ruby

Introduction

Behavior-driven Development (**BDD**) is an agile software development practice that enhances the paradigm of **Test Driven Development** (**TDD**) and acceptance tests, and encourages the collaboration between developers, quality assurance, domain experts, and stakeholders. Behavior-driven Development was introduced by Dan North in the year 2003 in his seminal article available at `http://dannorth.net/introducing-bdd/`.

Behavior-driven Development focuses on obtaining a clear understanding of desired application behavior through discussion with stakeholders using an ubiquitous language as described at `http://behaviour-driven.org/`.

It extends TDD by writing test cases in a natural language that non-programmers can read. Users describe features and scenarios to test these features in plain text files using Gherkin language in `Given`, `When`, and `Then` structure. You can find out more about Gherkin language at `http://en.wikipedia.org/wiki/Behavior-driven_development` and `https://github.com/cucumber/cucumber/wiki/Gherkin`.

The `Given`, `When`, and `Then` structures in the Gherkin language are described as follows:

- ▸   `Given`: This represents the initial context (precondition)
- ▸   `When`: This represents the user performing a key action (actor + action)
- ▸   `Then`: This ensures some kind of outcome (observable result)

In Behavior-driven Development, the process starts with users of the system and development team discussing features, user stories, and scenarios. These are documented in feature or story files using the Gherkin language. Developers then use the red-green-refactor cycle to run these features using the BDD framework, then write step definition files mapping the steps from scenarios to the automation code and re-running until all the acceptance criteria are met:

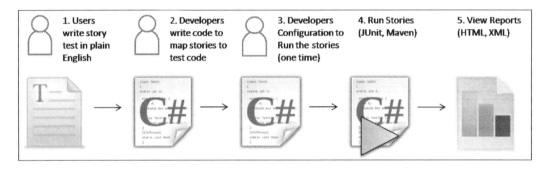

 Behavior-driven Development is also known as **Acceptance Test Driven Development (ATDD)** or **Story Testing**.

In this chapter, we will explore using frameworks like Cucumber-JVM, JBehave, SpecFlow.NET, and Capybara with Selenium WebDriver for Behavior-driven Development.

Using Cucumber-JVM and Selenium WebDriver in Java for BDD

BDD/ATDD is becoming widely accepted practice in agile software development, and Cucumber-JVM is a mainstream tool used to implement this practice in Java. Cucumber-JVM is based on Cucumber framework, widely used in Ruby on Rails world.

Cucumber-JVM allows developers, QA, and non-technical or business participants to write features and scenarios in a plain text file using Gherkin language with minimal restrictions about grammar in a typical `Given`, `When`, and `Then` structure.

This feature file is then supported by a step definition file, which implements automated steps to execute the scenarios written in a feature file. Apart from testing APIs with Cucumber-JVM, we can also test UI level tests by combining Selenium WebDriver.

In this recipe, we will use Cucumber-JVM, Maven, and Selenium WebDriver for implementing tests for the fund transfer feature from an online banking application.

Getting ready

1. Create a new Maven project named **FundTransfer** in Eclipse.

 You can refer to the recipes *Configuring Eclipse and Maven for Selenium WebDriver test development* or *Configuring IntelliJ IDEA and Maven for Selenium WebDriver test development* in the bonus chapter, *Integration with Other Tools*, available at `http://www.packtpub.com/sites/default/files/downloads/Integration_with_Other_Tools.pdf`, to create a Maven project.

2. Add the following dependencies to POM.XML:

```
<project xmlns="http://maven.apache.org/POM/4.0.0"
xmlns:xsi="http://www.w3.org/2001/XMLSchema-instance"
xsi:schemaLocation="http://maven.apache.org/POM/4.0.0 http://
maven.apache.org/xsd/maven-4.0.0.xsd">
        <modelVersion>4.0.0</modelVersion>
        <groupId>FundTransfer</groupId>
        <artifactId>FundTransfer</artifactId>
        <version>0.0.1-SNAPSHOT</version>
    <dependencies>
            <dependency>
                <groupId>info.cukes</groupId>
                <artifactId>cucumber-java</artifactId>
                <version>1.0.14</version>
                <scope>test</scope>
            </dependency>
            <dependency>
                <groupId>info.cukes</groupId>
                <artifactId>cucumber-junit</artifactId>
                <version>1.0.14</version>
                <scope>test</scope>
            </dependency>
            <dependency>
                <groupId>junit</groupId>
                <artifactId>junit</artifactId>
                <version>4.10</version>
                <scope>test</scope>
            </dependency>
            <dependency>
```

```
            <groupId>org.seleniumhq.selenium</groupId>
            <artifactId>selenium-java</artifactId>
            <version>2.25.0</version>
        </dependency>
    </dependencies>
</project>
```

How to do it...

Perform the following steps for creating BDD/ATDD tests with Cucumber-JVM:

1. Select the **FundTransfer** project in **Package Explorer** in Eclipse. Select and right-click on **src/test/resources** in **Package Explorer**. Select **New | Package** from the menu to add a new package as shown in the following screenshot:

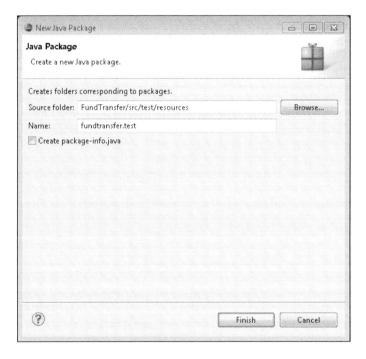

2. Enter `fundtransfer.test` in the **Name:** textbox and click on the **Finish** button.

3. Add a new file to this package. Name this file as `fundtransfer.feature` as shown in the following screenshot:

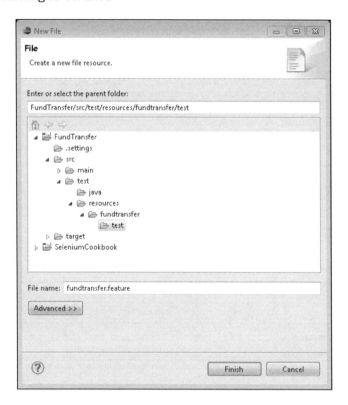

4. Add the `Fund Transfer` feature and scenarios to this file:

```
Feature: Customer Transfer's Fund
        As a customer,
        I want to transfer funds
        so that I can send money to my friends and family

Scenario: Valid Payee
        Given the user is on Fund Transfer Page
        When he enters "Jim" as payee name
        And he enters "100" as amount
        And he Submits request for Fund Transfer
        Then ensure the fund transfer is complete with "$100
        transferred successfully to Jim!!" message

Scenario: Invalid Payee
        Given the user is on Fund Transfer Page
        When he enters "Jack" as payee name
```

And he enters "100" as amount

And he Submits request for Fund Transfer

Then ensure a transaction failure message "Transfer failed!! 'Jack' is not registered in your List of Payees" is displayed

Scenario: Account is overdrawn past the overdraft limit

    Given the user is on Fund Transfer Page

    When he enters "Tim" as payee name

    And he enters "1000000" as amount

    And he Submits request for Fund Transfer

    Then ensure a transaction failure message "Transfer failed!! account cannot be overdrawn" is displayed

5. Select and right-click on **src/test/java** in **Package Explorer**. Select **New | Package** from menu to add a new Package as shown in the following screenshot:

6. Create a class named `FundTransferStepDefs` in the newly-created package. Add the following code to this class:

```
package fundtransfer.test;

import org.openqa.selenium.WebDriver;
import org.openqa.selenium.chrome.ChromeDriver;
import org.openqa.selenium.WebElement;
import org.openqa.selenium.By;

import cucumber.annotation.*;
import cucumber.annotation.en.*;

import static org.junit.Assert.assertEquals;

public class FundTransferStepDefs {
        protected WebDriver driver;

    @Before
    public void setUp() {
        driver = new ChromeDriver();
    }

    @Given("the user is on Fund Transfer Page")
    public void The_user_is_on_fund_transfer_page() {

        driver.get("http://dl.dropbox.com/u/55228056/fundTransfer.
        html");
    }

    @When("he enters \"([^\"]*)\" as payee name")
    public void He_enters_payee_name(String payeeName) {
        driver.findElement(By.id("payee")).sendKeys(payeeName);
    }

    @And("he enters \"([^\"]*)\" as amount")
    public void He_enters_amount(String amount) {
        driver.findElement(By.id("amount")).sendKeys(amount);
    }

    @And("he Submits request for Fund Transfer")
    public void He_submits_request_for_fund_transfer() {
        driver.findElement(By.id("transfer")).click();
```

```
    }

    @Then("ensure the fund transfer is complete with \"([^\"]*)\"
    message")
    public void Ensure_the_fund_transfer_is_complete(String msg) {
        WebElement message = driver.findElement(By.id("message"));
        assertEquals(message.getText(),msg);
    }

    @Then("ensure a transaction failure message \"([^\"]*)\" is
    displayed")
    public void Ensure_a_transaction_failure_message(String msg) {
        WebElement message = driver.findElement(By.id("message"));
        assertEquals(message.getText(),msg);

    }

    @After
    public void tearDown() {
        driver.close();
    }
}
```

7. Create a support class `RunCukesTest` which will define the Cucumber-JVM configurations:

```
package fundtransfer.test;

import cucumber.junit.Cucumber;
import org.junit.runner.RunWith;

@RunWith(Cucumber.class)
@Cucumber.Options(format = {"pretty", "html:target/cucumber-html-
report", "json-pretty:target/cucumber-report.json"})
public class RunCukesTest {
}
```

8. To run the tests in Maven life cycle select the **FundTransfer** project in **Package Explorer**. Right-click on the project name and select **Run As | Maven test**. Maven will execute all the tests from the project.

9. At the end of the test, an HTML report will be generated as shown in the following screenshot. To view this report open `index.html` in the `target\cucumber-html-report` folder:

> ▼ **Feature**: Customer Transfer's Fund
> *As a customer, I want to transfer funds so that I can send money to my friends and family*
>   ▼ **Scenario**: Valid Payee
>   **Given** the user is on Fund Transfer Page
>   **When** he enters "Jim" as payee name
>   **And** he enters "100" as amount
>   **And** he Submits request for Fund Transfer
>   **Then** ensure the fund transfer is complete with "$100 transferred successfully to Jim!!" message
>   ▼ **Scenario**: Invalid Payee
>   **Given** the user is on Fund Transfer Page
>   **When** he enters "Unmesh" as payee name
>   **And** he enters "100" as amount
>   **And** he Submits request for Fund Transfer
>   **Then** ensure a transaction failure message "Transfer failed!! 'Unmesh' is not registered in your List of Payees" is displayed
>   ▼ **Scenario**: Account is overdrawn past the overdraft limit
>   **Given** the user is on Fund Transfer Page
>   **When** he enters "Tim" as payee name
>   **And** he enters "1000000" as amount
>   **And** he Submits request for Fund Transfer
>   **Then** ensure a transaction failure message "Transfer failed!! account cannot be overdrawn" is displayed

How it works...

Creating tests in Cucumber-JVM involves three major steps: writing a feature file, implementing automated steps using the step definition file, and creating support code as needed.

For writing features, Cucumber-JVM uses 100 percent Gherkin syntax. The feature file describes the feature and then the scenarios to test the feature:

```
Feature: Customer Transfer's Fund
        As a customer,
        I want to transfer funds
        so that I can send money to my friends and family
```

You can write as many scenarios as needed to test the feature in the feature file. The scenario section contains the name and steps to execute the defined scenario along with test data required to execute that scenario with the application:

```
Scenario: Valid Payee
        Given the user is on Fund Transfer Page
        When he enters "Jim" as payee name
        And he enters "100" as amount
        And he Submits request for Fund Transfer
        Then ensure the fund transfer is complete with "$100
        transferred successfully to Jim!!" message
```

Team members use these feature files and scenarios to build and validate the system. Frameworks like Cucumber or JBehave provide an ability to automatically validate the features by allowing us to implement automated steps. For this we need to create the step definition file that maps the steps from the feature file to automation code. Step definition files implement a method for steps using special annotations. For example, in the following code, the `@When` annotation is used to map the step `"When he enters "Jim" as payee name"` from the feature file in the step definition file. When this step is to be executed by the framework, the `He_enters_payee_name()` method will be called by passing the data extracted using regular expressions from the step:

```
@When("he enters \"([^\"]*)\" as payee name")
public void He_enters_payee_name(String payeeName) {
    driver.findElement(By.id("payee")).sendKeys(payeeName);
}
```

In this method, the WebDriver code is written to locate the `payee  name` textbox and enter the name value using the `sendKeys()` method.

The step definition file acts like a template for all the steps from the feature file while scenarios can use a mix and match of the steps based on the test conditions.

A helper class `RunCukesTest` is defined to provide Cucumber-JVM configurations such as how to run the features and steps with JUnit, report format, and location, shown as follows:

```
@RunWith(Cucumber.class)
@Cucumber.Options(format = {"pretty", "html:target/cucumber-html-
report", "json-pretty:target/cucumber-report.json"})
public class RunCukesTest {
}
```

There's more...

In this example, step definition methods are calling Selenium WebDriver methods directly. However, a layer of abstraction can be created using the `Page` object where a separate class is defined with the definition of all the elements from `FundTransferPage`:

```
import org.openqa.selenium.WebDriver;
import org.openqa.selenium.WebElement;
import org.openqa.selenium.support.CacheLookup;
import org.openqa.selenium.support.FindBy;
import org.openqa.selenium.support.PageFactory;

public class FundTransferPage {

    @FindBy(id = "payee")
    @CacheLookup
```

```
public WebElement payeeField;

@FindBy(id = "amount")
public WebElement amountField;

@FindBy(id = "transfer")
public WebElement transferButton;

@FindBy(id = "message")
public WebElement messageLabel;

public FundTransferPage(WebDriver driver)
{
    if(!"Online Fund Transfers".equals(driver.getTitle()))
            throw new IllegalStateException("This is not Fund
            Transfer Page");
    PageFactory.initElements(driver, this);
}
}
```

See also

▶   The *Configuring Eclipse and Maven for Selenium WebDriver test development* recipe in the bonus chapter, *Integration with Other Tools*, available at `http://www.packtpub.com/sites/default/files/downloads/Integration_with_Other_Tools.pdf`

▶   The *Using the PageFactory class for exposing elements from a page* recipe in *Chapter 5, Using the Page Object Model*

Using SpecFlow.NET and Selenium WebDriver in .NET for BDD

We saw how to use Selenium WebDriver with Cucumber-JVM for BDD/ATDD. Now let's try using a similar combination in .NET using SpecFlow.NET. We can implement BDD in .NET using the SpecFlow.NET and Selenium WebDriver .NET bindings.

SpecFlow.NET is inspired by Cucumber and uses the same Gherkin language for writing specs. In this recipe, we will implement tests for the Fund Transfer feature using SpecFlow.NET. We will also use the Page objects for FundTransferPage in this recipe.

Getting ready

This recipe is created with SpecFlow.NET Version 1.9.0 and Microsoft Visual Studio Professional 2012.

1. Download and install SpecFlow from Visual Studio Gallery
   `http://visualstudiogallery.msdn.microsoft.com/9915524d-7fb0-43c3-bb3c-a8a14fbd40ee.`

2. Download and install NUnit Test Adapter from `http://visualstudiogallery.msdn.microsoft.com/9915524d-7fb0-43c3-bb3c-a8a14fbd40ee.`

This will install the project template and other support files for SpecFlow.NET in Visual Studio 2012.

How to do it...

You will find the `Fund Transfer` feature in any online banking application where users can transfer funds to a registered payee who could be a family member or a friend. Let's test this feature using SpecFlow.NET by performing the following steps:

1. Launch Microsoft Visual Studio.

2. In Visual Studio create a new project by going to **File | New | Project**. Select **Visual C# Class Library Project**. Name the project `FundTransfer.specs` as shown in the following screenshot:

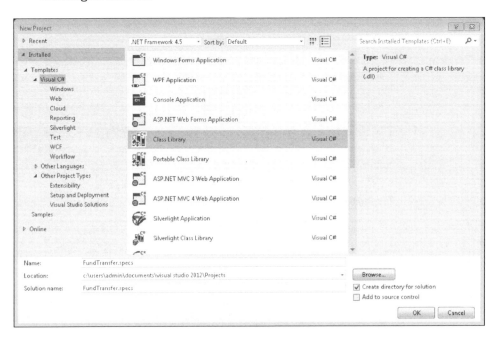

3. Next, add SpecFlow.NET, WebDriver, and NUnit using NuGet. Right-click on the `FundTransfer.specs` solution in **Solution Explorer** and select **Manage NuGet Packages...** as shown in the following screenshot:

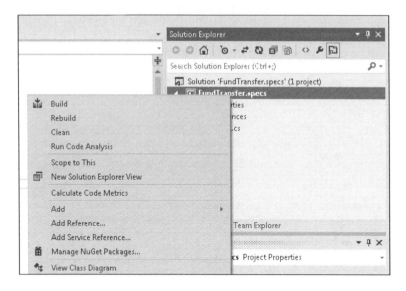

4. On the **FundTransfer.specs - Manage NuGet Packages** dialog box, select **Online**, and search for **SpecFlow** packages. The search will result with the following suggestions:

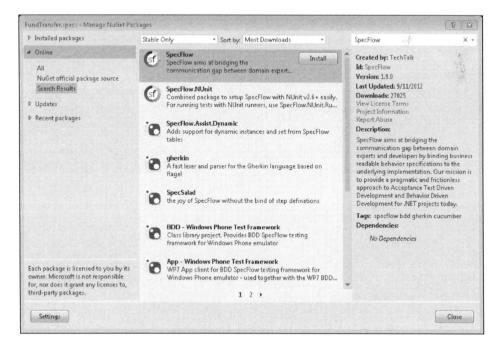

5. Select **SpecFlow.NUnit** from the list and click on **Install** button. NuGet will download and install **SpecFlow.NUnit** and any other package dependencies to the solution. This will take a while.

6. Next, search for the **WebDriver** package on the **FundTransfer.specs - Manage NuGet Packages** dialog box.

7. Select **Selenium WebDriver** and **Selenium WebDriver Support Classes** from the list and click on the **Install** button.

8. Close the **FundTransfer.specs - Manage NuGet Packages** dialog box.

Creating a spec file

The steps for creating a spec file are as follows:

1. Right-click on the FundTransfer.specs solution in **Solution Explorer**. Select **Add | New Item**.

2. On the **Add New Item – FundTransfer.specs** dialog box, select **SpecFlow Feature File** and enter FundTransfer.feature in the **Name:** textbox. Click **Add** button as shown in the following screenshot:

3. In the **Editor** window, your will see the `FundTransfer.feature` tab.

4. By default, SpecFlow will add a dummy feature in the feature file. Replace the content of this file with the following feature and scenarios:

```
Feature: Customer Transfer's Fund
        As a customer,
        I want to transfer funds
        so that I can send money to my friends and family


Scenario: Valid Payee
        Given the user is on Fund Transfer Page
        When he enters "Jim" as payee name
        And he enters "100" as amount
        And he Submits request for Fund Transfer
        Then ensure the fund transfer is complete with "$100
        transferred successfully to Jim!!" message


Scenario: Invalid Payee
        Given the user is on Fund Transfer Page
        When he enters "Jack" as payee name
        And he enters "100" as amount
        And he Submits request for Fund Transfer
        Then ensure a transaction failure message "Transfer
        failed!! 'Jack' is not registered in your List of Payees"
        is displayed


Scenario: Account is overdrawn past the overdraft limit
        Given the user is on Fund Transfer Page
        When he enters "Tim" as payee name
        And he enters "1000000" as amount
        And he Submits request for Fund Transfer
        Then ensure a transaction failure message "Transfer
        failed!! account cannot be overdrawn" is displayed
```

Creating a step definition file

The steps for creating a step definition file are as follows:

1. To add a step definition file, right-click on the `FundTransfer.sepcs` solution in **Solution Explorer**. Select **Add | New Item**.

2. On the **Add New Item - FundTransfer.specs** dialog box, select **SpecFlow Step Definition File** and enter `FundTransferStepDefs.cs` in the **Name:** textbox.

3. Click on **Add** button. A new C# class will be added with dummy steps. Replace the content of this file with the following code:

```csharp
using System;
using System.Collections.Generic;
using System.Linq;
using System.Text;
using TechTalk.SpecFlow;
using NUnit.Framework;
using OpenQA.Selenium;

namespace FundTransfer.specs
{
    [Binding]
    public class FundTransferStepDefs
    {
        FundsTransferPage _ftPage = new
        FundsTransferPage(Environment.Driver);

        [Given(@"the user is on Fund Transfer Page")]
        public void GivenUserIsOnFundTransferPage()
        {
            Environment.Driver.Navigate().GoToUrl("http://
            localhost:64895/Default.aspx");
        }

        [When(@"he enters ""(.*)"" as payee name")]
        public void WhenUserEneteredIntoThePayeeNameField(string
        payeeName)
        {
            _ftPage.payeeNameField.SendKeys(payeeName);
        }

        [When(@"he enters ""(.*)"" as amount")]
        public void WhenUserEneteredIntoTheAmountField(string
        amount)
        {
            _ftPage.amountField.SendKeys(amount);
        }

        [When(@"he enters ""(.*)"" as amount above his limit")]
        public void WhenUserEneteredIntoTheAmountFieldAboveLimit
        (string amount)
        {
            _ftPage.amountField.SendKeys(amount);
```

```
        }

        [When(@"he Submits request for Fund Transfer")]
        public void WhenUserPressTransferButton()
        {
            _ftPage.transferButton.Click();
        }

        [Then(@"ensure the fund transfer is complete with ""(.*)""
        message")]
        public void ThenFundTransferIsComplete(string message)
        {
            Assert.AreEqual(message, _ftPage.messageLabel.Text);
        }

        [Then(@"ensure a transaction failure message ""(.*)"" is
        displayed")]
        public void ThenFundTransferIsFailed(string message)
        {
            Assert.AreEqual(message, _ftPage.messageLabel.Text);
        }
    }

}
```

Defining a Page object and a helper class

The steps for defining a Page object and a helper class are as follows:

1. Define a Page object for the Fund Transfer Page by adding a new C# class file. Name this class FundTransferPage. Copy the following code to this class:

```
using System;
using System.Collections.Generic;
using System.Linq;
using System.Text;
using OpenQA.Selenium;
using OpenQA.Selenium.Support.PageObjects;

namespace FundTransfer.specs
{
    class FundTransferPage
    {
        public FundTransferPage(IWebDriver driver)
        {
            PageFactory.InitElements(driver, this);
```

```
        }

        [FindsBy(How = How.Id, Using = "payee")]
        public IWebElement payeeNameField { get; set; }

        [FindsBy(How = How.Id, Using = "amount")]
        public IWebElement amountField { get; set; }

        [FindsBy(How = How.Id, Using = "transfer")]
        public IWebElement transferButton { get; set; }

        [FindsBy(How = How.Id, Using = "message")]
        public IWebElement messageLabel { get; set; }
    }
}
```

2. We need a helper class that will provide an instance of WebDriver and perform clean up activity at the end. Name this class `Environment` and copy the following code to this class:

```
using System;
using System.Collections.Generic;
using System.Linq;
using System.Text;
using OpenQA.Selenium;
using OpenQA.Selenium.Chrome;
using TechTalk.SpecFlow;

namespace FundTransfer.specs
{
    [Binding]
    public class Environment
    {
        private static ChromeDriver driver;

        public static IWebDriver Driver
        {
            get { return driver ?? (driver = new
            ChromeDriver(@"C:\ChromeDriver")); }
        }

        [AfterTestRun]
        public static void AfterTestRun()
        {
            Driver.Close();
```

```
            Driver.Quit();
            driver = null;
        }
    }
}
```

3. Build the solution.

Running tests

The steps for running tests are as follows:

1. Open the **Test Explorer** window by clicking the **Test Explorer** option on **Test | Windows** on **Main Menu**.

2. It will display the three scenarios listed in the feature file as shown in the following screenshot:

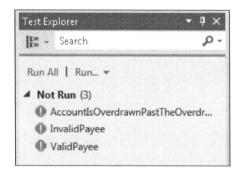

3. Click on **Run All** to test the feature as shown in the following screenshot:

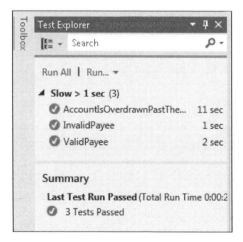

How it works...

SpecFlow.NET first needs the feature files for the features we will be testing. SpecFlow.NET supports the Gherkin language for writing features.

In the step definition file, we create a method for each step written in a feature file using the `Given`, `When`, and `Then` attributes. These methods can also take the parameter values specified in the steps using the arguments. Following is an example where we are entering the name of the payee:

```
[When(@"he enters ""(.*)"" as payee name")]
public void WhenUserEneteredIntoThePayeeNameField(string payeeName)
{
    _ftPage.payeeNameField.SendKeys(payeeName);
}
```

In this example, we are automating the `"When he enters "Jim" as payee name"` step. We used the `When` attribute and created a method: `WhenUserEneteredIntoThePayeeNameField`. This method will need the value of the payee name embedded in the step which is extracted using the regular expression by the SpecFlow.NET. Inside the method, we are using an instance of the `FundTransferPage` class and calling its `payeeNameField` member's `SendKeys1()` method, passing the name of the payee extracted from the step. Using the `Page` object helps in abstracting locator and page details from the step definition files, making it more manageable and easy to maintain.

SpecFlow.NET automatically generates the NUnit test code when the project is built. Using the Visual Studio Test Explorer and NUnit Test Adaptor for Visual Studio, these tests are executed and the features are validated.

See also

> ▶ The *Configuring Visual Studio for Selenium WebDriver test development* recipe in the bonus chapter, *Integration with Other Tools*, available at `http://www.packtpub.com/sites/default/files/downloads/Integration_with_Other_Tools.pdf`

Using JBehave and Selenium WebDriver in Java

JBehave is another famous framework for BDD/ATDD in Java. Similar to Cucumber-JVM, JBehave allows the writing of features as stories in the Gherkin language. Steps from the scenarios are later implemented in a step definition file.

In this recipe, we will explore using JBehave and Selenium WebDriver together for creating tests on a BMI calculator application.

Getting ready

You need to download and set up the JBehave Web extension, which is based on JBehave Core. It provides support for web-related access or functionality, including Selenium/WebDriver support.

The latest release of JBehave Web Distribution is available in JBehave's repository at Codehaus Nexus. You need to download the latest jbehave-web-distribution from `https://nexus.codehaus.org/content/repositories/releases/org/jbehave/web/jbehave-web-distribution/`.

Download the complete zip archive from the previously mentioned location. For this recipe, `jbehave-web-distribution-3.5-bin.zip` is used.

After downloading the JBehave Web, unzip the contents of this file on your machine. Locate the `lib` subdirectory; this directory contains all JAR files needed to create and run the following examples.

How to do it...

1. Create a new Java project and add all the JAR files to build a path from the `lib` subdirectory from the JBehave Web directory extracted earlier. This will add JBehave and Selenium support to the project. Also, add JUnit Library to this project.

2. We now need to prepare a story file, which will contain acceptance criteria for a user story written in the Given, When and Then structure. We will create a simple story file for the BMI Calculator Application; let's call this `Bmi.story`. Create this using the with following steps, in the source folder of your project.

   ```
   Narrative: I should be able to Calculate my Body Mass Index

   Scenario: I should see my BMI after entering Height and Weight

   When I open BMI Calculator Home Page
   When I enter height as '181'
   When I enter weight as '80'
   When I click on the Calculate button
   Then I should see bmi as '24.4' and category as 'Normal'
   ```

3. Next, we need to map steps from this story and create a step definition class. We will create a plain Java class that will extend the `StoryBase` class, which we will create shortly. For each step we will create a method with the `@When` and `@Then` annotations from the JBehave framework:

   ```
   import junit.framework.Assert;
   import org.jbehave.core.annotations.Then;
   import org.jbehave.core.annotations.When;
   ```

```java
import org.openqa.selenium.By;
import org.openqa.selenium.WebElement;

public class Bmi extends StoryBase {

    @When("I open BMI Calculator Home Page")
    public void IOpen()
    {
        driver.get("http://dl.dropbox.com/u/55228056/
        bmicalculator.html");
    }

    @When("I enter height as '$height'")
    public void IEnterHeight(String height)
    {
        WebElement heightCMS = driver.findElement(By.
        id("heightCMS"));
        heightCMS.sendKeys(height);
    }

    @When("I enter weight as '$weight'")
    public void IEnterWeight(String weight)
    {
        WebElement weightKg = driver.findElement(By.
        id("weightKg"));
        weightKg.sendKeys(weight);
    }

    @When("I click on the Calculate button")
    public void IClickOnTheButton()
    {
        WebElement button = driver.findElement(By.
        id("Calculate"));
        button.click();
    }

    @Then("I should see bmi as '$bmi_exp' and category as
    '$bmi_category_exp'")
    public void IShouldBmiAndCategory(String bmi_exp, String
    bmi_category_exp)
    {
        WebElement bmi = driver.findElement(By.id("bmi"));
```

```
        Assert.assertEquals(bmi_exp,
        bmi.getAttribute("value"));

        WebElement bmi_category = driver.findElement(By.
        id("bmi_category"));
        Assert.assertEquals(bmi_category_exp, bmi_category.
        getAttribute("value"));
        driver.quit();


    }
}
```

4. Finally, we will create a `Configuration` class that will be used by the step definition classes. In this class, we set up necessary configurations to execute the stories using JBehave and Selenium. We will name this class `StoryBase` and this will be extended from the `JUnitStory` class in the JBehave framework:

```java
import java.util.List;

import org.jbehave.core.configuration.Configuration;
import org.jbehave.core.configuration.MostUsefulConfiguration;
import org.jbehave.core.io.LoadFromClasspath;
import org.jbehave.core.junit.JUnitStory;
import org.jbehave.core.reporters.Format;
import org.jbehave.core.reporters.StoryReporterBuilder;
import org.jbehave.core.steps.InstanceStepsFactory;
import org.openqa.selenium.WebDriver;
import org.openqa.selenium.firefox.FirefoxDriver;

public abstract class StoryBase extends JUnitStory {

        protected final static WebDriver driver = new
        FirefoxDriver();

        @Override
        public Configuration configuration() {
                return new MostUsefulConfiguration()
                .useStoryLoader(new LoadFromClasspath(this.
                getClass().getClassLoader()))
                .useStoryReporterBuilder(
                                new StoryReporterBuilder()
                                .withDefaultFormats()
                                .withFormats(Format.HTML,
                                Format.CONSOLE)
                                .withRelativeDirectory
                                ("jbehave-report")
```

```
                                                    );
            }

        @Override
        public List candidateSteps() {
                return new InstanceStepsFactory(configuration(),
                this).createCandidateSteps();


        }
    }
```

How it works...

For creating tests in JBehave, we will need to first implement stories as the `.story` file using the `Given`, `When`, and `Then` structures. We need to add the `Narrative` section to describe the purpose of the story and the `Scenario` section, which contains the actual steps. We also pass the required test data from these steps:

```
Narrative: I should be able to Calculate my Body Mass Index

Scenario: I should see my BMI after entering Height and Weight

When I open BMI Calculator Home Page
When I enter height as '181'
...
Then I should see bmi as '24.4' and category as 'Normal'
```

Next, we map these steps using a step definition class. This class extends the `StoryBase` class, which will provide the necessary support to run the story in the JBehave framework, including an instance of WebDriver:

```
public class Bmi extends StoryBase
```

For each step, we use an annotation and implement a method to run that step. For example, for the step `When I enter height as '181'` we have defined the `IEnterHeight()` method as follows:

```
@When("I enter height as '$height'")
    public void IEnterHeight(String height)
    {
            WebElement heightCMS = driver.findElement(By.
            id("heightCMS"));
            heightCMS.sendKeys(height);
    }
```

We used the @When annotation here and also used '$height' for extracting the value mentioned in the .story file and passed this value to the IEnterHeight() method. In this method, we created an instance of WebElement for the height textbox and called its sendKeys() method, passing the value.

Along with a story file and a step definition class, a Configuration class needs to be created, which will be based on the JUnitStory class from the JBehave framework:

```
public abstract class StoryBase extends JUnitStory
```

The StoryBase class provides an instance of WebDriver to all the story or step definition classes:

```
protected final static WebDriver driver = new FirefoxDriver();
```

It also provides other configuration information, like the location of the story files and report settings, and format the JBehave framework. In this case, the .story files will be located using the path of the story or step definition classes:

```
@Override
public Configuration configuration() {
    return new MostUsefulConfiguration()
    .useStoryLoader(new LoadFromClasspath(this.getClass().
    getClassLoader()))
    .useStoryReporterBuilder(
                    new StoryReporterBuilder()
                    .withDefaultFormats()
                    .withFormats(Format.HTML, Format.CONSOLE)
                    .withRelativeDirectory("jbehave-report")
                );
}
```

We used the JUnitStory class so that we can execute these tests with JUnit Test Runner. At the end of the execution, JBehave generates an HTML report with a detailed status of the stories executed, stories passed, or failed.

See also

▶ The *Using Cucumber-JVM and Selenium WebDriver in Java for BDD* recipe

Using Capybara, Cucumber, and Selenium WebDriver in Ruby

Capybara is an acceptance test framework for web applications in Ruby. It integrates with Ruby-based BDD frameworks such as Cucumber and RSpec along with Selenium WebDriver for web testing capabilities. Capybara is widely used in testing Rails applications.

In this recipe, we will see how to use Capybara, Cucumber, and Selenium to test BMI Calculator application.

Getting ready

1. You need to install Capybara Gem by using the following command:

   ```
   gem install capybara
   ```

2. Additionally, you also need to install Cucumber and RSpec Gem on a fresh Ruby installation, as follows:

   ```
   gem install cucumber
   ```

   ```
   gem install rspec
   ```

How to do it...

In Capybara, we need to create a features file for the stories under test. These stories are written in Gherkin language with the Given, When, and Then structures in Cucumber format. Perform the following steps to create a feature and step definition file with Capybara:

1. Create a plain text file named BmiCalculate.feature, as follows:

   ```
   Feature: BMI Calculator has a Calculate Function

   Scenario: Calculate BMI
         Given I am on BMI Calculator
         When I fill in the following:
         | heightCMS | 181 |
         | weightKg | 80 |
         When I press "Calculate"
         Then I should see following:
         | bmi | 24.4 |
         | bmi_category | Normal |
   ```

2. Next, we need to create a step file for the feature file created earlier. This file maps each step from the feature file to a Capybara function to work on UI. Create a Ruby file with the following code and name it `BmiCalculate.rb`:

```
Given /^I am on BMI Calculator$/ do
    visit "http://dl.dropbox.com/u/55228056/bmicalculator.html"
end

When /^I fill in the following:$/ do |table|
        table.rows_hash.each {|field, value| fill_in field,
        :with => value }
end

When /^I press "([^"]*)"$/ do |button|
    click_button(button)
end

Then /^I should see following:$/ do |table|
        table.rows_hash.each {|field, value| find_field(field).
        value.should == value }
end
```

3. Finally, we need to create a configuration file that provides required support to run the features with Cucumber. Create a new file with the following code and name it `env.rb`:

```
require 'capybara'
require 'capybara/cucumber'
require 'selenium/webdriver'

Capybara.default_driver = :selenium
Capybara.register_driver :selenium do |app|
    Capybara::Selenium::Driver.new(app, :browser => :firefox)
end
```

How it works...

We need to copy all of these files together in a directory named `features` and use the cucumber command as follows:

cucumber

Since we are using Cucumber along with Capybara, it first needs feature files written in plain English. Cucumber allows defining feature files to enter data in web forms using a table-like format. In the following example, we have a step which will populate the `height` and `weight` fields in the BMI Calculator application:

```
When I fill in the following:
    | heightCMS | 181 |
    | weightKg | 80 |
```

The steps from a feature file are then mapped to Capybara commands using a step file written in Ruby. In the following example, the previously mentioned table format is mapped to a Capybara command, `fill_in`:

```
When /^I fill in the following:$/ do |table|
    table.rows_hash.each {|field, value| fill_in field, :with => value
}
end
```

To run these features with Cucumber we need a configuration file that will tell Capybara to use Selenium as a driver:

```
require 'capybara'
require 'capybara/cucumber'
require 'selenium/webdriver'

Capybara.default_driver = :selenium
Capybara.register_driver :selenium do |app|
  Capybara::Selenium::Driver.new(app, :browser => :firefox)
end
```

When Cucumber runs the features, a default report is generated in the following format:

See also

▶ The *Using Cucumber-JVM and Selenium WebDriver in Java for BDD* recipe

▶ The *Using SpecFlow.NET and Selenium WebDriver in .NET for BDD* recipe

▶ The *Using JBehave and Selenium WebDriver in Java for BDD* recipe

Index

getScreenshotAs() method 54
getScreenShotAs() method 191
getTestData() method 117, 128
getText() method 44, 176
Google Chrome
    used, for inspecting pages and elements 11,
        12
Google.new() method 141
GoogleSearch class 258
GraphicsEnvironment class 261
GUI (Graphical User Interface) tests 7

H

He_enters_payee_name() method 278
helper class
    defining 285, 286
highlightElement() method 183
hockwave Flash (SWF) movie file 266
HomePage class 157
HTML5 canvas element
    interaction, automating 250, 251
HTML5 video player
    automating 248, 249
HTML5 web applications, testing
    HTML5 video player, automating 248, 249
    interaction, automating on HTML5 canvas
        element 250, 251
    local and session storage, cleaning 255
    local storage, testing 252, 253
    session storage, testing 253, 254
HTML Archive (HAR) format 232
HTML frames 96
HttpWatch
    about 238
    downloading 239
    installing 239
    setting up, for Selenium WebDriver
        test 239, 240
    used, for measuring performance 238
    working 241
HttpWatch Controller class 241

I

id attribute
    about 16
    used, for locating elements 16

ID selector
    used, for finding elements 24
IEnterHeight() method 292, 293
IEnumerable property 132
IFRAME
    working with 101, 102
implicitlyWait() method 75
implicit wait
    used, for synchronizing test 74, 75
initElements() method 149
injectjQueryIfNeeded() method 37
Internet Explorer
    used, for inspecting pages and
        elements 12, 13
IPhoneDriver architecture 200
iPhone/iPad device
    iWebDriver App, setting up for 206, 208
iPhone/iPad simulator
    iWebDriver App, setting up for 202-205
isDisplayed() method 82
isElementPresent() method
    implementing 81
isEnabled() method 82
isLoaded() method 154, 155
isMultiple() method 58
isSelected() method 66, 68, 82
iWebDriver App
    configuring, for iPhone/iPad simulator 205
    setting up, for iPhone/iPad device 206, 208
    setting up, for iPhone/iPad
        simulator 202-204
iWebDriver App and iPhone driver
    used, for testing application 208-212

J

JavaScript alert
    handling 90-92
JavaScript code
    executing 51, 52
JavaScriptExecutor class 36, 184, 248
JavascriptExecutor interface
    about 51
    used, for executing JavaScript code 51, 52
Java String API methods
    contains() 45
    endsWith() 45

textContent attribute 31
text, element
  checking 44, 45
Timeouts Interface 75
timespan, between events
  calculating 228
tryToKillByName() function 70

U

UI state pseudo-classes
  :checked 34
  :disabled 34
  :enabled 34
  using 34
user action pseudo-classes
  using 34

V

Video playback 250
video showing test execution
  capturing 257
videos of tests
  recording, Monte Media Library used in Java
    258-262
  recording, using Castro in Python 266-268
  recording, using Microsoft Expression Encoder
    4 SDK in .NET 263-266
VNC
  enabling 267
  installing 267

W

wait.until() method 77
Watir-WebDriver-Performance gem
  about 242
  used, for client-side performance
    testing 242, 243
  working 245

WebElement class
  about 18
  getText() method 44
WebElementExtender class 182, 251
web page stores 252
WebTable constructor 172
WhenUserEneteredIntoThePayeeNameField
  method 288
Windows processes
  controlling 70
Windows registry value
  modifying, from Selenium WebDriver 72
  reading, from Selenium WebDriver 71
WindowsUtils class 70
workflow, data-driven approach 106
writeStringRegistryValue() method 72
writeTo() method 234

X

XPath
  about 26
  partial match, performing on attribute
    values 28
  used, for locating elements 26
  working 30
XPath axis
  ancestor 30
  descendant 30
  following 30
  following-sibling 30
  preceding 30
  preceding-sibling 30
  URL 30
  used, for locating elements 29
XPath functions
  contains() 28
  ends-with() 28
  starts-with() 28
xpath() method 31

Thank you for buying
Selenium Testing Tools Cookbook

About Packt Publishing

Packt, pronounced 'packed', published its first book "*Mastering phpMyAdmin for Effective MySQL Management*" in April 2004 and subsequently continued to specialize in publishing highly focused books on specific technologies and solutions.

Our books and publications share the experiences of your fellow IT professionals in adapting and customizing today's systems, applications, and frameworks. Our solution based books give you the knowledge and power to customize the software and technologies you're using to get the job done. Packt books are more specific and less general than the IT books you have seen in the past. Our unique business model allows us to bring you more focused information, giving you more of what you need to know, and less of what you don't.

Packt is a modern, yet unique publishing company, which focuses on producing quality, cutting-edge books for communities of developers, administrators, and newbies alike. For more information, please visit our website: www.packtpub.com.

About Packt Open Source

In 2010, Packt launched two new brands, Packt Open Source and Packt Enterprise, in order to continue its focus on specialization. This book is part of the Packt Open Source brand, home to books published on software built around Open Source licences, and offering information to anybody from advanced developers to budding web designers. The Open Source brand also runs Packt's Open Source Royalty Scheme, by which Packt gives a royalty to each Open Source project about whose software a book is sold.

Writing for Packt

We welcome all inquiries from people who are interested in authoring. Book proposals should be sent to author@packtpub.com. If your book idea is still at an early stage and you would like to discuss it first before writing a formal book proposal, contact us; one of our commissioning editors will get in touch with you.

We're not just looking for published authors; if you have strong technical skills but no writing experience, our experienced editors can help you develop a writing career, or simply get some additional reward for your expertise.

Selenium 1.0 Testing Tools: Beginner's Guide

ISBN: 978-1-84951-026-4   Paperback: 232 pages

Test your web applications with multiple browsers using the Selenium Framework to ensure the quality of web applications

1. Save your valuable time by using Selenium to record, tweak and replay your test scripts

2. Get rid of any bugs deteriorating the quality of your web applications

3. Take your web applications one step closer to perfection using Selenium tests

4. Packed with detailed working examples that illustrate the techniques and tools for debugging

Python Testing Cookbook

ISBN: 978-1-84951-466-8   Paperback: 364 pages

Over 70 simple but incredibly effective recipes for taking control of automated testing using powerful Python testing tools

1. Learn to write tests at every level using a variety of Python testing tools

2. The first book to include detailed screenshots and recipes for using Jenkins continuous integration server (formerly known as Hudson)

3. Explore innovative ways to introduce automated testing to legacy systems

4. Written by Greg L. Turnquist – senior software engineer and author of Spring Python 1.1

Please check **www.PacktPub.com** for information on our titles

NetBeans IDE 7 Cookbook

ISBN: 978-1-84951-250-3   Paperback: 308 pages

Over 70 highly focused practical recipes to maximize your output with NetBeans

1. Covers the full spectrum of features offered by the NetBeans IDE

2. Discover ready-to-implement solutions for developing desktop and web applications

3. Learn how to deploy, debug, and test your software using NetBeans IDE

4. Another title in Packt's Cookbook series giving clear, real-world solutions to common practical problems

NetBeans Platform 6.9 Developer's Guide

ISBN: 978-1-84951-176-6   Paperback: 288 pages

Create professional desktop rich-client Swing applications using the world's only modular Swing application framework

1. Create large, scalable, modular Swing applications from scratch

2. Master a broad range of topics essential to have in your desktop application development toolkit, right from conceptualization to distribution

3. Pursue an easy-to-follow sequential and tutorial approach that builds to a complete Swing application

Please check **www.PacktPub.com** for information on our titles

33109804R00184

Made in the USA
Lexington, KY
13 June 2014